JESUS OR NIETZSCHE

VIBS

Volume 259

Robert Ginsberg
Founding Editor

Leonidas Donskis
Executive Editor

Associate Editors

G. John M. Abbarno
George Allan
Gerhold K. Becker
Raymond Angelo Belliotti
Kenneth A. Bryson
C. Stephen Byrum
Robert A. Delfino
Rem B. Edwards
Malcolm D. Evans
Roland Faber
Andrew Fitz-Gibbon
Francesc Forn i Argimon
Daniel B. Gallagher
William C. Gay
Dane R. Gordon
J. Everet Green
Heta Aleksandra Gylling
Matti Häyry
Brian G. Henning

Steven V. Hicks
Richard T. Hull
Michael Krausz
Olli Loukola
Mark Letteri
Vincent L. Luizzi
Hugh P. McDonald
Adrianne McEvoy
J.D. Mininger
Peter A. Redpath
Arleen L. F. Salles
John R. Shook
Eddy Souffrant
Tuija Takala
Emil Višňovský
Anne Waters
James R. Watson
John R. Welch
Thomas Woods

a volume in
Ethical Theory and Practice
ETP
Olli Loukola, Editor

JESUS OR NIETZSCHE
How Should We Live Our Lives?

Raymond Angelo Belliotti

Amsterdam - New York, NY 2013

Cover photo: Dreamstime

Cover Design: Studio Pollmann

The paper on which this book is printed meets the requirements of "ISO 9706:1994, Information and documentation - Paper for documents - Requirements for permanence".

ISBN: 978-90-420-3659-8
E-Book ISBN: 978-94-012-0925-0
© Editions Rodopi B.V., Amsterdam - New York, NY 2013
Printed in the Netherlands

For

Marcia, Angelo, and Vittoria

Supra lu majuri si 'nsigna lu minuri.
("We learn by standing on the shoulders of the wise.")

CONTENTS

Editorial Foreword by Olli Loukola		ix
Preface		xi
Acknowledgments		xv
List of Abbreviations		xvii
Introduction		1
	1. Introduction	1
	2. Nietzsche's Life	5
	3. Problems of Interpretation in Nietzsche	7
	4. My (Mis)Interpretation of Nietzsche	9
One	Jesus: The Nature of Our World and Our Mission in It	13
	1. Family Relations	13
	2. Associating and Identifying with Undesirables	17
	3. Unsettling Established Rituals	19
	4. Interrogating Prevailing Norms of Just Distribution	20
	5. Material Minimalism	31
	6. Jesus and the Concept of Forgiveness	34
Two	Nietzsche: The Nature of Our World and Our Mission in It	51
	1. Perspectivism	51
	2. Genealogical Critiques	63
	3. Crafting a Worthy Self	64
	4. Values	65
	5. Nietzsche's Glad Tidings	66
	6. Master and Slave Moralities	69
	7. Going Beyond Good and Evil	80
	8. Eternal Recurrence	84
	9. Philosophy and Psychology	100
	10. Style and Rhetoric	105
	11. Tragic View of Life	110
	12. Jesus and Nietzsche	114

THREE	Fundamental Understandings of Human Beings: Unconditional Love and the Will to Power	115
	1. The Power of Unconditional Love	115
	2. The Paradoxes of Agapic Love	119
	3. Parental Agape	123
	4. The Will to Power	126
	5. The Last Man and The Overman	131
	6. Nietzsche on Jesus	136
	7. Nietzsche on St. Paul and Christianity	141
	8. Nietzsche's Understanding of Jesus	143
	9. Jesus and Engagement in this World	145
	10. Daunting Normative Ideals	149
FOUR	The Perfectionism of Jesus	151
	1. Perfectionism and Unconditional Love	151
	2. Extending Unconditional Love	154
	3. Unconditional Love and Abstraction	158
	4. A Summary of the Perfectionism of Jesus	159
	5. The Ethic of Jesus and Contemporary Philosophy	161
	6. Jesus' Enduring Message	180
FIVE	The Perfectionism of Nietzsche	181
	1. Nietzsche's Vision	181
	2. Aristocratic Privilege	187
	3. A Summary of the Perfectionism of Nietzsche	194
	4. The Perfectionism of Nietzsche and Contemporary Philosophy	195
	5. Jesus and Nietzsche: Toward a Synthesis	205
NOTES		211
BIBLIOGRAPHY		219
INDEX		225
ABOUT THE AUTHOR		231

EDITORIAL FOREWORD

Ethical Theory and Practice (ETP) is a special series in the Value Inquiry Book Series, and it is dedicated to works which attempt to close the gap between ethical theory and practice. One of the goals of *Jesus or Nietzsche: How should we live our lives?* is to examine the tension between the ways we theorize our moral ideals and the practicalities of human life. Jesus and Nietzsche were both sincere followers of the original Socratic mission of moral philosophy, that is, how to live the good human life not only in some distant idealized future, but also within mundane human existence. It is surely here that Jesus and Nietzsche have made a lasting impact in the history of morality, and most certainly in everyday life.

These two thinkers share an important starting point. They cast a critical eye on everyday circumstances, especially as they are regulated, dictated and controlled by established, traditional moral rules and beliefs. They both interrogate the point and purpose of this realm. They search for sense and purpose outside the conventional moralities of their day, and yearn to understand the role of moral reformation in pursuing the good human life. Yet their thinking reaches for the everlasting and transcendent.

Religion has probably been the single most influential element in the history of Western moral thought after the Greek philosophers, and it has continuously sculpted our moral reasoning, judged our motives, and dictated our goals. As such it has tended to calcify into prejudiced dogmatism and blind following of the arbitrary commands of omnipotent beings and of systems of power, backed up by all-encompassing fears of punishment. In the light of such extremism, it is easy to sympathize with the Nietzschean project of dismantling these practices and institutions, and stripping them of their undeserved dominance in defining human autonomy and potentials. Nietzsche offers an alternative image of how we might direct our lives and fashion the persons we might become.

In its reformative aspirations, Nietzsche's project bears similarities to Jesus's radical moral message. But the two part company: Nietzsche announces the death of God, while Jesus supplies a forceful rejoinder. As Raymond Angelo Belliotti convincingly shows in this book, Jesus and Nietzsche are not merely historical icons or galvanizers of power-hungry institutions. Instead, they are inspiring visionaries whose works can inform our existential choices and energize our lives today.

Olli Loukola, Editor
Ethical Theory and Practice

PREFACE

Three stories explain the origins of this work.

The First Story

I was raised a Roman Catholic. I attended parochial school from kindergarten through eighth grade. During my religious training—and religion was always the focus of the first session of every school day—we spent considerable time on the parables of the New Testament. This was unsurprising in light of the moral lessons contained in those stories. The transmission of moral lessons was, of course, the raison d'être of parochial school.

One day, when I was in fifth grade, we were ruminating over the Parable of the Laborers in the Vineyard. During recess, I sidled over to our teacher, a nun in the order of St. Joseph and enthusiastically offered my judgment, "Sister, I think that Jesus was wrong on this one." The nun made no effort to conceal her shock. As Jesus could never be wrong, just who was I to call his teachings into question.

A wiser student would have apologized for his impertinence, marched resolutely back to his seat, and cut his losses. Unfortunately, a ten-year-old boy with a big mouth and a curious, undisciplined mind rarely recognizes much less embraces prudent strategy. Predictably, I doubled down on what I took to be my wisdom. First, I outlined the reasons, expressed exquisitely and articulately in my judgment, why I thought that Jesus' conclusions were erroneous. Second, I accepted the nun's challenge, and provided an account of how Jesus could be wrong: given by Catholic theology that he was at once the son of God and a human being, he was susceptible to mistake when and only when his human side was in play. Thus, he could be wrong when enunciating a parable if and only if during the rendering his human fallibility clouded his typically flawless divine judgment. This, undoubtedly, must have occurred during his account of the Parable of the Laborers in the Vineyard.

You must remember that this encounter occurred in the 1950s, when the Catholic Church was even less accommodating to quasi-heretical utterances than it is today. The nun acted swiftly; she convened a meeting which was attended by the parish priest, herself, my parents, and me. This unpleasant religious intervention had only one agenda item: a host of authority figures would confront an incorrigible youth and get his mind straight.

As always, my parents privately counseled a pragmatic stance: Maybe you are on to something, but do not get kicked out of school; make whatever atonements you must and get on with your education; for goodness sake (that was not the phrase they used), do not turn stubborn on this matter. So I sat, listened, was unconvinced, but feigned contrition, and returned to the good graces of the parish. The Church was always a sucker for a sinner who had seemingly seen the light and offered repentance. But I remained unconvinced that Jesus' conclusions were right. (I now understand that one of the paramount points of the parable is its reformative aspiration: the story is not designed to reflect the conventional economic wisdom of society but to call for the transformation of dominant ideas. Thus, that I, using conventional economic wisdom, concluded that Jesus was "wrong" is unsurprising. What I missed then was Jesus' enjoinment to renounce conventional economic wisdom for a nobler standard. Even if we decide, all things considered, to reject the loftier norm, Jesus was not "wrong" for the reasons I advanced when I was ten years old.)

In any event, I always enjoyed contemplating the parables of the New Testament, whether inspired by a priest's sermon or the classroom instruction of my nuns (who throughout the remainder of my parochial school years cast suspicious glances my way whenever parables were recounted in class; word about me spread quickly).

About fifteen years later, I was enrolled as a graduate student in philosophy at the University of Miami. My chosen specializations within that field were ethics, political philosophy, and philosophy of law. At some point in my matriculation, one of my professors remarked that every philosopher that he knew who specialized in ethics had a strong religious background. Perhaps they had later strayed from organized religion or were even strident atheists, but they all shared at least one characteristic: they were exposed thoroughly to religion and its theological underpinnings throughout their formative years.

My years as a philosophy professor have only confirmed my mentor's view. I have retained my appreciation of the parables and find that when I recall them today they raise uncommonly interesting philosophical issues. Jesus challenged the conventional moral wisdom of his own time and examining now his prescriptions for the good human life interrogates the conventional moral wisdom of our time.

The Second Story

When I was an undergraduate, the work of Friedrich Nietzsche was beginning to undergo rehabilitation in the United States which was animated mainly by Walter Kaufmann's stunningly thorough scholarship of the early 1950s. Although Kaufmann viewed him as a master philosopher and psychologist, Nietzsche had been more frequently portrayed as a cultural prophet with a strikingly eccentric literary style. This dominant portrayal, however, was a step up from Nietzsche's earlier caricature as a philosopher of Nazism.

My first exposures to Nietzsche's work were typically accompanied by a host of professorial disclaimers: Nietzsche is not really a philosopher because he rarely advances arguments; his aphorisms may be stimulating but they certainly are not susceptible to critical analysis; Nietzsche is important as an historical figure, perhaps as a precursor of European existentialism, but his work is fatally flawed by pervasive self-contradictions; he embodied stylistic flair and a poetic temperament, but his writing is unrigorous and undisciplined; Nietzsche's work too often degenerates into abusive ad hominem, genetic fallacies, and self-referential paradoxes; and he too frequently provokes and irritates readers by his rhetoric excess and by his idiosyncratic subjectivism.

From the standpoint of the analytic strains of philosophy pervasive in Anglo-America during the 1950s through the 1990s, such charges were and are devastating. Nietzsche was permitted into the cherished enclaves of Anglo-America philosophy more as an amusing side show than as a full-fledged member.

Upon becoming a philosophy professor, I often taught Nietzsche in my undergraduate classes but I did so only in introductory courses, as a way of stirring the imagination of those still untutored in analytic philosophy, and as a challenge to the stultifying conformity embodied by most freshmen.

But that changed in the spring semester of 1996, when I taught an advanced undergraduate seminar on Nietzsche. Spurred on by a group of bright students and by other compulsions, I immersed myself in Nietzsche's thought, voraciously reading most of his published work and a sizeable amount of the secondary literature. The Nietzsche Seminar became part of my regular teaching rotation. I found Nietzsche unique among philosophers: he was impossible to ignore.

The Third Story

On June 24, 2011, a former student wrote the following, "You may not remember me, but I took a couple of your courses at SUNY Fredonia-*Philosophy of Sex and Love*, and the *Socrates Seminar* about 6 years ago. I am at a very transitional point in my life and career and what happens for me at these points in my life is that I begin to get nostalgic as I reflect on what has led me 'here.' I am writing you to tell you that you have influenced me. I completed my Masters in Social Work, and I am nearly done with my Masters in Marriage and Family Therapy, and as I am working with my clients, or thinking about my own happiness or fulfillment, I hear your voice in my head asking the question, 'How should I live my life?' I only minored in philosophy, but I want you to know that through these two classes, you taught me how to be a critical thinker. At my clinic, I get labeled as the therapist who 'thinks outside the box,' when really I am just being a philosopher. I am a philosopher because of my connection to you. I tell people all the time: 'I am not just a therapist. I am and will always be a Psychologist, a Social Worker, a Philosopher and a student.' Thank you so much for your inspiration."

I remembered her well. She was uncommonly bright, graced with a warm personality and a strong work ethic. Her success after graduation was due entirely to her own efforts. That six years later she would be so thoughtful as to attribute some reflected credit to me speaks more about her generosity than it does about the value of my teaching.

But she reminded me of that enduring, paramount question, "How should I live my life?" and thereby inspired the subtitle of this work. This question, along with cosmological inquiries about the nature of the world, animated Western philosophy in its earliest recorded years. Given that belief in the Greek and Roman gods failed to provide substantive guidelines for everyday living, philosophy arose in large measure as practical instruction in the art of living the good human life. Thus, the predominant Greek philosophical schools—The Academy (originally Platonic), The Peripatetics (originally Aristotelian), Stoicism, and Epicureanism—offered different definitions of the good life; diverse recipes for attaining such a life; and competing accounts of why those recipes were successful.

That Jesus and Nietzsche provide vastly different answers to the question of "How should I live my life?" is well known. By studying carefully their definitions, recipes, and accounts of what constitutes the good human life we can understand better who we are and who we might be. Moreover, by writing this book I can keep faith with my former student's conviction that we should all strive to be lifelong learners. Such is the genesis of this work.

ACKNOWLEDGMENTS

Numerous people contributed to this work directly or indirectly. As always, my family comes first. My wife, Marcia, as always, provided immeasurable emotional support and critical commentary as I undertook this project. An eighteenth-century Italian playwright, Carlo Goldoni, wrote "*Muore per meta chi lascia un' immagine di se stesso nei figi*." ("He only half dies who leaves an image of himself in his sons.") I am fortunate to have spawned and raised a son, Angelo, who extravagantly exceeds my image in every important way. I am blessed twice by having also a daughter, Vittoria, whose unwavering sense of justice, boundless capability to love, and intense family pride are prized by all who know her. As always, that this book will long outlive its author and my words will be available to torment my children when I am no longer here warms my spirit.

Thanks to Kathryn Glenwright, the former student who six years after graduation thoughtfully posted me, for granting permission to reprint her message here. Thanks also to Olli Loukola, editor of the Ethical Theory and Practice series at Rodopi, who steadfastly supported this project and was an ongoing source of sound advice and good cheer. I deeply appreciate Olli's contribution of a generous Foreword to this work. Thanks to Eric van Broekhuizen, acquisitions editor for the Value Inquiry Book Series at Rodopi, who, as always, added his expertise to the production process and who dealt patiently and considerately with an author, who was too often impatient and annoying. Finally, thanks to Joanne Foeller, the wizard of book formatting who corrected my numerous errors and prepared the final manuscript with unmatched efficiency, grace, and excellence.

The author and publisher gratefully acknowledge permission to reprint, adapt, or revise material from my book, *Stalking Nietzsche* (Westport, CT: Greenwood Press, 1998).

LIST OF ABBREVIATIONS

As is the common practice in Nietzsche and Biblical scholarship, when I have cited from Nietzsche's writings or from the canonical scripture, the references in all cases have been given immediately in the text and not in the notes. I used multiple versions of the texts. All references are to sections, not page numbers. I have used the following abbreviations:

AC	*The Anti-Christ* (1895)
BGE	*Beyond Good and Evil* (1886)
BT	*The Birth of Tragedy* (1872)
D	*The Dawn* (1881)
EH	*Ecce Homo* (1908)
GM	*On the Genealogy of Morals* (1887)
GS	*The Gay Science* (1882)
HAH	*Human, All-Too-Human* (1878)
NCW	*Nietzsche Contra Wagner* (1888)
TI	*Twilight of the Idols* (1889)
UM	*Untimely Meditations* (1873–1876)
WP	*The Will to Power* (unpublished notebooks, 1883–1888)
WS	*The Wanderer and His Shadow* (1880)
Z	*Thus Spoke Zarathustra* (1883–1885)
Matt.	The Gospel of Matthew
Mark	The Gospel of Mark
Luke	The Gospel of Luke
John	The Gospel of John

INTRODUCTION

1. Introduction

Unlike academic philosophers, religious reformers and custodians of societal traditions do not craft sophisticated deductive arguments to prove their moral conclusions. They do not seek to persuade through logical legerdemain; instead, these influential paragons tell stories. Thus, the Bible is rich with imaginative parables that press themselves upon our minds, stir our deepest emotions, and teach us moral lessons in unforgettable contexts. Likewise, Aesop's fables cascade through generations with greater social impact than any syllogism or categorical moral imperative. The power of parables and folklore arises from their accessibility, colorful cast of characters, and magical allure. Events occur in stories that transcend the natural laws of reality: animals are active moral agents, supra-human beings intervene, and miracles spring up at propitious occasions. Moreover, comedic and tragic artistic considerations often demand the inclusion of episodes that require the audience to execute astounding leaps of faith. After all, parables and folklore are exquisitely more entertaining than a painstaking, pedantic philosophical demonstration.

Friedrich Nietzsche was not a fan of academic philosophers, whom he scorned as at best "scholarly oxen" (EH, "Why I Write Such Great Books," 1) and at worst timid minions of the status quo who served as "frontier guards and spies of the sciences" (UM III.8). Nietzsche distanced himself from traditional philosophical discourse by expressing his views in aphorisms, short passages, extended parodies, and autobiography. He, too, freely uses members of the animal kingdom to illustrate critical points.

However, the colorful, evocative, seductive dimensions of such writing and speaking styles exact a price. Parables, folklore, aphorisms, and narratives are less rigorous than refined philosophical arguments: conflict, tension, and outright contradiction pervade Biblical parables, Aesop's fables, and Nietzsche's compositions when each set of moral messages is brought together as a whole. Perhaps that is their greatest lesson: the human condition resists neat, fully coherent explanations and principles that might capture the full complexity of our moral lives.

Understanding Jesus' teachings and trying to apply them to contemporary contexts require some comment on how to perceive the historical Jesus. This is no easy task. The historical Jesus has been interpreted in numerous ways. For example, Jesus has been viewed as a Jewish Cynic peasant philosopher firmly convinced that embracing material minimalism and dismissing conventional societal values were required for personal salvation;[1] as an apocalyptic prophet who was convinced that the arrival of a cosmic judge, the Son of Man, was imminent on earth and that he would render judgment, transvalue the dominant values of the world, and inaugurate the Kingdom of God;[2] as the Son of God, sent as savior to suffer and die in order to redeem all human beings;[3] as an advocate of violent revolution who aspired to liberate the Jews from Roman domination;[4] as a politically leftist social reformer who urged his followers to strive for a radically egalitarian society in which goods were distributed according to need;[5] as a proto-feminist concerned with gender equality and easing the oppression of women;[6] as an accomplished magician capable of performing extraordinary deeds;[7] and as a teacher in the Essene Jewish tradition.[8]

How a person interprets the historical Jesus affects numerous issues, including how much in the canonical Gospels can be understood as the words of Jesus and how much should be viewed as embellishments crafted by early Christians to advance their religious fervor. In any case, the parables contained in the Gospels are among the teachings attributed to Jesus that are among the most uncontroversial in this regard: under every plausible interpretation of Jesus offered by scholars, the parables are taken to be among the words most likely to have been spoken by Jesus and not concocted by well-meaning followers. Thus, the parables provide ripe fruit from which to harvest Jesus' moral message. Accordingly, I use interpretations of the parables as my main source for reconstructing Jesus' advice on how to live our lives.

Jesus invokes the "Kingdom of God" throughout his preaching. Interpreters understand the precise meaning of that phrase in accord with how they view the historical Jesus. For example, those who take the historical Jesus to be a Jewish Cynic peasant philosopher conclude that the Kingdom of God is a metaphor for the good human society, the ultimate salutary human community. Some interpreters in this camp take the phrase to be purely secular. Thus, Don Cupitt writes:

> [The Kingdom of God] is a dream of all-round freedom and dignity for the ordinary citizen . . . a dream that continues as a guiding ideal in the present and as a future hope . . . a human world in which people live without ressentiment, and are completely easy with each other . . . a world in which God has disappeared into human hearts . . . a human social world in which we are all of us in fully open communication—indeed, communion—with each other.[9]

On this view, the Kingdom of God is not intended to advance doctrinal teachings about divinity, but instead describes the better world to arrive on earth through the social transformation of putting into practice Jesus' moral message.

Others who view the historical Jesus as a Jewish Cynic peasant philosopher take a slightly different approach. They understand the Kingdom of God as an ethical condition such that human beings live in the present as if God's force and will were fully in control. John Dominic Crossan describes the present vision of the Kingdom of God thusly:

> [Wisdom is required] for discerning here and now in this world, one can so live that God's power, rule, and dominion are evidently present to all ob-

servers. One enters the kingdom by wisdom or goodness, by virtue, justice, or freedom. It is a style of life for now rather than a hope of life in the future. This is therefore an ethical kingdom . . . [Jesus] taught and acted, theorized and performed against social oppression, cultural materialism, and imperial domination.[10]

Those who understand the historical Jesus to have been an apocalyptic prophet interpret the Kingdom of God as a future eventuality where God will rule on earth as God already rules in the transcendent realm. A cosmic judge, the Son of Man, would soon arrive to render judgment and transvalue values—those enjoying power and privilege will be humbled and those who are currently oppressed and disenfranchised will be exalted—as a prelude to the establishment of the Kingdom of God on earth. In this vein, Bart Ehrman writes:

> When Jesus talks about the Kingdom [of God], he appears to refer principally to something here on earth—where God will at some point begin to rule as he already does rule up above . . . Jesus . . . evidently thought that God was going to extend his rule from the heavenly realm where he resides down here to earth. There would be a real, physical kingdom here, a paradisal world in which God himself would rule his faithful people, where there would be eating, drinking, and talking, where there would be human co-regents sitting on thrones and human denizens eating at banquets. This future kingdom stands over against the present evil kingdoms to which God's people are now subjected, kingdoms of hatred, want, and oppression. In the future kingdom, God's people will be rewarded with a utopian existence.[11]

On this approach, the Kingdom of God is neither metaphorical nor extant. Instead, its future inauguration is assured and human beings are advised to live now in ways that prefigure the ideals of the coming kingdom. That is, understanding the nature of the coming Kingdom of God allows human beings to derive proper courses of conduct today.

> In the Kingdom there would be no more war. Jesus' disciples were not to engage in acts of violence now. In the Kingdom there would be no more poverty. Jesus' disciples were to give away all they had and give to the poor now. In the kingdom there would be no more oppression or injustice. Jesus' disciples were to treat all people equally and fairly now—even the lowest classes, the outcasts, the destitute; even women and children . . . The ways Jesus' disciples were to live in the present in preparation for the coming Son of Man reflected life as it would be when the Kingdom fully arrived.[12]

Mainstream Christians who understand the historical Jesus as the Son of God sent to redeem the world from sin by the sacrifice of his life take the Kingdom of God to embody love, peace, and harmony. The Kingdom began with Jesus' death and resurrection, is expanded by human beings who live by Jesus' example and teachings, and will attain perfection when Jesus returns at the end of time. Jesus will then render Final Judgment: only those who are judged righteous will enjoy God's reign forever, while the wicked shall be punished. At Final Judgment, the forces of evil will be forever extinguished. As such, the Kingdom of God can be viewed as God's ultimate intention.

For my purposes, regardless of how one understands the historical Jesus, how one interprets the Kingdom of God, and how one views the timing of the Kingdom of God (as present in those acting according to God's will, as an inevitable future wrought by the Son of Man and God, or as beginning with the death and resurrection of Jesus and expanding through the actions of people of good will), the critical conclusion is that human beings in the present should act in accordance with the supposed values and ideals of the Kingdom. Thus, regardless of one's allegiances to the perplexing questions surrounding the true understanding of the historical Jesus, the values and ideals of the Kingdom of God that Jesus articulated should guide human action today, at least for those who accept Jesus as an exemplary moral teacher (if not more).

Although numerous early Christians, including St. Paul and the writers of the canonical Gospels, stressed that belief in Jesus (and especially in his death and resurrection) was critical for a felicitous entrance into the Kingdom of God, Jesus emphasized appropriate action to alleviate the oppression of the poor, needy, and disenfranchised. For example, "For I was an hungred, and ye gave me meat; I was thirsty, and ye gave me drink; I was a stranger, and ye took me in . . . as ye have done it unto one of the least of these my brethren, ye have done it unto me" (Matt. 25: 35, 40); "I say unto you, Inasmuch as ye did it not to one of the least of these [those in need], ye did it not to me" (Matt. 25: 45). There is an ongoing Christian debate about the relative importance of belief in the salient parts of Jesus' life and death, the performance of praiseworthy deeds for the needy, and the receipt of saving grace for entering eternal life. However, to deny that the historical Jesus highlighted the role of human compassion for and action to benefit the oppressed in attaining the Kingdom of God is difficult.

Debate also centers on the meaning of the phrase the "Son of Man" and on whether the historical Jesus actually used that expression or whether the phrase was attributed to him by early Christians as an expression of their conviction that Jesus was divine. Those who interpret Jesus as an apocalyptic prophet take the phrase to connote the cosmic agent of divine judgment who will ensure soon the total victory of the forces of good over the forces of evil presently dominating the world and who will begin the process through which the Kingdom of God will be realized. Those who interpret Jesus as a Jewish Cynic peasant philosopher take the "Son of Man" to be Jesus' way of identifying himself with his audience, as sharing their common identity as oppressed human beings. Christians who interpret Jesus as divine take the "Son of Man" as Jesus' assurance that he will return to render final judgment and inaugurate the Kingdom of God. In short, whether Jesus was referring to himself as the Son of Man in those instances where the words are attributed to him in the canonical Gospels and whether he uttered the expression at all are highly disputed issues.

In this work, I take no position on the proper way to understand the historical Jesus. Instead, I reconstruct the cornerstones of his moral teachings about how to lead a good, even exemplary, human life. I do so in a way that is compatible with the most prominent, competing versions of the historical Jesus. I also contrast Jesus' understanding of the best way to lead our lives with that of Nietzsche. Both Jesus and Nietzsche were self-consciously moral revolutionaries. Jesus refashioned the imperatives of Jewish law to conform to what he was firmly convinced was the divine will. Nietzsche aspired to transvalue the dominant values of his time—which themselves were influenced greatly by Christianity—in service of what he took to be a higher vision. The interplay of these radical versions of the good human life, seasoned with critical commentary emerging from modern findings in the sciences and humanities, opens possibilities and lines of inquiry that can inform our choices in answering that enduring, paramount question, "How should I live my life?"

2. Nietzsche's Life

Nietzsche makes his own life an issue for examination by insisting that great philosophy is autobiographical. Born in Prussia in 1844, his father was a Lutheran minister, as were both his grandfathers.[13] He was his parents' first child and was named in honor of the reigning king of Prussia. Nietzsche sometimes claimed his paternal line descended from Polish noblemen, but that is unclear. His father became mentally ill by the time Nietzsche was four years old, and died a year later. Nietzsche's childhood household consisted of his mother, sister, paternal grandmother, and two maiden aunts. Nietzsche had apparently loved his sister, Elisabeth, deeply as a child, but as an adult often found her avid German nationalism, anti-Semitism, penchant for meddling, and husband virtually impossible to bear.

Near-sighted and often plagued by migraines, Nietzsche was an excellent student. At age 20, he graduated from a renowned Protestant boarding school and then studied theology and classical philology at the University of Bonn. By 1865 he gave up theology and went to Leipzig, following his philology lecturer, Friedrich Wilhelm Ritschl. There he read Schopenhauer for the first time and was greatly impressed. One strain of philosophical gossip holds that Nietzsche contracted syphilis in Cologne while he was a student at Bonn, and untreated or improperly treated syphilis is what eventually drove him insane. Nietzsche was in military service from 1867-1868, being discharged because of an injury suffered when riding a horse.

In 1868, he first met renowned German composer and poet, Richard Wagner and his wife Cosima. For more than eight years, Nietzsche extolled Wagner as a paradigm of artistic genius, and apparently was infatuated with Cosima. In 1869, Nietzsche, upon strong recommendation of Ritschl, was appointed associate professor of classical philology at University of Basel. Soon thereafter he was awarded his doctorate by Leipzig without examination, on the basis of his published work. In 1870, he received a leave to volunteer as a medical orderly in the Franco-Prussian War. Within less than two months, he returned to Germany with dysentery and diphtheria. Another strain of philosophical gossip holds that Nietzsche contracted syphilis while ministering to ill soldiers. In any event, Nietzsche had few sexual encounters. The most that has been claimed is that as a student he may have visited a brothel once or twice. Throughout his life, he cultivated an exquisitely polite, soft-spoken, reserved manner, and suffered poor health.

In 1872, Nietzsche accompanied Wagner on the latter's 59th birthday to the laying of the foundation stone of the Bayreuth theater, a proposed cultural center. Early in April 1876, Nietzsche traveled to Geneva and spent a few days with Hugo von Senger, a conductor whom he had met in Bayreuth. At Senger's house, Nietzsche met Mathilde Trampedach. She apparently made a stunning impression on Nietzsche: he wrote her a letter on April 11th in which he proposed marriage. She swiftly declined his invitation.

In the summer of 1876, the First Bayreuth festival marked the beginnings of his estrangement from Wagner. Nietzsche sensed Bayreuth was fast becoming a center of rabid German nationalism, anti-semitism, and Christian idolatry. He left Bayreuth with Paul Ree, a friend whom he had first met in Basel in 1873. By 1878, Nietzsche received from Wagner the score of Parsifal, which Nietzsche derided. His friendship with Wagner had ended.

Nietzsche's classes attracted relatively few students, but several of them chronicled their high regard for him. By 1879, he retired from the University of Basel due to ill health. For the next ten years, he wandered and wrote, mostly in France, Switzerland and Italy. Nietzsche generally stayed in hotel rooms and modest resorts. He suffered severe migraines, painful vomiting spells, near blindness, and a variety of stomach and lung ailments throughout this period. It is said that his lodgings would contain one table for his writing and another table for the numerous medicines and potions he used to moderate the symptoms of his illnesses.

In 1882, Ree met Lou Salome in Rome and apparently fell in love with her. Nietzsche later met her and was greatly impressed. Some writers claim Nietzsche proposed marriage to Lou Salome either in person or through Paul Ree, was turned down, but eventually settled for an intellectual ménage a trois. Other writers claim Nietzsche never proposed marriage to her, although Lou was apparently waiting for him to do so. In any event, it is clear that Nietzsche was attracted to her and regarded Lou Salome as uncommonly gifted. It is also clear that the two remained chaste and by the end of 1882, Nietzsche was estranged from both Ree and Salome, partly due to the intrigues and meddling of Elisabeth.

In 1889, at age 45, Nietzsche collapsed in a street in Turin while embracing a horse that had been flogged by a coachman. Nietzsche's friend, Franz Overbeck brought him back to Basel and took him to a psychiatric clinic. Nietzsche's mother soon arrived and placed him in the Jena Psychiatric Clinic. In May 1890, Nietzsche was permitted to leave the clinic and live in Naumburg with his mother. There he was cared for by his mother and a maidservant. From early 1894, Nietzsche was unable to leave the house. His mother died in 1897. From the moment of his collapse in Turin until his death in 1900, Nietzsche was insane.

Elisabeth, after the suicide of her husband in Paraguay where they aspired to nurture a racially pure Aryan colony, returned home to find that Nietzsche's fame was spreading. She took control of Nietzsche's care during his final three years. She also acquired publishing rights to all his work. In the last three years of Nietzsche's life, Elisabeth sometimes dressed him in flowing white robes and orchestrated showings for visitors. Ironically, Nietzsche became famous only after he had gone insane. Elisabeth nurtured the Nietzsche legend, a combination of solitary visionary and saintly prophet, as a way to earn prominence in German society. She also apparently loved her brother deeply.

After Nietzsche's death, his sister continued to exploit his fame, including editing and publishing passages from Nietzsche's notebooks, and telling Hitler that he was precisely what Nietzsche had in mind when he discussed the Übermensch. Although Elisabeth claimed special insight into her brother's motivations and intentions, she lacked refined analytic and critical skills. Several unscrupulous Nazi interpreters, such as the notorious Alfred Baumler, pictured Nietzsche as an apologist for the Third Reich despite the extensive textual evidence that Nietzsche despised German nationalism, anti-Semitism, and the idolizing of the state over culture. The Nazi interpretation of Nietzsche damaged his reputation in the Anglo-American world for decades.

3. Problems of Interpretation in Nietzsche

To interpret Nietzsche is to invite a legion of problems. Nietzsche tells us that the philosophical is the personal: all great philosophy is autobiographical. Thus, the connection between Nietzsche's life and his work assumes an importance that is obscured in other philosophers. Also, there is an oxymoronic character to his writing. He enjoys talking, for example, about "false truths," "selfish altruism," "irreligious religion," "compassionate contempt," and the like. Such linguistic puzzles add interpretive difficulties.

Nietzsche uses a variety of literary styles and embraces a multiplicity of critical perspectives. Aphorisms, metaphors, calculated exaggerations, genealogical critiques, and personal invectives coalesce uneasily in his work. Both the forms and contents of Nietzsche's writing may strike novice readers as hopelessly contradictory. He cultivates this reaction by relishing self-referential paradoxes, passages where he seemingly self-consciously contradicts his earlier positions. Nietzsche tells us that multiplicity forms the core of the human spirit. Thus, according to his own conviction, there is no fixed, final way to read and interpret Nietzsche, only many plausible ways.

Writing a book which interprets Nietzsche makes it virtually impossible not to entomb his thought in a non-Nietzschean metaphysical language of explanation. An interpreter cannot make a rational system of Nietzsche's thought without falsifying Nietzsche's guiding impulse. To fulfill readers' expectations to read the "truth" about Nietzsche in unequivocal terms is to domesticate his literary style and to defeat Nietzsche's central aspirations. Readers must confront Nietzsche's work directly to experience the episodic rhythms and psychological drives that constitute his thought.

Interpreters must grapple with the relationships between Nietzsche's broad themes, his critique of mainstream philosophy, his general musings on living life, his specific background views which energize his general musings on living life, his world views which often embody warrior rhetoric, his genealogical suspicions about conventional wisdom, and his (vague) vision of the future.

By Nietzsche's "broad themes" I mean his most fundamental recurring convictions: the inescapability of inner conflict; the perspectival nature of truth; the links between psychological types of human beings and their acceptance of different truth claims; the need to perceive reality from multiple perspectives; the connection between writing and life; the inability of language to capture life's complexities and fluidity; the denial of absolutism; the need to impose order and meaning on the world of Becoming; the salutary rhythms of deconstruction, reimagination, and re-creation; the need to recognize and welcome the tragedy and contingency that constitute life; replacing the task of objectively disproving truth claims with the project of casting suspicion upon their origins and the psychology of those who embrace them; the importance of self-overcoming, which includes subjecting one's own theoretical and practical commitments to the strictest scrutiny; and the call to luxuriate in the immediacy of life. These broad themes, taken as a whole, resist unambiguous, doctrinal exposition.

There is also the problem of Nietzsche's avowed experimentalism. How much of what he says is provisional and discarded, implicitly or explicitly, later in his work? How much shows a mind in flux? To what extent is the central character in one of his major books, Zarathustra, a projection of Nietzsche's own thoughts and to what extent is Zarathustra only a literary character
meant to represent a variety of attitudes and stages of life, some decidedly un-Nietzschean? Nietzsche has a penchant for self-parody, warns us not to regard his work as the redemptive final word, and insists that the only disciples worth addressing are those who seek to surpass, not abjectly parrot, their teacher.

Finally, to what extent are Nietzsche's Nachlass, his voluminous unpublished writings, admissible as evidence of Nietzsche's philosophical convictions? By far the best-known part of the Nachlass is a volume, The Will to

Power, first edited and published by Nietzsche's sister, Elisabeth Forster-Nietzsche, in 1901. The volume contains selections from Nietzsche's notebooks of the years 1883-1888. The arrangement and numbering of selections were done by his sister, not by Nietzsche. Subsequent editions, with inclusions by various editors, were published in 1904, 1906, 1911, 1930, 1940, and 1956. Walter Kaufmann published a version of The Will to Power in 1967 with a warning: "These notes were not intended [by Nietzsche] for publication in this form . . . this book is not comparable to the works Nietzsche finished and polished, and we do him a disservice if we fudge the distinction between these hasty notes and his often gemlike aphorisms" (WP xv-xvi).

Some philosophers, such as Martin Heidegger, regard the Nachlass as the key to Nietzsche's thought. Heidegger took Nietzsche's published work to be the mask of an author who insisted on the need for disguises. The interpreters in this camp are likely to render Nietzsche more philosophically, metaphysically, systematically and doctrinally than other interpretations see him. Other philosophers, such as Bernd Magnus, distinguish sharply between Nietzsche's published work and the Nachlass. Under the commonsense assumption that unpublished thoughts scribbled into notebooks during long walks should not be regarded on a par with polished, published work, such philosophers rule material from the Nachlass inadmissible. The interpreters in this camp are likely to portray Nietzsche as an early postmodern, nonrepresentational philosopher and psychologist who paved the way for contemporary thinkers such as Derrida, Foucault, and Rorty.

4. My (Mis) Interpretation of Nietzsche

I make use of The Will to Power sparingly, using selections, I hope, only when they support passages cited from Nietzsche's published work. However, I also portray Nietzsche more philosophically and systematically than postmodernists, and perhaps Nietzsche himself, would like.

This book is in part an introduction to Nietzsche's thought with special attention to those who, having been influenced by numerous popular renderings of Nietzsche, approach his work with grave skepticism. The book is accessible to nonspecialists and does not presuppose extensive philosophical training or previous reading of Nietzsche's work. It concentrates on, and its literary style exemplifies, the connection between philosophy and living, and between the teachings of Jesus and those of Nietzsche: How can reading Nietzsche and Jesus change one's life? What links are there between accepting Nietzsche's broad philosophical themes and practical conduct? What lessons, if any, can Nietzsche teach us about the human condition?

I write from the perspective that the power of Nietzsche's thought resides in his broad themes, not in his specific pronouncements. While the indeterminacy of those themes annoys many interpreters, I find it liberating and challenging. Nietzsche's "system" is a framework of commitments and historical interpretations that counsels accelerated self-revision, robust acceptance of radical contingency, and grave suspicion of conventional wisdom.

As are all attempts to mediate Nietzsche's work for readers, mine is a (mis)interpretation. Only direct confrontation with Nietzsche's thought conveys his spirit. Still, (mis)interpretations are important because they exemplify Nietzsche's broad themes and permit communication among readers. Perhaps we can all appropriate something from Nietzsche's work for our lives, even if we cannot—as Nietzsche said we could not—freeze his ideas into doctrines, stable theories, and truths.

When I immersed myself in Nietzsche's writings, I found, just as I did with Jesus' words, that I could not treat him the way I treat so many philosophers, as academic signposts in the history of ideas. Nietzsche, like Jesus, challenges the way we live and forces us to interrogate the person we are becoming. Certainly other philosophers ask the same questions that Nietzsche and Jesus do, but most can still be treated in the established academic fashion: at a distance, with detachment, safely confined within the university classroom. Nietzsche and Jesus, by contrast, follow me home. Nietzsche screams and preens, he prods and irritates, he breaks all the rules of academia and laughs about it, and then he laughs at himself. Jesus reminds us of a nobler vision of community, a way of life that elevates the need to cultivate our souls and minimize our zeal for false, material comfort. Neither Nietzsche nor Jesus will be ignored. They both refuse anonymity and vigorously resist marginalization.

In Chapter One, I outline and critically assess Jesus' moral message on proper family relations, associating and identifying with undesirables, unsettling established rituals, interrogating prevailing norms of just distribution, material minimalism, and the concept of forgiveness. Although Jesus was uninterested in deriving moral conclusions mechanically and formalistically from general normative principles, his moral message resonates with three recurrent themes: extending unconditional love to everyone, including strangers and those perceived as enemies; nurturing an almost default mindset of forgiveness and mercy toward the shortcomings and transgressions of others; and providing aid to those in need regardless of their tribe, religion, ethnicity, or level of antecedent righteousness.

Along the way, I introduce the individual-community continuum. An existential tension is at the heart of human experience: our yearning for intimate connection with others and the recognition that others are necessary for our identity and freedom coalesces uneasily with the fear and anxiety we experience as others approach. If we experience too much individuality we risk alienation, estrangement, and psychological isolation. If we experience insufficient individuality we court emotional suffocation, loss of self-esteem, and unhealthy immersion in the collectivity. This disharmony may never be fully reconciled once and forever, and so we find ourselves making uneasy compromises and adjustments during our life's journey as we oscillate along the continuum whose endpoints are 'radical individuality' and 'thorough immersion in community,' respectively. Jesus champions the community side of the continuum, while Nietzsche prizes the individual side.

In Chapter Two, I explain and critically assess Nietzsche's major philosophical themes: the nature and implications of perspectivism; his use of genealogical critiques; his obsession with creating a worthy self; his understanding of value; his proclamation that god was dead; his interpretation of the master and slave moralities; his efforts to go beyond conventional notions of good and evil; his doctrine of eternal recurrence; his linkage of philosophy to psychology; his convictions regarding philosophical style and rhetoric; and his tragic view of life. Nietzsche, too, was uninterested in deriving moral conclusions mechanically and formalistically from general normative principles, but his normative message echoes three recurrent themes: the need for people of potential greatness to distance themselves from dominant, conventional understandings; the connection between different types of human beings and the convictions they embrace; and the importance of the process of self-realization, captured by the metamorphoses of construction-deconstruction-reimagination-re-creation, in a radically contingent world.

In Chapter Three, I more carefully examine Jesus' understanding of the power of unconditional love. In so doing, I confront the paradoxes of agapic love in the contexts of divine and parental affection. I then unravel Nietzsche's notion of the will to power and how it relates to two images of human beings: the exemplary dispositions of the overman and the banal aspirations of the last man. Also, I state, explain, and critically examine Nietzsche's interpretation of the life and character of Jesus and St. Paul. Finally, I discuss Jesus' description of the best way to engage the world and outline the most demanding features of the respective normative ideals of Jesus and Nietzsche.

In Chapter Four, I thoroughly confront Jesus' perfectionist ethic. I first connect his perfectionist ideal with his invocation of unconditional love; then I examine and reject the possibility that Jesus' notion of love is hopelessly abstract; and I summarize the foundational themes of Jesus' perfectionism. After alluding to the difficulties attending Jesus' perfectionism, I introduce the work of contemporary moral philosophers, Peter Singer and James Rachels. Singer's work is relevant to the issue of how much we owe to those in dire need, while Rachels addresses the topic of how impartial we should be when allotting our resources, time, energies, and affections to other people. Finally, I argue that even if we conclude that Jesus' moral message can be implemented only by heroes, martyrs, and saints, we can nevertheless incorporate portions of his teachings to improve our own lives.

In Chapter Five, I examine carefully Nietzsche's aristocratic vision, his idea that the justification of the human species lies in its highest exemplars, and his principle of nobility. I explain why Nietzsche adopts an averaging approach to perfectionism and detail the difficulties such a method confronts. I point out the most repugnant features of Nietzsche's perfectionism and introduce the work of contemporary philosophers Roberto Unger and Robert Nozick as points of departure to sketch a refashioned image of Nietzsche's grand striver. Finally, I sketch the beginnings of reconciliation between the moral message of Jesus and Nietzsche's normative conclusions.

This book is an attempt to tell different sides of Nietzsche's and Jesus' stories, without a happy ending, indeed, with no final solution, but only a trajectory toward a synthesis of the respective strengths in their teachings. My hope is that Jesus and Nietzsche will follow you home, too.

One

JESUS: THE NATURE OF OUR WORLD AND OUR MISSION IN IT

Jesus' moral message was radical in several respects, among which were his views on the importance of close family relations; associating and identifying with social undesirables; unsettling established rituals; interrogating prevailing notions of just distribution; embracing material minimalism; and the importance of forgiveness.

1. Family Relations

In the Mediterranean world during Jesus' time, the family was firmly entrenched as the fundamental social unit. Jesus apparently had as many as four brothers and more than one sister (Matt. 13: 55-56; Mark 6: 3).[1] Yet Jesus often distances himself from family affiliations in deference to wider community membership. For example, when informed that his mother and brothers have arrived, Jesus replies that those who comply with God's will are his brothers and mother (Mark 3: 31-35). When a woman in a crowd proclaims how fortunate his mother was to have born and raised him, Jesus responds that "rather blessed are they that hear the word of God, and keep it" (Luke 11: 27-28). Jesus informs a multitude of people that he has not come to confer peace on earth, but division among families: "The father shall be divided against the son, and the son against the father, and the daughter against the mother; the mother-in-law against her daughter-in-law, and the daughter-in-law against her mother-in-law" (Luke 12: 51-53; Matt. 10: 35). He instructs followers that they must "hate" (probably meaning "abandon") their families and their own lives in order to be genuine disciples (Luke 14: 26-27; Matt. 10: 37). Moreover, scripture alleges that Jesus' own family did not fully believe in what Jesus was doing and were even offended by him: "A prophet is not without honor, but in his own country, and among his own kin, and in his own house" (Mark 6: 3-4; Matt. 13: 55-57).

Several explanations for Jesus' repudiation of established family values are available. First, Jesus may be underscoring his conviction that nothing, not even the supposed fundamental social unit of the family, is more important than proper worship of God and compliance with God's will. If allegiance to family takes on the role of idolatry, it, too, is an obstacle to salvation. Second, a corollary of that conviction is Jesus' commitment to opening the boundaries of community. The Parable of the Good Samaritan (Luke 10: 25-37) instructs us that our "neighbors" are not simply those who share our religion, ethnicity, race, and tribe. So too, our family is not restricted merely to parents, siblings, and blood relatives. All "those who comply with God's will" are our siblings, parents, and relatives. The community of God is accessible in principle to everyone. Thus, everyone in principle is our kin. Third, abandoning one's family may entail more than merely leaving one's home. It may mean that we discard conventional notions of hierarchy, authority, and deference in order to more closely emulate the salutary relationships embodied in the Kingdom of God. As the family is the initial locus of socialization, it is most likely to reflect the dominant societal ideas that Jesus aims to unsettle. As such, tight allegiance to the established family ethos promotes parochialism and conformity, both of which are antithetical to Jesus' revolutionary moral message.

Fourth, some commentators argue that the key to understanding Jesus' attack on family values is the passage in which Jesus declares his intent to divide families. The passage is often misread to mean that some family members will believe in Jesus' message, while others will not, and the resulting division will be ideological. But John Dominic Crossan points out that all the divisions mentioned are generational (older fathers, mothers, and mothers-in-law to younger sons, daughters, and daughters-in-law, respectively). He concludes that Jesus' repudiation of the traditional family is an effort to dislodge entrenched relationships of power: "The attack is on the Mediterranean family's axis of power, which sets father and mother over son, daughter, and daughter-in-law . . . The family is society in miniature . . . It is not just a center of domestic serenity; since it involves power, it invites the abuse of power and it is at that precise point that Jesus attacks it.[2]

Of course, the unsettling of established power relations as such cannot be the genuine goal of Jesus' efforts. Instead, it is better viewed as a means or instrument through which either wider social transformation becomes possible or greater access to the Kingdom of God blossoms for more people. Viewed in this light, established power relations are an obstacle to Jesus' revolutionary moral message and must be dissolved in order for that message to resonate with more people.

Fifth, those who interpret Jesus as an apocalyptic prophet deny that wider social transformation was his goal. Rather, they argue that Jesus' view of the family was predicated, as always, on his immediate concern: that people prepare for the imminent arrival of the Kingdom of God.[3] On this view, Jesus' motivation for repudiating established family values (and much else) was purely expedient: nurturing family relations was a trivial pursuit given the impending apocalypse. Because the Son of Man would soon arrive and elevate the impoverished, meek, and oppressed, while deflating the wealthy and hitherto powerful, tending to long-range concerns such as family, occupation, and material accumulation was pointless. Now was the time to prepare spiritually for the coming age.

Still, in my judgment, those who are convinced that Jesus was "only" an apocalyptic prophet must concede that the way to prepare spiritually for the coming age was to prefigure the values and ideals of the Kingdom of God now. Regardless of whether the arrival of that Kingdom is imminent or sometime in the unknown future, those of good will should model their behavior on the appropriate values and ideals as soon as these are revealed. Thus, we have no reason to think that Jesus' moral message, particularly his views on proper family relations, would be different had he believed that the arrival date of the Kingdom of God was unknown or in the distant future. That is, I am not persuaded that the content of Jesus' moral message was driven by his alleged conviction that the Kingdom of God was imminent. Are we to believe that if Jesus was convinced that the arrival of the Kingdom of God was in the distant future that he would have counseled those of faith to adhere closely to traditional family values, to nurture assiduously their retirement pensions, to accumulate fervently wealth, and to pursue excitedly their secular careers? I do not think so. Whether the historical Jesus was only an apocalyptic prophet, a Jewish Cynic peasant philosopher, or the Son of God as understood by mainstream Christians, he would have extolled the values and ideals of the Kingdom of God and urged disciples to embrace and exemplify those values and ideals enthusiastically and immediately.

From a contemporary standpoint, we can advance a strong defense of traditional family values.[4] Conventional morality permits us to advance the interests of family over those of a stranger when we cannot fulfill the interests of everyone. As always, Jesus' contrary conclusion is grounded in his ethic of unconditional love and uttered from the moral standpoint of an Ideal, Impartial Observer, namely God. But human beings firmly seated in this world cannot easily ascend to such an Archimedean point. We are concrete individuals with specific biologies and biographies that largely constitute our identities; we are often grateful for and aspire to reciprocate past benefits that others have bestowed upon us; we develop personal relationships that facilitate our self-realization; we love a few other people in ways that cannot be extended to all human beings indiscriminately; and we understand well that but for the efforts of family we might well not even exist.

Families, cultural traditions, and national heritages are valuable because of their role in constituting personal identity. Human beings are also valuable but vulnerable: without social attachments and connections, of which some arise nonvoluntarily, we would all stand alone, naked before a terrifying and seemingly all-powerful universe. Not to belong to a nation, tribe, or parents—to be stripped of our metaphysical constituents—is to be nobody. We all draw strength from and are constituted by our inherited legacy and to be uprooted, to belong to no place, is the great tragedy of displaced persons, refugees, and aliens. Such people suffer grave and frightening identity crises because they have lost some of their most valuable characteristics, those pertaining to membership and belonging. Thus our inherited legacy helps fulfill necessary psychological functions. A large measure of our inherited biological and biographical legacy often involves our families.

The self is given in and through a social context, and is not a fixed and complete entity at a certain specified time. We enter the world already laden with history, traditions, prejudices, and community structures. Others make us who we are; we share and participate in a common identity and tradition which comprises one segment of the human heritage. Our concrete context of community memberships, cultural heritage, historical circumstances, core aspirations, attachments, and commitments are not always possessions or attributes we choose; instead, they partly constitute who we are. Their moral force results from the recognition that they are indispensable in forging the particular people that we are and in constituting the particular value we embody. At their best, certain interpersonal relations are characterized by intimate feelings—love, deep mutual affection, recognition that the interests of family members are part of my good as we experience forming subjectivities wider than ourselves.

We are also typically better placed to advance the interest of family members than we are to nurture the interests of strangers. To say that a moral agent is in a favored position to preserve and maintain value might suggest criteria relevant to resources such as wealth, or the possession of special skills and abilities, or situational advantages such as geographical proximity or being privy to certain information not accessible to everyone. But the more fundamental criterion here is one's metaphysical constitution. The values of a certain inherited legacy *are* "me" and as the repository of such values I am better placed than others to understand and preserve them simply by being who I am. In my view, one bears a special responsibility to the particular segment of the shared human heritage that one embodies and thus is in a position to cherish.

Our noninherited attachments, commitments, and properties are also important constituents of self. If others contribute to our personal identities intentionally, positively, and significantly—if they extend themselves in uncommon ways to us—then we are permitted to advance their interests over strangers in conflict situations. One ground for these moral requirements is a contractualist appeal to reciprocity; another arises from acknowledging the value of individuals. We all embody value—regardless of whether we are precisely who we would like to be, who we might have been, and in some cases regardless of the presence or absence of affection toward those who have contributed to our identities. We owe more to those who intentionally, voluntarily, and knowingly (and often at considerable sacrifice) made beneficial contributions to the person that we are and the value we thereby embody, as a demand of justice—returning value for value. Thus, our metaphysical constitution and our embodiment of certain value have moral implications in concert with generally accepted liberal principles of justice.

Our familial and other relationships are the core of life and morality. They provide the context for our deepest convictions, values, and normative moorings. The more radical and implausible versions of impartialism secure their universal prescriptions by plundering individuals of their distinctive metaphysical constituents and they thereby impoverish our concept of personhood. Charges along these lines could be issued by the apostles of conventional morality against the unconditional love ethic of Jesus.

I must not, however, overly sentimentalize the tribalism of Mediterranean families prevalent during Jesus' life. Families then (and now) form bulwarks against the excesses of oppressive governments, hostile circumstances, and unreliable social relations. But they also reinforce to some degree the very estrangement from wider community from which their tribal ethic arose. Families both contribute to and mediate wider social injustice. The moral irony of family tribalism—its simultaneous promotion in the family and repression on other social levels of the cardinal virtues—is accompanied by a psychological irony: on the one hand such family codes provide spiritual sustenance and the foundations of personal identity in an otherwise hostile world, while on the other hand the code facilitates lingering dependencies and helps ensure that the outside world will remain hostile.

In Jesus' view, softening family bonds was an important part of his general program of extending unconditional love, practicing impartial benevolence, and prefiguring the values of the impending Kingdom of God. Those who are skeptical of the possibility of loving strangers and enemies unconditionally, those who are convinced that impartial benevolence is untrue to the reality of our duties within concrete personal relationships, and those who doubt that the Kingdom of God will ever arrive will be unconvinced by Jesus' prescriptions.

While I have emphasized the value of robust family relations, Jesus insists that these sentiments must be tempered by awareness that the family requires numerous myths, taboos, and tribal conventions that sometimes cultivate psychological distortions and impede full spiritual development. Accordingly, in Jesus' view, human beings must distance themselves from their families, at distinct times and often to extreme degrees, to actualize fully their potentials. Typically, Jesus' moral message will not be hostage to conventional understandings. His revolutionary view of the role of the family in attaining personal salvation resists my philosophical labors in defense of family values.

2. Associating and Identifying with Undesirables

Tax collectors exacted tribute from the Galilean population to be forwarded to Rome as payment for maintenance and security. Many were undoubtedly dishonest, charging excessive amounts from which they skimmed for their own benefit. All were in service of an imperialistic overseer, Rome, that had assumed dominion over land that God had presumably bequeathed to the Jews. As such, tax collectors, taken collectively, were not perceived as righteous. Yet Jesus consorted with them easily (Mark 2: 15-16; Luke 19: 1-10; Matt. 11: 19). So, too, Jesus associated with other people stigmatized as undesirables such as demoniacs (Mark 5: 1-20), lepers (Mark 1: 40-42; Luke 17: 12-19), Samaritans

(Luke 17: 12-16; John 4: 4-40), and prostitutes (Luke 7: 36-48; Matt. 21: 31). Anticipating the ideals and values embodied by the Kingdom of God, wherein the haughty would be humbled and the oppressed would be exalted, Jesus ministered to those spurned as undesirables who both required and could benefit from his instruction the most.

In that vein, Jesus laments that John the Baptist was derided as demonic or demented for appearing on the scene austerely, neither drinking wine nor eating bread. But Jesus appears eating and drinking and he is criticized as a glutton, a drunk, and a crony of tax collectors and sinners: "You say, Behold a glutton and a drunkard, a friend of tax collectors and sinners" (Luke 7: 34; Matt. 11: 19). In part, this was a reaction to another aspect of Jesus' ministry: his proclivity for and encouragement of eating and socializing with people without regard for existing social distinctions (Matt. 22: 1-13; Luke 14: 15-24). Prefiguring an egalitarian ideal of the Kingdom of God, Jesus refused to comply with the Jewish tradition of reflecting social hierarchy and division while eating: the recognized rules and customs of dining were microcosms of the more general regulations of association and socialization. Jesus softens the Jewish tradition in this regard by advocating "an open commensality, an eating together without using table as a miniature map of society's vertical discriminations and lateral separations . . . Jesus lived out his own parable, [and] the almost predictable counteraccusation to such open commensality would be immediate: Jesus is a glutton, a drunkard, and a friend of tax collectors and sinners. He makes, in other words, no appropriate distinctions and discriminations.[5]

The radical egalitarianism of Jesus' theory and practice with regard to commensality, material possessions, and class structures threaten established social hierarchies and divisions that are so common that they are typically viewed as necessary to orderly social life. Imprisoned in what Jesus would take to be a false necessity, citizens too often conclude that the familiar is the inevitable. As such, they unwittingly collaborate in further entrenching the social forces that ensure their oppression. Jesus' invocation of love insisted that such distinctions are impediments to anticipating the ideals of the Kingdom of God. A precondition of opening our hearts to genuine love and loving is to break through false necessity and see social hierarchies for what they are: artificial barriers to creating robustly meaningful human relationships. As always, for Jesus, transforming our hearts and souls supersedes formalist renderings of traditional law and conventional social understandings of appropriate conduct: a new kind of human being is required in the Kingdom of God.

Jesus' proclamations about the transvaluation of values in the Kingdom of God, particularly the exaltation of the downtrodden and the humbling of the powerful, were not received warmly by the established community leaders. Moreover, Jesus' invocation to bestow unconditional love upon everyone (especially to those antecedently scorned as enemies) and forgiveness of all debts and transgressions (sometimes even in the absence of the perpetrator's repentance) threatened the foundations of society. Would not indiscriminant forgiveness condone past and encourage future wrongdoing? Would not unconditional love embolden enemies to amplify their malevolent schemes? Would not wholesale waiving of debts undermine the justice of restitution and retribution?

Jesus may have been swayed by his conviction that moral accounts would be squared during Final Judgment. Instead of despising one's enemies now and responding to their malevolence in kind, we are better served by anticipating the ideals of the Kingdom of God, which require that we tend to the condition of our own hearts and souls, and strive to encourage our enemies to act likewise. Should our enemies rebuke our efforts, we would still retain our internal harmony while they will presumably meet cosmic justice during Final Judgment. In any case, we would not have committed the most serious moral error—collaborating with or participating in evil that harms our soul. Moreover, by exemplifying the ideals of the Kingdom of God now we maximize our prospects for a felicitous judgment from the Son of Man in the future: to forgive others their trespasses now heightens the probability that our moral shortcomings will be forgiven later.

Jesus' moral message is stunning and undeniable. Beware of society's proclivity for labeling those who do not neatly fit established categories as "undesirables." Such people need our concern and care more than those who have been warmly embraced by the wider community. Moreover, the "undesirables" may have been wrongly defined by only certain aspects of their being. In any case, they retain their humanity from which a legitimate call upon our allegiance arises.

3. Unsettling Established Rituals

As attested to by the Parable of the Good Samaritan, Jesus was willing to stray from the established Jewish purity rituals of his time. For example, the Pharisees and most other Jews always washed their hands prior to eating, as well as cups, containers, and cookware. This was not in deference to sanitation concerns, but to established traditions that stressed purity and cleanliness as critical for proper worship of God. Upon observing that Jesus and his disciples did not comply with the purity ritual, the Pharisees took Jesus to task (Mark 7: 1-5). Jesus' response, in effect, is that what is more important than observing the purity rituals is how a person speaks, acts, and chooses: "There is nothing outside a man which by going into him can defile him; but the things which come out of a man are what defile him" (Mark 7: 15; Matt. 15: 11); "Woe to you, scribes and Pharisees, hypocrites! For you cleanse the outside of the cup and of the plate, but inside are full of extortion and rapacity. You blind Pharisee! first cleanse the inside of the cup and plate, that the outside also may be clean" (Matt. 23: 25-26: Luke 11: 39-40). In sum, Jesus accuses the Pharisees, as usual, of not seeing the forest for the trees: they miss the big picture of what compliance with God's law entails because they are preoccupied with the minutiae of formalist renderings of traditions and conventions.

This instruction is reinforced in the Parable of the Good Samaritan where the story's hero is an unclean Samaritan and the less noble figures are the priest and Levite who are overly scrupulous about observing the purity traditions. By refusing to act compassionately, the priest and Levite reveal that their internal condition does not match their external cleanliness; whereas the Samaritan, by acting compassionately, demonstrates that his heart and soul glisten even if he is judged by conventional Jewish standards to be externally contaminated.

Unlike the Pharisees, Jesus did not believe that fastidious compliance to formalist renderings of the laws of Torah was paramount to earning salvation in the Kingdom of God. Unlike the Sadducees, Jesus did not believe that scrupulous adherence to the rituals of worship and sacrifice in the Temple of Jerusalem was most important. Although Jesus may well have shared some of the Essenes' apocalyptic views and conviction that the Jews of the age had morally degenerated, he was not concerned with forming isolated communities focused primarily on maintaining their own purity. His rejection of the Sadducees, aristocratic leaders of the Temple, and his prophecy that God would soon destroy the Temple and transvalue existing values in the Kingdom of God—including humbling the self-righteous leaders of the Jewish sects—along with the threat Roman authorities perceived when he failed to deny that he was King of the Jews, undoubtedly led to his crucifixion by the Romans.

Underscoring his concern with inner motives and intentions, Jesus implicitly appeals to the philosophical distinction between reality and appearance. A soul that seems pure and righteous may in fact be narrow and ungenerous. Those who obsess over following rule-book understandings of law and tradition may be insufficiently caring. As always, the crucial barometers of our inner merit are our willingness to bestow unconditional love, our efforts to extend ourselves in service of those in need, and our indifference to the false glitter of the surrounding world.

4. Interrogating Prevailing Norms of Just Distribution

That Jesus distanced himself from conventional understandings of justice defined by the principles of desert and retribution is clear. In the Parables of the Prodigal Son (Luke 15: 11-32) and the Laborers in the Vineyard (Matt. 20: 1-16), the mean-spiritedness, jealousy, and envy of the older son and the first hired, respectively, are highlighted and repudiated. To assume that the undeserved good fortune of others amounts to an injustice to yourself is wildly misguided, especially when you have received all to which you were entitled. Jesus teaches that in order to nurture our hearts and souls properly we must go beyond strict adherence to justice as defined by the principles of desert and retribution.

To understand the principle of personal desert we should begin with a few general principles:[6]

- If people deserve something they do so on the basis of some prior performance or by virtue of some possessed characteristic.
- If someone deserves something then that is a good reason for giving that something to him or her but not always a sufficient or conclusive reason.
- The nature of the something to be distributed—whether it is a prize, reward, blame, punishment, praise, or the like—will determine, at least partially, the nature of the basis that warrants the person's claim of deserving that something.

Typically, for someone to claim to deserve something he or she must point to some prior performance that might warrant the claim: The person must have done something in the past. We deserve something in virtue of prior acts for which we are responsible. In some cases, though, we may justifiably claim to deserve something based on our possession of a relevant characteristic and not on a prior performance.[7] For example, I deserve equal consideration of certain of my interests, along with those of other human beings, based only on my possession of humanness. However, a person who lacks both a relevant past performance and a relevant characteristic has no legitimate claim based on desert. For example, we cannot justifiably claim that we deserve to win the New York State Lottery or that we deserve our natural talents. In the case of the lottery, merely purchasing a ticket and wishing on our lucky stars that we might win are past performances that are not enough to support a justified claim of desert. In the case of natural talents, we possess them due only to the genetic lottery; we did nothing, we were nothing, prior to our birth.

Claims of desert are typically, although not always, connected to the results of voluntary actions over which we have major control. The notion of desert is often invoked to treat human beings appropriately given that they are responsible for their actions. Having no control over the amount and type of natural talents we possess or over who wins the New York State Lottery, we can assert no credible claim of desert in either case. If a person deserves something that provides a reason, but not always a conclusive consideration, why she ought to receive it.

Claims of desert must be distinguished from claims of entitlement, another principle of justice. Consider the following example: The Buffalo Bills play the Miami Dolphins for the right to enter the Super Bowl. The Bills prove conclusively that they are the better team and also that they exerted the most effort on this particular Sunday. However, because of a stunning series of lucky breaks, fortuitous decisions by the game officials, and cooperation of the weather, the Dolphins win the contest, 21–20. To claim that the Bills *deserved* to win—Should not the better team that tries harder be declared the more deserving?—is reasonable. But even if the Bills are unanimously deemed the more deserving team, they are neither *entitled* to play in the Super Bowl nor do they have a *right* to play in the Super Bowl. The Dolphins, the less deserving squad, are entitled and have a right to compete in the Super Bowl. By the same token, the winner of the New State Lottery did not deserve to win, but is entitled to the prize.

- Someone is *entitled* to a prize if and only if he or she has fulfilled the qualifying conditions specified by the rules determining who receives that prize.
- Someone *deserves* to win a prize if and only if he or she demonstrated to a higher degree than all other competitors the skill and effort set forth as the basis of the competition.

Accordingly, one may be entitled to something but not deserve it, and one may deserve something but not be entitled to it. For example, children may work steadfastly to support their elderly, disabled parents and observers may well conclude that the children deserve a reward for their effort, commitment, and contribution, but there may simply not be a reward for which they qualify and thus none to which they are entitled. Having been legally designated in a will, Jones may be entitled to a huge inheritance that observers might accurately conclude Jones does not deserve based on their examination of Jones's life. Desert and entitlement, then, are two distinct claims of justice that sometimes conflict when others determine what one *ought* to receive as his or her just due.

- If someone deserves something it does not follow that he or she has a right to that something.
- If someone is entitled to something then he or she has a right to that something.

Again, a person may deserve something although not be able to lodge a justified claim to it either because there is no prize or award to be claimed or, even if there is such a prize or award, because he or she has not fulfilled the qualifying conditions to receive it. Entitlement is a consideration of justice that applies only to things that people desire or ought to desire. In contrast, desert is a consideration of justice that sometimes applies—in the cases of punishment and blame—to things that people typically do not desire. In that vein, to claim that someone has a right to praise or reward is compelling under the appropriate circumstances, but to claim that someone has a right to blame or punishment is peculiar. Accordingly, the notion of rights is tightly connected to the concept of entitlement, but not to the concept of desert. In that vein, the notion of personal desert is mainly or entirely pre-institutional; it is a natural moral notion that is not conceptually tied to political institutions, social structures, and legal rules. The notion of entitlement is mainly or entirely institutional; it is an institutional notion that is logically linked to political institutions, social structures, and legal rules.

This distinction, though, is far from iron-clad. Several desert claims do presuppose a sociopolitical context because of the nature of the treatment or object at stake. For example, to say that Mary deserves a Pulitzer Prize, Vito deserves the Medal of Honor, and John deserves a long stretch in prison are all legitimate assertions under the appropriate circumstances, and they all presuppose the existence of different social, military, and legal institutions. Still, claims of desert, unlike those of entitlement, do not arise merely by fulfilling the conditions specified in an institutional system of political or legal rules. Mary, Vito, and John may have satisfied the conditions laid down for their respective treatments, but doing so is not the basis of their desert claims. That there are such things as the Pulitzer Prize, the Medal of Honor, and imprisonment is a function of institutional arrangements. But desert claims, unlike entitlement claims, related to these awards and treatments must be grounded on bases other than satisfying the qualifying conditions specified for them. The basis of desert, then, remains certain qualities that Mary, Vito, and John embodied and how those qualities animated their respective actions.

Numerous bases have been offered in support of claims of desert. For example, a person may lodge a claim of desert based on moral worth; on success in contributing to society; on general productivity; on effort expended in seeking to contribute to society or to general productivity; or on the possession of relevant characteristics. Of course, these considerations do not always coalesce easily. Who deserves the prize—the person who made the most effort or the person who demonstrated the most skill and produced more? The nature of the object at stake and a series of value judgments will typically determine the appropriate basis of the desert claim. For example, if a scarce medical resource can be administered to only one of two equally needy patients, one of the possible recipients might be more deserving of the resource based on her superior contributions to society. Of course, that she ought, all things considered, to receive the resource based only on the fact that she is more deserving is another matter. In other contexts, claims of desert based on greater societal productivity are irrelevant. For example, a renowned, stunningly productive citizen is not allowed to vote more times in a national election than an ordinary person.

Controversy swirls around the question whether need is a legitimate basis for desert claims. We might see need as the type of personal characteristic that grounds desert claims to, say, medical treatment or allocation of food.

But need is less a personal characteristic and more a (hopefully) temporary condition or situation. A person is needy not because of his or her inherent personal attributes but because of a series of describable choices, causes, and events. In fact, we are all antecedently needy until our biological, psychological, and material desires are satisfied to one degree or another. But what of a person whose needs flow from an extraordinary run of misfortune, none of which is due to her misdeeds or shortcomings? To conclude that she deserves a break or some good fortune is not misplaced. We would be assuming that nonculpable people should not be subject to a disproportionate amount of bad luck. We hope that luck would finally even out or at least occasionally smile on those it had unduly assaulted. Such a desert claim would underscore the disparity between a person's blameless performance and massive misfortune. Having not deserved relentless battering from lady luck, the person now deserves a squaring of accounts. Of course, such a claim appears platitudinous. Having no control over the whims of fortune, we are casting only a hope into the wind.

Suppose you had one delicious slice of pizza to bestow and two possible recipients. Both were strangers who were equal in all respects—contributions, effort, productivity, and the like. However, one had been the constant victim of bad luck, while the other was unremarkable in that regard. Would you conclude that the nonculpable victim deserved the food more than the other person and you now had a chance to reverse the cycle of misfortune, at least to a small extent? Although the two possible recipients are equally needy in terms of food, they are unequally needy in terms of reversing past outrageous fortune. Neither is entitled nor do they have a right to the slice, but a review of past circumstances might well impel you to decide in favor of the unfortunate pilgrim. Still, the case is not clear cut. If the two famished people are equal in respect to contributions, effort, and productivity, then more credit might be given to the person who battled through more adverse circumstances; perhaps effort is not equal after all. Or perhaps the more unfortunate of the two was blessed with greater (undeserved) innate talents that permitted her to equal the production of her more fortunate but less naturally gifted colleague. If so, attributions of desert are more ambiguous. In any event, appeals to need are better severed from appeals to desert. The two types of appeals often constitute conflicting claims to just distribution of social goods. However, innocent suffering and bad luck can affect a person's desert claims in indirect ways.

The mere possession of desirable character traits flowing from the genetic lottery such as high intelligence, willingness to work, physical strength, natural wit, and the like do not produce genuine desert claims. Lacking the animation provided by effort, such desirable characteristics produce little or nothing. Possessing desirable characteristics as innate gifts is one thing, but exercising those characteristics is quite another. Thus, even if *willingness* to work is a character trait that a person embodies because of the luck of the genetic lottery, *actual* work and effort may still underwrite a genuine claim of desert. Manifesting and exercising desirable character traits requires concentrated effort that vivifies legitimate desert claims. To treat people as they deserve is to respond to them as autonomous, free beings responsible for their actions. Doing so also heightens our understanding that by crafting our actions in certain ways, we can strongly influence how others will respond to us. When others treat us as we deserve they are responding to us according to our deeds, commensurately to what we have earned.

Of course, even if a person does not deserve something it does not follow that he ought not to receive it or even that he is not entitled to it; it follows only that the notion of desert cannot provide him with any claim to it. While a person may well deserve certain things, it is typically impossible to calculate what she genuinely deserves and this epistemological problem often renders the notion of desert a feckless practical guide to the distribution of social goods. To calculate what accomplishments, exertions of effort, notable deeds, and the like flow from characteristics that a person deserves or has earned and what arises from undeserved initial social position and innate talents is virtually impossible.

Aristotle observed that "Friendship unites the state. When men are friends, there is no need of justice, but when even if men are just, friendship is still necessary. Friendship is not just necessary, but also noble."[8] Expand "friendship" to "love" and Aristotle's sentiments resound throughout the teachings of Jesus. To love our neighbor unconditionally requires that we go beyond appealing to justice, as defined by the principles of desert and retribution, when allocating goods and when responding to wrongdoing. Jesus points out that loving someone who loves you and benefiting someone who has aided you are not major accomplishments (Matt. 5: 44, 46-47; Luke 6: 27, 32-33). Instead, we should reflect God's willingness to be generous to the ungrateful and the wicked (Matt 5: 45; Luke 6: 35). In sum, lavishing unconditional love upon our neighbors requires an abundance of understanding, compassion and affection that exceeds the imperatives of justice as defined by the principles of desert and retribution. Our typical notions of justice spawn resentment, competition, and invidious comparison. Moreover, as Aristotle intuited, our notions of justice are insufficient for robust human community. Where there is friendship (and unconditional love of neighbors) justice may be superfluous.

In the Parable of the Laborers in the Vineyard (Matt. 20: 1-16), the group of workers first hired and the owner of the vineyard had agreed orally to a standard contract of that time and place. Those first hired would labor for 12 hours and receive a denarius for their service. The other sets of workers, agreed to work 9, 6, 3 hours and 1 hour, respectively, for "whatever is right." The terms of payment were vague, but the various sets of workers either trusted the vineyard owner to be fair or they simply had no alternative or both. We must conclude that they assumed that their wages would be proportionate to the hours they worked. Certainly, none of these workers could have reasonably expected to receive a full-day's wage, the amount the vineyard owner doled out to them at the end of the day.

From a contemporary standpoint, the workers first hired and the vineyard owner were exercising their *freedom of contract*: they had agreed voluntarily to a wage-labor exchange. Freedom of contract presumably honors and encourages the exercise of individual liberty and autonomy, thereby recognizing the inherent dignity and worth of the bargainers; facilitates efficient allocation of resources, as market forces, particularly the supply of workers and the demand for labor, determines wage-labor exchanges; and thereby promotes economic growth.

But the principle of freedom of contract is not absolute. Numerous voluntary agreements will not be enforced by modern courts.[9] For example, contracts to perform illegal acts, such as embezzlement or prostitution, under state or federal criminal law are not enforceable. More important, the doctrine of unconscionability allows courts to refuse to enforce contracts on grounds of unfair surprise, disparity of bargaining power, and procedural or substantive unfairness. Procedural unconscionability includes the presence of duress, fraud, undue influence, failure to comply with the duty to disclose, obscure terms, vastly unequal bargaining power in adhesion contracts, and the like.[10] Substantive unconscionability includes the presence of contractual terms that are strikingly immoral (for example, the sale of a baby) that contravene public policy (for example, contracts that include penalties of physical punishment for breach or delay), or that unjustifiably subvert a party's purposes for contracting (for example, radically one-sided contracts).

We must assume that the contract forged by those first hired and the vineyard owner in the parable would be a permissible, enforceable wage-labor contract given the standards of the time and place. The elements of procedural and substantive unconscionability are absent. No illegal or immoral acts are in play. One might argue that the vast disparity in bargaining power between the vineyard owner and day laborers suggests that the agreed-upon wage was meager and thus exploitive. But the lessons of the parable work best when we brush this aside. Moreover, to make such a claim about an ancient economic transaction from contemporary standards reeks of anachronism.

Assuming the general propriety of the contract, the *entitlements* of the parties vest. The vineyard owner is entitled to 12 hours of labor from each of those first hired, who is in turn entitled to receive a denarius at the end of the workday. The notion of desert fades into the background. We need not and should not make assessments of what the vineyard owner and those first hired deserve. Upon consummating their contract, each party has vested rights and duties based on the entitlements flowing from their agreement. From the standpoint of distributive justice, the murkier, more contestable judgment as to what they deserve becomes unnecessary.

The principle of equal pay for equal work often conflicts with freedom of contract. This notion of *proportionate reward* is grounded in a straightforward claim of personal desert: if two people work equally—as judged by productivity and amount of time expended—they deserve to receive the same wage, all other relevant things being equal. The desert claim is based on effort, time, and results. Under such circumstances, any inequality in pay must be justified by a relevant difference between the two workers. Some examples of permissible differences that could justify unequal pay for two workers who labored the same number of hours: one worker might earn a higher salary based on seniority, years worked on the job; one worker might have produced more in a reward system based on merit; or one worker might earn more to offset a previous distributive injustice he or she endured. From a contemporary standpoint, however, differential pay based on group characteristics such as gender, race, religion, or ethnicity is impermissible. In such cases, unequal pay for equal work is redolent with the stench of discrimination, prejudice, and bias.

Thus, the entitlements flowing from freedom of contract and the desert-based claims grounding the principle of proportionate reward may conflict. To argue that freedom of contract permits differential pay for similar work—after all, the workers agreed to the terms of their respective contracts without fraud or duress—will be unsuccessful in many cases, especially those wherein previously disenfranchised groups receive lower pay in the absence of justifying relevant differences.

The allegation of unjustified unequal remuneration lodged by the workers first hired in the parable must be viewed as a claim grounded in desert: We worked 11, 9, 6, and 3 hours more, respectively, than the other groups of workers, yet we received the same wage. Those first hired ("the stalwarts") received precisely that to which they were *entitled*, but they feel shortchanged in terms of what they *deserved*: they expended more effort, as judged by hours labored; they did so under more trying conditions—under the piercing sun; and they produced more through their efforts. Accordingly, even though they deserved more than the other groups, they received the same wage. They are alleging that they should receive more pay than the other groups because they worked longer hours and produced more than those groups. The stalwarts' claim is that the vineyard owner was paying the various groups equally for unequal work. While the *entitlements* of the stalwarts are defined by their wage-labor contract with the vineyard owner, what they *deserve* must take into account the comparative effort, time expended, and productivity of the different groups of laborers. To judge the stalwarts as merely casting an "evil eye" on the beneficence of the vineyard owner may well be harsh. On the contrary, they do seem to have a plausible, prima facie claim that they have not been treated in accord with the principle of desert.

If my analysis rings true, then the standard interpretation of the parable must be adjusted. Again, the typical analysis concludes that people should not receive less than they deserve; but some people will receive more than they deserve because of the generosity and bestowal of grace of the agent doing the distributing. These two axioms produce another moral principle: where no one has received less than he or she deserves any resentment or envy or jealously directed at those who have received more than they deserve is misplaced and demonstrates a deficiency of character. Instead, everyone should rejoice in that no one has been short-changed and some have been especially fortunate. The adjustment I offer is that the parable more precisely stands for the following propositions:

- People should not receive less than that to which they are *entitled*
- But some people will receive more than they *deserve* because of the generosity of the distributing agent
- Where no one has received less than he or she is *entitled* any resentment toward those who received more than they *deserved* is misplaced and demonstrates a deficiency of character
- Instead, everyone should rejoice in that no one has been short changed and some have been especially fortunate

Now imagine that each group of workers in the parable agreed to a wage-labor contract with the vineyard owner. The facts of the agreement involving the stalwarts remain the same. Three hours later, the vineyard owner offers the next group of workers ("the back-ups") a denarius each for 9 hours work; they would, presumably, be pleased to accept the terms as they would receive a standard full-day's pay for three-fourths of a day's labor. Later, the vineyard owner returns and offers the third group ("the nooners"), the fourth group ("the penultimates"), and the fifth group ("the fortunate sons") of workers a denarius each for 6 hours, 3 hours and 1 hour of labor, respectively. Presumably, each set of workers would be increasingly thrilled to accept the terms as they would be earning a full day's pay for a fraction of a day's labor. Under the hypothetical, each set of workers has vested entitlements upon formally agreeing to the terms offered by the vineyard owner. At the end of the work day, when the vineyard owner presents each worker with one denarius, all entitlements under the respective contracts have been fulfilled. No worker would have a legitimate complaint that the wage he had received was insufficient with regard to his *entitlements*.

Of course, the stalwarts could still lodge a plausible complaint based on the principle of *desert*: in the absence of justifying differences among the various groups of workers, the principle of desert implies that those who worked longer hours, thereby expending more effort and producing more, should receive higher wages than the other groups of workers. That is, the principle of desert supports allocation based on proportionate reward.

Still, under the hypothetical, the principle of desert provides only a reason, and not automatically decisive evidence, for morally appropriate conclusions. The vineyard owner could point out that the differential contracts were not grounded in discrimination or prejudice against disenfranchised groups; on the contrary, the workers in one group were indistinguishable from those in the other groups in terms of gender, religion, ethnicity, and the like. Moreover, no group was exploited in that even the stalwarts received what was taken to be a fair wage for a full day's labor. Thus, in this case, distributive justice is served where entitlements are fulfilled precisely.

We might conclude that claims grounded in the principle of desert seem more abstract here and should not trump entitlement requirements. But a critic could retort that had the stalwarts known in advance that the other groups would be receiving the same wage as they were offered even though working fewer hours they would have refused the owner's offer and bargained for a higher wage. Advocates of the vineyard owner, however, could rebut this charge, citing two considerations: first, when the owner initially approached the stalwarts he was unaware that he would be returning to contract for more workers—hence, he could not have made the stalwarts aware of what he himself did not know at the time; second, the owner offered the stalwarts the standard agreement for day laborers—he had not sought to short change them given established labor practices of the day and place. Moreover, the stalwarts would have been unlikely to refuse to work given that their alternative would be idleness.

The situation in the parable, however, is different from my hypothetical. There no group of workers has set entitlements other than the stalwarts. The other groups have agreed to work for 9 hours, 6 hours, 3 hours and 1 hour, respectively, for "whatever is right." While they undoubtedly assumed that they would receive wages proportionate to their hours worked, they ended up receiving a standard full day's pay. The parable includes no evidence that, say, the back-ups objected that they had been short changed because the fortunate sons, who had labored eight fewer hours, received the same wage as they had. We must assume that all members of groups other than the stalwarts were overjoyed at receiving higher wages than they had expected.

But a problem emerges. The last four groups of workers lacked fixed entitlements because they labored without a clear contract. By offering to pay "whatever is right," the owner explicitly allows wider moral considerations—than those arising from the principle of entitlement—to come into play. Thus, the stalwarts might well have argued that proportionate reward underwritten by the principle of personal desert should determine economic distribution. Unlike the case of the previously considered hypothetical, in the parable the principle of entitlement should not clearly control moral conclusions for two reasons: first, among the various groups of workers, only the stalwarts have fixed entitlements; and, second, by invoking the phrase "whatever is right," the vineyard owner has invited wider moral assessment.

To demean the character of the stalwarts by asking accusatorily "Is your eye evil because I am good?" seems harsh. The stalwarts are not envious of gifts that the vineyard owner has bestowed generously and independently of wage-labor agreements. Instead, a charitable interpretation would conclude that the stalwarts question the vineyard owner's allocations in the context of a series of wage-labor agreements *wherein the owner had tacitly accepted the relevancy of moral considerations beyond strict entitlements.* Of course, the vineyard owner might have offered moral considerations that could have justified his policy of disproportionate reward. For example, perhaps the members of the other groups were needier than the members of the stalwarts; perhaps they had fewer opportunities to be employed, and the like. But in the absence of such moral considerations, the vineyard owner's icy rebuke of the stalwarts seems excessive.

Again, my analysis understands the parable only at the level of human economics. Those who insist plausibly that we should analyze the story only in terms of Jesus' need to soften the growing pretensions of the apostles or of Jesus' efforts to defend his associations with and acceptance of sinners or of Jesus' message that God's grace of salvation is a gift that is not subject to human expectations will be unmoved.

Nevertheless, I offer my analysis from the assumption that the parables are also designed to provide moral lessons for leading a good human life. To the extent possible, the parables are invoked to guide human beings in their efforts to prefigure the Kingdom of God—in whatever form we understand that Kingdom—by our actions today in our world. As always, Jesus' prescriptions in the Parable of the Laborers in the Vineyard transcend the conventional wisdom of his time and place. As ever, Jesus forces us to reassess the received opinion of our time and place.

In the Parable of The Laborers in the Vineyard, from the standpoint of justice understood as distribution according to the principle of desert, the workers first hired have a strong case. But Jesus insisted that unconditional love does not bow before that principle of justice. Agape is not constrained by or reducible to the respective deeds of the beloved: the merits of the beloved are irrelevant to the distribution of social goods. However, I am troubled that the vineyard owner demonstrated his generosity in connection with wage labor—he allotted the money to each of the groups hired at the end of the day and apparently for services rendered. I would think that had he paid each group of workers proportionate to the hours they worked but later gave monetary gifts to the last groups hired that equalized what each group received overall then the first hired would have no basis for complaint. Instead, the vineyard owner muddled distribution according to (a) proportionate desert with (b) distribution according to need and (c) distribution as gift. From a contemporary standpoint that conflation was unnecessary and leads to moral confusion. But from Jesus' vantage point the point of the parable may simply be the superiority of unconditional love to any humanly-contrived principle of justice. Even where unconditional love and justice overlap, such as distribution according to need, it is the power of unconditional love that is paramount in determining how to proceed. The trajectory of unconditional love does not require identical treatment of everyone, but it does privilege needs over merits, spurns social hierarchy and division, and marginalizes factual differences among persons.

Of course, the problem is that we do not operate from a condition of universal friendship and unconditional love. Although it may well be true that should everyone adopt and act in compliance with Jesus' teachings our conventional notions of justice would be superfluous, what are we to say about our actual social condition—where only a tiny percentage of the population actually lives in accord with Jesus' teachings?

5. Material Minimalism

In the Kingdom of God a transvaluation of values will occur: "many that are first will be last; and the last first" (Mark 10: 31; Matt. 20: 16; Luke 13: 30). When the Son of Man renders judgment on our corrupt world, many of those who now revel in economic, social and political power and privilege will be ousted and replaced by those who are now oppressed and disenfranchised. The implication is that many of those who now enjoy hierarchical advantage have benefited from and contributed to the evil that pervades the world.

As always, Jesus instructs that human beings should prefigure the Kingdom of God by unsettling the dominant values and social understandings that underwrite current corruption. Thus, instead of aspiring to the conventional indicia of a successful life—the accumulation of material resources, the attainment of political power, and the exercise of privilege—genuine disciples should dedicate their lives to community service. By relinquishing the competitive and material desires so common among human beings and by focusing our energies and efforts on service to other people, we can transform our own souls and anticipate social relations in the Kingdom of God: "For whoever would save his life will lose it; and whoever loses his life for my sake and the gospel's will save it" (Mark 8: 35). Instead of seeking to amplify and glorify ourselves as superior to others, we should humbly strive to advance the interests of other people, especially those paramount interests that nurture their souls. Alleviating the oppression and easing the exploitation of disenfranchised people is a prelude to facilitating the enrichment of their spirits.

Accordingly, material aggrandizement is either superfluous or an obstacle to personal well-being. Beyond garnering minimal material necessities, the pursuit of wealth distracts us from more important concerns. Jesus' message mirrors moral wisdom that generously predates his birth. About four centuries earlier, Socrates argued along similar lines (much of which reflected the spade work of Pythagoras): purifying the soul is the most important human mission; pursuit of society's rewards—wealth, honor, reputation, and privilege—distracts from or prevents the success of that mission; genuine harm is that which unsettles the harmony of the soul; service to others, in the form of philosophical illumination, is paramount; and those who ignore their souls and who lust for society's rewards will be barred from entering the everlasting bliss of the World of Forms.

Imagine, though, a world, nation, or community that self-consciously embraced the moral message of Jesus or Socrates. Would science and technology suffer? Would accumulated knowledge progress robustly? Would life be too simple and drab? Would the world, nation, or community be akin to an uninspiring Mennonite or Amish conclave?

To be fair, Socrates certainly emphasized the value of knowledge. Indeed, if knowledge truly does equal virtue (it doesn't) then the good human life and the purified soul depend on the pursuit of truth. While Jesus stresses only knowledge required to prefigure the values forthcoming in the Kingdom of God, surely he does not preclude the pursuit of non-religious truth. Still, Socrates and Jesus are utterly indifferent to economic growth, scientific understanding, and even earnest labor. They clearly oppose the mindset of the consumer society, which is grounded in value largely determined by goods that cannot be shared: "There is nothing in the teaching of Jesus as understood in the earliest days of the church or in the days of Jesus himself to give comfort to any kind of system that subordinates people to capital and to markets. Neither state, worker, nor 'free enterprise' capitalism can draw any valid support from this Jesus."[11]

Both Jesus and Socrates were convinced that their societies were firmly rooted in unfertile soil. Both concluded that a transformation of the human soul (or heart) was critical for personal salvation and societal advance. But the utopianism in both visions, and particularly in Jesus' anticipation of the Kingdom of God, rests uncomfortably with the exigencies of everyday life.

For example, Jesus' Sermon on the Mount includes, among other pieces of moral instruction the following: "Whoever then relaxes one of the least of these commandments and teaches men so, shall he be called least in the kingdom of heaven"; "But I say to you that everyone who is angry with his brother shall be liable to judgment"; "If your right eye causes you to sin, pluck it out and throw it away . . . And if your right hand causes you to sin, cut it off, and throw it away"; "If any one strikes you on the right cheek, turn to him the other also"; "Love your enemies and pray for those who persecute you" (Matt. 5: 19, 22, 29, 30, 39, 44). Moreover, Jesus advises followers to sell all of their possessions and distribute the proceeds to the poor (Matt. 19: 21; Luke 12: 33, 18: 22). These bits of moral instruction are wrapped within Jesus' most general imperative: unconditional love for everyone.

Jesus' moral instruction is devoid of self-executing bright-line rules that might be applied mechanically to individual cases. His life of the interior, embodying the injunctions of love, must inform our judgments when applying his thoughts to particular circumstances. But we may well be wary of relying totally only on human judgment when seeking correct moral decision. Surely we must interpret Jesus' words as providing the guiding trajectory of moral decisionmaking. Moreover, in borderline cases, we should incline toward the decision that better promotes the health of our souls and those of our neighbors.

Given the apparent utopianism in his teachings, the question arises whether the totality of Jesus' moral message can be universalized. Supposing that everyone desires to follow Jesus' moral instructions, is it practically possible to do so? As Don Cupitt observes,

> [Jesus' ethic] seems to be economically impossible. We cannot all live like holy vagabonds . . . and we cannot all of us sell up everything we have. Who would there be to sell to? There has to be settled life, there has to be land tenure, there has to be social infrastructure, there has to be economic exchange, and of course there has to be Piers Plowman, toiling away in the fields every day and carrying the rest of the world on his back. And in view of all this, is it not obvious that there will have to be some sort of compromise between the two moralities? The old theological morality of religious law binds everyone into maintaining the existing social order, while the dream morality is kept as 'pie in the sky' and as a distant hope of future blessedness. . . . Economic necessity versus utopian humanism.[12]

Universal acceptance of Jesus' radical moral message has not occurred, even among those who describe themselves as Christians. Relatively few people are willing to distance themselves from their families; to renounce material goods and the pursuit of robust careers; to nurture forgiveness and mercy as their virtually default mindset and response to those who transgress against them; to abrogate or at least soften appeals to retributive and restitutional justice; to seek out and minister to societal outcasts; to transcend distributive justice grounded in personal desert and production; to acknowledge the aggression and violence of others by offering compassion; to bestow unconditional love upon strangers and even those who perceive themselves as enemies; to promote impartial and thoroughly egalitarian relationships; and to understand harm as related primarily to injury of one's inner condition.

Jesus-inspired socialist movements in Europe during the late 19th century met an all too predictable response: they were squashed by the governing military forces.[13] Encircled by those who have internalized the dominant social conviction that zero-sum contests pervade international and national relations, those who embrace Jesus' moral message may well appear to be well-intentioned, pure of spirit, but ultimately doomed by their naiveté. At least when laboring outside of established religious orders, such disciples may seem to be abject gulls in a wider society firmly entrenched in a much different ethos. If so, then Jesus' moral message is designed only for the personal salvation of those accepting the metaphysical background that animates Jesus' teachings: the existence of an all-knowing, all-powerful, all-benevolent God; the impending inauguration of the Kingdom of that God; and a human telos designed to exalt the inner citadel of the self by embracing and acting according to the imperatives of the divine will.

In any case, efforts to portray Jesus as an apostle of laissez-faire capitalism or patriarchal privilege or military adventurism are invariably strained. The words attributed to Jesus neither anticipate the economic wisdom of George Whatley, nor echo Aristotle's paean to patriarchy, nor paraphrase Homer's encomia to the warrior virtues.

We can speculate on Jesus' reaction to the branches of Christianity prevalent in our world, especially those that have accumulated vast chests of wealth by trading on his name. In the 1960s, an uncharitable slogan proclaimed that, "Billy Graham saves, saves every darn penny he can get his hands on." But the same could be said for other Christian denominations, televangelists, and a host of enterprising capitalists masquerading as religious prophets. While many Christian institutions and leaders do much charitable work that alleviates the recurring hardships of the least fortunate among us, we may wonder whether Jesus would approve of the amount of wealth they often amass.

Conventional moral wisdom, in Jesus' time and in our own, cannot ratify his moral message. Dominant social ideas and practices will judge much of Jesus' teachings in the parables and elsewhere in scripture as inadequate. But no surprise, that. Unsettling dominant understandings was one of Jesus' paramount purposes. Accordingly, each set of ideas and practices will be viewed suspiciously by the other. Human beings are invited to choose one set or the other, or broker a compromise between them, or re-imagine and remake the possible combinations. As ever, no light matter is at stake, but the very fashion in which we will craft our souls and marshal our lives.

6. Jesus and the Concept of Forgiveness

The paramount questions surrounding the concept of forgiveness are these: What is involved when one person forgives another? What is the relationship between wrongdoers and their transgressions? Is forgiving others a moral duty or a supererogatory act? Must the transgressing party repent his wrongful deed in order to earn forgiveness? What sort of attitude is required in order for one person to forgive another? What is the relationship between retributive justice and forgiveness? Does forgiving wrongdoing condone past and encourage future transgressions? Why should we forgive wrongdoers and why is forgiveness important? What is the difference, if any, between forgiving a wrongdoer and forgetting his wrong? Is Jesus' view of forgiveness unique in some respects?[14]

Let's begin by describing the elements of forgiveness. In order for one person to forgive another we must identify a wrong that has been committed by the latter of which the former is aware. If no wrong has been committed then there is nothing to forgive. Moreover, if a wrong has been committed but the victim is unaware of that act then she is not in a position to forgive. Furthermore, if a wrong has been committed, the victim is aware of the wrong, but she does not know the identity of the wrongdoer then she cannot forgive the wrongdoer. Bear in mind also that not all misdeeds are legal wrongs punishable by the judiciary nor are all moral wrongs grave and significant. A moral wrong as simple and relatively minor as speaking ill of a friend to another person is a misdeed subject to possible forgiveness. Thus, our *first element: a transgressor wronged a victim and the victim acknowledges that the transgressor wronged him.*

However, sometimes people transgress against others under circumstances where they are not fully responsible for their acts. That is, the transgressor has a legitimate excuse or justification for his act. An excuse would mitigate or erase the transgressor's moral culpability for the act. Perhaps the transgressor was subject to an irresistible impulse, or was coerced into acting by an external force, or was deceived into thinking that the act was actually permissible, or was otherwise not responsible for what he did. A justification would demonstrate that the act was not in fact a wrong because the agent performed it because of a public necessity, in deference to a higher duty, in self-defense, or the like. If the transgressor acted with justification then he committed no wrong that is subject to forgiveness; if he acted with a legitimate excuse then he may not be morally culpable for the act and, again, he is not subject to forgiveness. Thus, our *second element: the transgressor is fully responsible and morally culpable for his action and the victim acknowledges these facts.*

If a transgressor is to be forgiven the only person in a position to forgive is the person who was wronged, her agents, and, perhaps, those uncommonly close to her who were also wronged to some extent. This is the case at least where we are discussing interpersonal forgiveness. In cases of judicial forgiveness, we can view the decision makers as the legal agents of the victim or, probably better, we can consider such instances legal forgiveness independent of the victim. Surely, a judge might forgive a miscreant under circumstances where the victim of the wrongdoer's transgression remains obdurate and vice versa. Moreover, after coming to understand the relevant facts, the public at large may feel sympathy for the wrongdoer, but unaffected third parties are not in a position to forgive the wrongdoer. Thus, our *third element: Only the victim, his explicitly empowered agents, and, perhaps, those uncommonly close to the victim who were also wronged to some extent by the transgressor are in a position to forgive the transgressor.*

In order to forgive, the victim does not accept or condone the past wrong, or encourage future wrongs. Instead, the victim continues to acknowledge that the transgressor is fully responsible for his wrongful action. What forgiveness requires is that the victim surrenders all negative feelings and attitudes toward the transgressor that arose from the wrongdoing. Forgiveness, then, is a function of how the victim regards the transgressor. Thus, our *fourth element: In order to forgive the transgressor, the victim must relinquish his negative feelings and attitudes toward the transgressor that arose from the transgressor's wrongdoing.*

But how can the victim attain such a state? How can the victim retain his conviction that he has been wronged and that the perpetrator is fully responsible for that wrong yet relinquish his negative feelings of the perpetrator that sprung from that event? It would seem that the victim must distinguish the wrongful deed from the value of the fully responsible agent who performed it. That is, the victim cannot *define* the perpetrator by the wrongful deed at issue. The victim must perceive the perpetrator as more and better than the wrongful deed that gave rise to the understandably negative attitudes toward the perpetrator that the victim initially embodied. In effect, the victim must distance the perpetrator from his wrongful action or, perhaps more precisely, the victim must evaluate the perpetrator from a wider, more charitable perspective. At first blush, the victim judges the perpetrator only by the instant wrong he has committed; in order to forgive the perpetrator, the victim must either separate the perpetrator from the wrongful deed or assess the perpetrator from a broader, more sympathetic vantage point. Thus, our *fifth element: In order to forgive the transgressor, the victim must distinguish the wrongful deed from the value of the fully responsible person, the transgressor, who performed it.*

This is easier stated than achieved. What could lead the victim to separate so neatly the wrongful deed from the value of the fully responsible perpetrator who performed it? After all, evaluating the perpetrator from a wider perspective may well result in learning about a host of other, even more horrifying, misdeeds that the person has wreaked upon other victims. One possibility is that the perpetrator sincerely repents his wrongdoing. Under such circumstances, the perpetrator distances himself from his wrongful deed. He invites the victim to no longer define him by his wrongdoing and to judge his value as higher than he had demonstrated by his mischief. Here the victim does not need to *create* a distance between the perpetrator and the wrongful deed, but merely *recognize* the distance that the perpetrator himself has forged through his repentance.

Suppose a perpetrator of a wrong has sincerely repented. Does this imply that the victim of that wrong is obligated to forgive the perpetrator? From the vantage point of conventional moral wisdom, the answer is "no." Forgiving the perpetrator would be a supererogatory act (a virtuous deed that goes beyond the requirements of morality) on the part of the victim, not the discharge of a moral duty. The question, however, is more difficult to answer from the vantage point of Jesus. For example, Jesus instructs his disciples, "Take heed to yourselves; if your brother sins, rebuke him; and if he repents, forgive him; and if he sins against you seven times in the day, and turns to you seven times, and says, 'I repent,' you must forgive him" (Luke 17: 3-4); and when the apostle Peter inquired, "how often shall my brother sin against me, and I forgive him? As many as seven times?" Jesus answered, "I do not say to you seven times, but seventy times seven" (Matt. 18: 21-22). In the Parable of the Unforgiving Servant: "And in anger his lord delivered him to the jailers, till he should pay all his debt. So also my heavenly Father will do to every one of you, if you do not forgive your brother from your heart" (Matt. 18: 34-35).

The force of such passages appears to hold that a perpetrator's repentance is a sufficient condition for the victim's forgiveness. Moreover, the passages from Matthew do not seem to require repentance on the part of the perpetrator; the victim must forgive even trespassers who are recidivists. On this interpretation, a perpetrator's repentance triggers a moral duty on the part of the victim to forgive; here forgiveness is not a supererogatory act. Moreover, these passages hold open the possibility that even if the perpetrator does not repent and continues to transgress against the same victim that victim *must* forgive. In effect, even where the perpetrator has not distanced himself from his misdeed, the victim must somehow create that distance between the agent and his wrongful act.

Nicholas Wolterstorff resists such an interpretation. He is concerned that understanding a perpetrator's repentance as sufficient condition for the victim's forgiveness would imply that such a transgressor would have a vested right to be forgiven once he repented. Thus, a victim who refused to forgive would have wronged the repentant perpetrator. This is unacceptable for Wolterstorff so he offers two possible alternative interpretations of the Biblical passages.

One possibility is that Jesus' words set forth an ideal toward which to strive, one that goes beyond the requirements of moral duty and retributive justice:

> One possibility is that Jesus is setting before them a better way to go, a way that goes beyond what duty and justice require, a way in tune with the ways of our Father in heaven, the way of supererogatory love.[15]

I find this possibility unpersuasive for two reasons. First, the language of the Biblical passages is not aspirational. Jesus informs his disciples that they *shall* forgive those trespassers who repent. If Jesus was setting forth a series of supererogatory suggestions we would expect the term "should" instead of "must" and "shall." Second, Jesus is not "setting before them a better way" in the sense of offering them an alternative moral wisdom that they might emulate. Instead, Jesus appears to be informing them of *the* proper way to act in the world. His words are neither equivocal nor wavering.

The second possibility that Wolterstorff offers is that the duty to forgive does not vest a right in the repentant perpetrator but, instead, vests a right in third-parties: Jesus and God the Father. Thus, a victim who refused to forgive a repentant transgressor would not be wronging the transgressor, but would be wronging God.

> The other possibility is that he is declaring that they have an obligation toward Jesus and our Father in heaven to forgive the repentant wrongdoer. This would be a so-called third-party duty; they have a duty *toward* Jesus and the Father *with respect to* their fellows to forgive them. Correlative to this third-party duty would be a third-party right: Jesus and the Father have a right against them with respect to their fellows, to forgive their fellows. If they did not forgive the brother who has wronged them and is repentant, they wrong not the brother but Jesus and the Father.[16]

In my view, this is by far the stronger of the two possibilities that Wolterstorff presents for at least two reasons. First, the language of the Parable of the Unforgiving Servant (Matt. 18: 23-35) suggests that God takes special umbrage at those who refuse to forgive their trespassing neighbors. Without being blasphemous, God apparently takes the refusal to forgive personally—as if God has also been wronged by the refusal. Second, this interpretation permits what I take to be the gist of Jesus' position on forgiveness: where there is repentance there is no option, we must forgive. As is typical, Jesus' view goes beyond the conventional moral wisdom of his day as well as that of our time.

I would, however, add to Wolterstorff's second possibility. Why does God take the refusal to forgive a repentant wrongdoer so personally? I suspect that not only does God sense that God's rights have been infringed but also that the repentant wrongdoer has also in some sense been short changed. I would offer the following: once the wrongdoer repents he *deserves* to be forgiven by the victim of the wrong, but he is not *entitled* to be forgiven. That is, the repentant wrongdoer lacks a vested right to be forgiven; he is not in a position to claim that he must be forgiven because he possess such a right. Thus, a victim who refuses to forgive the repentant wrongdoer has not violated his rights. But the repentant wrongdoer *deserves* to be forgiven because he has distanced himself from his misdeed. Claims based on desert do not always vest a right and this is one such case. The desert claim in this case provides a moral reason why the victim should forgive the repentant wrongdoer. Such reasons are not automatically conclusive, but where, as here, there are no countervailing moral reasons then they should determine moral action. In refusing to forgive, the victim would be unjustifiably giving the repentant less than he deserved. Accordingly, God's ire is twice raised: one of his human creatures is receiving less than he deserves and God's third-party rights have been infringed. In this fashion, we can preserve our intuition that the repentant wrongdoer is not in a position to demand forgiveness as his right yet underscore Jesus' conviction that forgiveness in such cases is mandatory. Thus, our *sixth element: From the standpoint of human conventional moral wisdom, the transgressor's sincere repentance is one way that he can distance himself from his wrongful action. Under such circumstances, from the standpoint of conventional morality, the victim's forgiveness is not morally required but is recommended as a supererogatory act. From the standpoint of Jesus' revolutionary moral message, the transgressor's sincere repentance creates an obligation such that the victim must forgive the transgressor. Should the victim refuse to forgive the transgressor under such circumstances he would have failed to discharge his moral duty in that he would have given the transgressor less than he deserved and he would have infringed on God's third-party rights.*

But suppose that the perpetrator of a wrong does not repent and thus does not distance himself from his transgression. Is it possible for the victim to create unilaterally a distance between the wrongdoer and his wrong? If so, under what circumstances would such a creation of distance occur?

One set of possibilities are wrongdoings that seem out of character. Here the victim might conclude that the misdeed does not reflect the overall worth of the perpetrator because the wrongful action is aberrational. For example, if a person has an otherwise acceptable record of past behavior and the instant wrong is a first offense. If so, the first offense may well be judged as out of character for the perpetrator. Under such circumstances, the victim might create unilaterally a distance between the wrongful deed and the value of the perpetrator. Even in the absence of the perpetrator's repentance, the victim may decide to forgive the transgressor even though the victim continues to recognize that the transgressor is fully responsible for wronging her. But why would the perpetrator not repent in such a case? At the extreme, he might have died prior to having the chance to repent. Forgiving the dead for their transgressions remains possible. Even if the perpetrator has not died, he might not repent because he mistakenly believes that his act was permissible. Here he would remain fully responsible for the wrong and also responsible for his mistaken belief. Moreover, another case occurs where the perpetrator does repent his wrong but the victim is unaware of that fact and thus cannot take it into account. Another possibility is that the perpetrator lives under the fatuous code of never regretting any of his acts and never apologizing for them. Following this stringent principle rigidly, the perpetrator does not consider repentance a live option.

Another example of wrongdoings that seem out of character is the perpetrator who has enjoyed a salutary relationship with the victim and whose current wrong seems minor by comparison to the past benefits of the relationship. Even in the absence of repentance, the victim may well create unilaterally a distance between the instant wrong and the overall character of the perpetrator and forgive the misdeed.

Beyond wrongdoings that seem out of character, other possibilities for forgiving in the absence of repentance can be advanced. For example, suppose I am having difficulties in an intimate relationship that has hitherto brought me great joy. I have a well-intentioned but somewhat inept friend who is greatly concerned for my well-being. She tries to intercede in my problem and facilitate reconciliation between my lover and me. However, by officiously intermeddling in my affairs she makes the problem worse. She wrongs me by insinuating herself into my situation without my permission and by making an unpleasant situation much worse. She would remain fully responsible for her wrongful deed—her worthy intentions are neither excuses nor justifications for her actions. Still, even in the absence of repentance, I may well forgive her because her actions were well-intentioned although poorly executed.

Yet another case for forgiving in the absence of repentance centers on the suffering of the perpetrator. If the transgressor has already suffered significantly, perhaps even disproportionately to the gravity of the wrong, then the victim may choose to forgive. For example, suppose a prominent person commits a wrong that becomes highly publicized. As a result, the transgressor suffers a host of humiliations including loss of reputation, fading business opportunities, family dissolution, and the like. As the victim of that wrong, I might well conclude that the transgressor has suffered sufficiently and forgive him even in the absence of repentance.

Does forgiving unrepented transgressions unjustifiably condone wrongdoing? I think not. Remember, by creating a distance between the agent and his wrongful act, the victim can still deplore the wrong but reconcile with the wrongdoer. Remember that in all the cases of the victim unilaterally creating distance between the wrongdoer and his deed that I have presented the perpetrator remains fully responsible for his action which remains a wrong.

However, I do not want to oversell the notion that victims can create unilaterally a distance between wrongdoers and their misdeeds. Clearly, that will depend on the gravity of the misdeed, the antecedent character of the transgressor, what happens after the offense, and how the transgressor conducts himself in the aftermath. That the transgressor has the opportunity to repent his wrong but fails to do so cannot, all other things being equal, count in favor of forgiveness.

Moreover, the neat separation of agents from their acts can be dangerous. Just as in the case of agapic love, when we begin stripping people of their choices, actions, and deeds they begin to fade away as concrete individuals and appear more as abstract exemplars of humanity. To forgive the person requires, among other things, that enough constitutive attributes remain that we can distinguish among individuals. These remarks are intended as cautions to those who are tempted to forgive as a matter of course.

But is this not what Jesus requires? Does Jesus not insist that we forgive others who trespass against us and that we do so even if they do so repeatedly? Does Jesus not hold that repentance is a sufficient but not a necessary condition of forgiveness?

Whether Jesus requires that the perpetrator of an offense repent his wrongdoing in order to gain the forgiveness of his victim is unclear. If Jesus' moral message is that we should forgive only repentant sinners then his teaching in this regard only underscores Jewish tradition. If Jesus teaches that we should forgive even unrepentant sinners—that we can create unilaterally the distance between sinner and sin that is necessary for forgiveness—then his approach is characteristically novel. Moreover, understanding Jesus this way coheres neatly with numerous other aspects of his moral message: bestowing generosity and grace even where those gifts are not strictly deserved; prefiguring the ideals of the Kingdom of God now; and forgiving the trespasses and debts of other people just as we hope that God will forgive our moral shortcomings.

But we should not take this observation too far because to do so would make the act of repentance insignificant. Jesus also implores us to repent our sins as a step toward personal transformation. To be forgiven automatically creates a disincentive for perpetrators of offenses to distance themselves from their sins as a prelude to invigorating their hearts and souls. In fact, just as in the Parable of the Prodigal Son, Jesus rejoices in the personal transformation of repentant sinners more effusively than he does in the presence of even the steadfast rectitude of the morally upright: "Just so, I tell you, there will be more joy in heaven over one sinner who repents than over ninety-nine righteous persons who need no repentance" (Luke 15: 7); "Those who are well have no need of a physician, but those who are sick; I came not to call the righteous, but sinners" (Mark 2: 17).

The most reasonable conclusion to draw is that repenting our sins is paramount, both to begin to repair our relationship with the person whom we have wronged and also to begin our internal transformation. That is, perpetrators of wrongs should do for their part the work required to distance themselves from their misdeeds. But on at least some occasions, injured parties should create unilaterally the distance between sin and sinner required for genuine forgiveness. To do so as a matter of course would nullify much of the incentive to repent and could even encourage more wrongdoing, but to do so on appropriate occasions brings glory to a host of concerns critical to Jesus' moral message. At times, even where the perpetrator of a wrong against us does not repent his misdeed, we should forgive him even while recognizing the severity of his wrong. Knowing when to render such forgiveness, like most of Jesus' moral teaching, requires practical moral wisdom and is not susceptible to adjudication by applying bright-line rules or formalist reasoning.

Thus, although some Biblical passages may suggest such a stance, we should not conclude that Jesus requires human beings to always forgive their trespassers even in the absence of repentance. While I do accept that Jesus holds the strong view that repentance by a perpetrator of a wrong is a sufficient condition for forgiveness, I do not conclude that Jesus held the even stronger view that victims must always forgive as such. After all, Christian theology is clear that even God typically requires repentance of sins. While God may bestow grace and confer more upon some human beings than they deserve or to which they are entitled, God presumably does not do this as a matter of course. Moreover, if Jesus required all victims to forgive automatically their trespassers, repentance would in effect be irrelevant for forgiveness—merely an interesting sidebar to the required story.

Thus, our *seventh element: Even if the transgressor does not repent his wrongful deed, the victim can create unilaterally a distance between the transgressor and his wrong such that the victim can forgive the transgressor. Some relevant circumstances that may energize that unilateral creation: the instant wrong is perpetrator's first offense; the perpetrator's wrong was grounded in good intentions; the perpetrator and the victim enjoyed a prior salutary relationship; or the perpetrator suffered sufficiently in the aftermath of his wrong. Should the victim forgive the transgressor on the basis of the victim's unilateral creation of distance between the transgressor and the transgressor's wrong then the victim's forgiveness is a supererogatory act. Jesus' revolutionary moral message seems to confirm this analysis generally, but suggests that sometimes morality requires that victims forgive those who wrong them even in the absence of repentance.*

What is the metaphysical result of forgiving a wrongdoer? Where the transgressor repents and the victim forgives, we can talk in terms of reconciliation. Neither party views the other as alien or estranged. Each has made an effort to mend the rupture between them. Even if they did not enjoy a prior relationship, once the instant misdeed established them as victim and transgressor they were involved with each other. At that point, hard feelings ensued: the victim, understandably, joined the transgressor to his wrongdoing and judged the transgressor negatively. Once the transgressor repents and the victim forgives, the victim relinquishes his hard feelings toward the perpetrator and the transgressor separates herself from her wrongful deed. This opens the way for reconciliation and renewal.

The Parable of the Prodigal Son provides a classic example: the father apparently forgives the wrong that his younger son has inflicted upon him; recognizes that his son has repented; refuses to judge his son based on his worst moments; and immediately offers reconciliation and renewal of their relationship. Of course, from the narrative, the father did not relinquish retributive feelings toward his son because the father never gives evidence that he bore such sentiments. Either the father never fully recognized his son's actions as wrongs or he acknowledged his son's actions as wrongs but refused from the start to harbor retributive emotions toward his son.

But what occurs when the victim unilaterally creates the distance between the transgressor and her misdeed? Here the transgressor has not separated herself from her misdeed. How can reconciliation and renewal take place unilaterally? A relationship requires at least two parties. Where the transgressor refuses to repent her wrongful act, to talk of reconciliation and renewal is misplaced. To be more precise, I would think that the victim's forgiveness in the absence of repentance is an offer of reconciliation that can occur only if the transgressor reciprocates in kind. Even in the absence of the transgressor's repentance, the victim has relinquished his hard feelings, but that is insufficient for reconciliation. The transgressor must bring something to the table.

Some reasons why the victim might be inclined to forgive transgressors are epistemological: Human beings are flawed, fallible creatures; we all err at times; we cannot know fully the background socialization of transgressors; we cannot arrive at fully accurate judgments about the characters of other people; and we rarely are fully aware of the social circumstances other people endure. A principle of charity suggests that judging other people by their worst moments and by their most immoral acts is unwise. Instead, a wider assessment is recommended and the opportunity to atone for one's worst moments should be offered.

Thus, our *eighth element: Should the victim forgive a repentant transgressor, the metaphysical result is reconciliation and renewal. Should the victim forgive an unrepentant transgressor, the metaphysical result is an offer of reconciliation and renewal from the victim to the transgressor. To accept that offer, the transgressor must distance himself from his wrongful act or otherwise reach out to the victim.*

What is the relationship between forgiveness and punishment? Is forgiveness compatible with fully exacting the requirements of retributive justice? Or does forgiveness imply the waiving of all punishment?

Forgiveness is personal between the transgressor and the victim (or her agents or, perhaps, those especially close to her), and involves the victim's positive change of *feelings* toward the transgressor. Punishment is typically a legal notion whereby rightful authorities exact deprivation on the transgressor for a host of purposes: retribution, restitution, deterrence, rehabilitation, or incarceration. Retributive punishment implies depriving the transgressor of his freedom and many of his privileges in order to balance moral scales: the transgressor deserves to be retributively punished because he is responsible for wrongdoing. Restitution implies forcing the transgressor to make his victim whole by restoring, to the extent possible, the *status quo ante* through monetary compensation. Deterrence implies depriving the transgressor of his freedom and many of his privileges in order to deter him or others from committing similar offenses. Rehabilitation implies depriving the transgressor of his freedom and many of his privileges in order to reform him. Incarceration implies depriving the transgressor in order to protect society from his possible mayhem in the future.

Should the victim forgive the transgressor, she relinquishes her retributive feelings and her fantasies of vengeance. That is, the victim surrenders all thoughts of retaliation along with her harsh evaluation of the transgressor. The victim may, however, still conclude that institutional punishment of the (convicted) transgressor is appropriate on grounds of deterrence, rehabilitation, or incarceration. Moreover, forgiveness is compatible with seeking and accepting restitution from the transgressor. Indeed, making restitution is one way that a transgressor can facilitate the process of reconciliation and renewal.

Consider the following scenario: a perpetrator transgresses against a victim. After the perpetrator repents his wrong, the victim forgives him. She pleads with the legal authorities to forego punishing the perpetrator because she is convinced that he poses no future danger to others. The court, nevertheless, sentences the convicted perpetrator and cites retributive grounds. That the court has retributively punished the offender does not vitiate the victim's forgiveness of that offender. The victim's forgiveness is personal and involves her surrendering feelings of revenge and retribution. That the rightful authorities decide to punish the offender does not alter the victim's state of mind toward her transgressor.

One might argue that once the offender has served his sentence, once he has "paid his debt to society," then his wrong is expunged and there is nothing for the victim to forgive. In my judgment, that view is mistaken. Yes, the offender should now be allowed to rejoin society and enjoy freedom, but the victim's feelings toward the offender are still at issue. For example, suppose a negligent or reckless driver of a motor vehicle seriously injures a pedestrian. The victim was not targeted by the motorist; the harm was accidental. But the reckless driver is still culpable for his wrong and the victim, we will suppose, is paralyzed by his malfeasance. The driver sincerely repents his actions, pleads guilty, and is sentenced to a significant term in prison. He serves his time as a model prisoner and is eventually released.

Does it follow that the moral universe is now balanced and there is nothing for the victim to forgive? Hardly. In such a case, the *status quo ante* is impossible to restore. The victim has been and remains paralyzed. That the reckless driver has been retributively punished registers no effects on the victim's condition. She could have, of course, forgiven the transgressor at the time he repented and pled guilty, but suppose that she did not. Her career as an Olympic skier was ruined and she harbors ill will toward an obtuse motorist who was texting while driving at a high speed. Once the offender serves his sentence and is released, her feelings may or may not change. But the point is that forgiveness is still an option. That the convicted motorist has served his sentence does not imply that his wrongdoing has been expunged and that there is no wrong that might be forgiven.

This is in fact the case even in those situations where restitution does seem to restore the *status quo ante*. Suppose a reckless motorist slams into your parked car which is occupied by you and your small child. Miraculously, although your vehicle is severely damaged, you and the child suffer no significant injuries. Neither you nor the reckless driver has car insurance, but he makes full restitution and your car is returned to its former condition. Does it follow that forgiveness is impossible because restitution has expunged the reckless driver's wrong? No. You have still suffered great fear at the time of the collision, terror at the thought of the injuries that might have occurred, and major inconvenience during the period when your car was being repaired. The reckless driver's restitution cannot alter those facts. You may or may not decide to forgive his recklessness, but the point is that the possibility of forgiveness is not eliminated by his act of restitution—restitution does not expunge the wrong in the sense that there is nothing remaining that might be forgiven.

Jesus has an important addition to this analysis. Let's imagine a recidivist wrongdoer who never repents his deeds. In fact, he consistently reaffirms his connection to his transgressions. After every offense, even after those for which he is apprehended by the authorities, he brays, "I am proud of my mischief. These acts are true to my character. I apologize for nothing. I hope to increase my mayhem in the future. I've got to be me." In other words, by refusing to recant his actions and by pledging more of the same if possible, he utterly refuses to distance himself from his wrongdoing. Let's also assume that the typical ways that victims can unilaterally distance perpetrators from their wrongs are unavailable in this case. That is, the victim is not the subject of the perpetrator's first offense; the perpetrator's wrong was not grounded in good intentions; the perpetrator and the victim did not enjoy a prior salutary relationship; and the perpetrator cannot reasonably be judged as having suffered sufficiently in the aftermath of his wrong. Under these circumstances, it does not seem that the victim can forgive his transgressor because the required distance between the offender and his wrongful deed has not been established by the offender and cannot be created by the victim.

What would Jesus say? Even where forgiveness is not possible (as in the case above), the victim must still love his offender and advance his good. For example, "If you love those who love you, what credit is that to you? For even sinners love those who love them. And if you lend to those from whom you hope to receive, what credit is that to you? For even sinners do the same . . . But love your enemies, and do good, and lend, expecting nothing in return, and your reward will be great" (Luke 6: 32-35); "You have heard that it was said, 'An eye for an eye and a tooth for a tooth.' But if any one strikes you on the right cheek, turn to him the other also . . . Love your enemies and pray for those who persecute you" (Matt. 5: 38-39, 44).

This means, in part, relinquishing retributive feelings and banishing vengeful attitudes. Victims are enjoined to advance the good of even their offenders who remain "enemies." While it is easy to love those who love us and to benefit those who benefit us, the genuine test of our humanity is our response to those who transgress against us. We should not respond to transgressors precisely as they have treated us or even with the proportionate punishment that they deserve. Instead, we should aspire to a taxing ideal: loving those who have injured us. Perhaps the victim can also forget about the transgression, at least in time. Still, these approaches do not rise to the level of forgiveness because the required distance between offender and offense has not been established or created.

Is it humanly possible to love our unrepentant "enemy," seek to advance his good, and, perhaps, forget about his transgressions? Let's return to the hypothetical case I sketched. The recidivist offender, apparently lacking all redeeming social value, who, after being convicted of a major crime, snarls churlishly and sputters that he desires only to inflict more mayhem in the future. Can the mother of the young man, who was the murder victim of this lowlife, genuinely love the murderer, forego feelings of revenge, and seek his good? Although she probably will never forget what the murderer has done and cannot forgive him in the fullest philosophical sense of that term, I must admit that some victims—in this case, the mother of the victim—can achieve Jesus' ideal.

I say this because I was once an attorney in New York City and witnessed precisely such an event on a few occasions. Obviously, this does not occur as a matter of course, but only rarely. But I have seen and heard victims and their parents profess love for those who have grievously transgressed against them; they seemingly surrendered all thoughts of vengeance. Moreover, some of these paragons have tried to advance the good of these offenders after their convictions. Obviously, such a response is wildly counterintuitive, radically at variance with conventional moral wisdom, and fiercely at odds with human instincts. That some victims and their parents acted in such a manner can be explained only by their embrace of Jesus' revolutionary moral message.

We might wonder at the object of love in such cases. Is it the recidivist offender, in all his brutish ignobility? Is it some aura of humanity in which the offender shares by virtue of being a member of the human species? Is it love of Jesus, as a sort of third party beneficiary?

In any event, our *ninth and final element: Should the victim forgive the transgressor, he would abandon his retributive feelings and his fantasies of vengeance. The victim would surrender all thoughts of retaliation along with his harsh evaluation of the transgressor. However, the victim may still conclude that institutional punishment of the (convicted) transgressor is appropriate on grounds of deterrence, rehabilitation, or incarceration. Moreover, the victim's forgiveness is compatible with his seeking and accepting restitution from the transgressor. In fact, the transgressor's restitution is one way that he can facilitate the process of reconciliation and renewal with the victim. Moreover, neither the transgressor's repentance, nor his punishment by rightful authorities, nor his restitution expunges his wrongdoing such that there is nothing remaining for the victim to forgive. Finally, Jesus' revolutionary moral message enjoins victims to relinquish their retributive feelings and banish their vengeful attitudes even where forgiveness is not philosophically possible because the required distance between offender and offense is absent. Victims should aspire to the ideal of loving those "enemies" who have injured them and of enhancing their good.*

Perhaps we should not oversell the virtues of forgiveness. We should, at least, mention the dangers of forgiveness too easily bestowed. When victims forgive perpetrators of wrongs too facilely, they may increase the possibility of serial transgressions. If we are all free moral agents, responsible for our actions, then we must also accept the consequences of our mistakes. To be forgiven automatically may encourage wrongdoers to continue or amplify their wayward approach to life. For example, family members who continually forgive a spouse's or parent's abuse or aggressive actions may be unwitting collaborators in or unsuspecting enablers of future escalations of that violence. Moreover, just as we have epistemological problems in determining the mindsets of perpetrators of wrongs, we have similar problems when assessing the sincerity of their repentance. Surely, the chronicle of wrongdoing is replete with fraudulent expressions of remorse by perpetrators who understand well that victims and legal authorities welcome such demonstrations. To reward such false repentance with forgiveness brings no honor to either victim or perpetrator. We might insist on a type of moral symmetry: if we lack epistemological certitude about the intentions and motives of perpetrators of wrongs such that we are in a poor position to judge them, so too, we lack certitude regarding the sincerity of their expressions of repentance and are thus in a poor position to forgive them. Finally, those who forgive too easily might suffer from a lack of self-esteem; because of intense guilt or feelings of inferiority, they may on some level think they deserve to be transgressed upon. Accordingly, to conclude that some instances of forgiving are appropriate and some are inappropriate is reasonable.

From another vantage point, it may seem that those who forgive others arrogate to themselves the positions of judge and moral superior. Despite Jesus' injunction to avoid judging others (Matt. 7: 1), forgiving others presupposes that the victim has judged that a perpetrator has wronged him or her and the perpetrator is fully responsible for that transgression. The victim has judged that something bad has happened that might be forgiven. The victim, one might well argue, then places himself or herself in a position of moral superiority: although the victim initially harbors resentment and, probably, thoughts of retaliation, the victim will forego those sentiments in the interests of magnanimity. In effect, the victim has turned the tables on the perpetrator in that the perpetrator may well sense that the victim believes that the act of forgiveness places the perpetrator in the victim's debt. Behind the apparent purity of the victim's motives may lay a repressed resentment and subtle moral retaliation that is masked by high-minded rhetoric. Perhaps victims who forgive do so in service of their own empowerment: they assume the role of divine judge and generously bestow forgiveness upon their moral subordinates. The act of forgiveness, then, may at least sometimes be laced with moral condescension; to forgive another person may be a way to elevate oneself and to underscore that person's moral inferiority. This is especially true in cases where the quality of the perpetrator's act is somewhat contestable or where the perpetrator's responsibility for that act is ambiguous.

A truly stellar individual, such as the father in the Parable of the Prodigal Son, who does not respond to supposed slights with resentment and negative judgments, lacks the prerequisites of forgiveness. In that parable, I would argue that the father, a paragon of unconditional love, does not truly forgive his wayward son because he never judged that his son had wronged him. Lacking negative sentiments toward his son, the father could not relinquish them in order to forgive.

My point is not that all acts of forgiveness mask mendacious motives, but only that not all acts of forgiveness are morally pure. Assuming we had full access to the inner spirits of other people, we would need to evaluate fully the motives and intentions of forgiving people to assess the moral quality of their acts; the act of forgiveness as such is not morally self-ratifying. As Jesus taught, inner motives and intentions are critical to moral assessment. Of course, that places us, again, in the role of judge, a position that Jesus instructs us to avoid. The deeper conceptual problem, then, is this: Is Jesus' injunction to avoid judging others compatible with his imperative to forgive the transgressions and shortcomings of others? How can we forgive others without judging the quality of their actions and motivations?

If Jesus is enjoining human beings to forgive in the same fashion as God forgives us then we might point out that the judgments of God have advantages that those of human beings lack, one of which is epistemological infallibility.

In any case, the foundations of how Jesus views our world and our mission in it consist of his recurring general themes: he makes moral judgments from an Archimedean point of the Ideal Observer, God; as such, Jesus privileges the universal and the unconditional over the particular and contingent; from this perspective, what is common among human beings—their supposed spark of divinity and shared membership in the human community—is more important than factual inequalities that they embody; from this arises a commitment to radical egalitarianism such that we should extend our love and concern to everyone, especially to those with special needs. Jesus is suspicious of formalistic and mechanical application of moral law to specific cases. He cautions us against pursuing the flimsy glitter of material accumulation and celebrity in this world. He is suspicious of moral claims grounded in the principle of desert and his is a virtue ethic that places great emphasis on inner motives and intentions.

Throughout history, many writers have argued that existential tension is at the heart of human experience: our yearning for intimate connection with others and the recognition that others are necessary for our identity and freedom coalesce uneasily with the fear and anxiety we experience as others approach.[17] We simultaneously long for emotional attachment yet are horrified that our individuality may evaporate once we achieve it. If we experience too much individuality we risk alienation, estrangement, and psychological isolation. If we experience insufficient individuality we court emotional suffocation, loss of self-esteem, and unhealthy immersion in the collectivity. This disharmony may never be fully reconciled once and forever, and so we find ourselves making uneasy compromises and adjustments during our life's journey as we oscillate along the continuum whose endpoints are 'radical individuality' and 'thorough immersion in community', respectively. This existential tension replicates itself at numerous levels: the individual confronts family, the family confronts wider community, communities confront society, and society confronts the state.

By stressing our joint project of redemption and salvation, and through his relentless call for unconditional love and forgiveness, Jesus places himself squarely on the communitarian side of the continuum. However, Friedrich Nietzsche has a radically different approach to our existential predicament. We shall now turn to Nietzsche's invocation of power and self-actualization.

Two

NIETZSCHE: THE NATURE OF OUR WORLD AND OUR MISSION IN IT

His commitments to perspectivism, genealogical accounts, the connection between knowledge and crafting the self, and the nature of values underwrite Friedrich Nietzsche's substantive normative conclusions.

1. Perspectivism

Nietzsche's perspectivism denies the existence of absolute, transcendent truths and affirms the need for perspectival interpretations. Nietzsche rejects the distinction between the true world and the seeming or false world. The phenomenal world—the world as it is commonly experienced by human beings—is the only world that matters. The notion of an external, objective reality is unintelligible in his view because any experience of a part of this alleged reality would be distorted by being filtered through the prism of one's subjectivity. For Nietzsche, no things-in-themselves stand above space, time, and our grasp of causality. Language and conventional discourse, which reflect the needs, interests, and psychology of different types of human beings, mold our beliefs about the world. We embrace perspectives to cope with, impose order on, and make sense of our context. Accordingly, the perspectives we select are connected to our character, experiences, and powers. We cannot access brute facts that are independent of our perspectival interpretations; we cannot legitimately appeal to foundational justifications for our truth claims. Thus, we lack access to a specific account or a privileged perspective that could uniquely capture the complexities of physical reality: we are unable to access an Archimedean point. Perspectivism, then, is the fundamental condition of human life.

Nietzsche rejects the self-defeating conclusion that all perspectival interpretations are equally sound. Some perspectives are better than others because they are more comprehensive; open to revision; self-consciously adopt fallibilism; better reflect the available evidence; flow from nobler origins; are not infected by resentment and dishonesty; have greater style and unity; increase power more than other perspectives; and the like. Nietzsche accepts a deflated version of "objectivity": knowing objects by employing a variety of perspectives that reflect more interests; filtering out distorting psychological factors such as resentment and nationalistic fervor; and being aware of and controlling our antecedent biases. Thus, Nietzsche aspires to attain as complete a vision of objects as is humanly possible. On this view, truth is what we are warranted in believing on the basis of the best available evidence. However, the findings we derive are not the objective truths extolled in conventional discourse: pure, dispassionate, transcendent conclusions arising from contemplations unaffected by interests. Under this general framework, Nietzsche cannot independently *prove* perspectivism, but he takes perspectivism to be the most warranted belief based on the best available evidence.

Lacking the capability to create firm, fixed foundations for our epistemological and moral theories, we are advised by Nietzsche to regard those theories as aesthetic creations—ways of purposefully engaging the world that are always susceptible to challenge and revision. However, one recurring difficulty for Nietzsche is describing the status of his own conclusions. Given his broad themes such as perspectivism, the inability of language to capture life's complexities and fluidity, and the denial of absolutism, his own findings may seem no more binding than anyone else's subjective musings. That is, Nietzsche's own conclusions seem to wither in significance when judged by Nietzsche's broader philosophical themes. Thus, a critic might well argue that Nietzsche's work is fatally ensnared by self-referential paradox. As much as he rails against dogmatism and absolutism, he ends up advancing his own positive theses—indeed he must—as if they were unconditional insights. So he presents his convictions—that "all truths are conditional," "there is no aperspectival truth," "there are no things-in-themselves," "the world is inherently undifferentiated chaos," "the judgments of the herd nurture mediocrity," and all the rest of his views—as if they are "really" true. He underscores what he himself takes to be the stench of unconditionality when he asserts his conclusions with such self-promotion and such rhetorical stridency.

But such an objection to Nietzsche's perspectivism assumes that stability of meaning, explaining away conflict, the principle of identity, and the entire objective world are the framework within which Nietzsche must work in order to convince his audience. But how could he possibly do that, at least through reason, when he denies from the start all those presuppositions? Of course, from within a different set of language games from those within which Nietzsche operates, Nietzsche's views will seem deficient, for it is precisely the metaphysical and logical basis of those language games that Nietzsche calls into question.

Nietzsche understands well the conditionality of his own views; he does not hold them as aperspectival or absolute truths. His multiple literary styles, his appreciation of ambiguity, his calculated reversals of meanings—which critics would call equivocations, his embrace of flux and conflict as definitive of life, all exemplify his most deeply held convictions: the need for self-overcoming, institutional deconstruction and re-creation, going beyond one's own current convictions. His real message, I think, is not in specific recommendations, but in these broad themes. He is not a closet absolutist seeking to impose fixed doctrines on humanity; he remains the apostle of contingency.

Critics will not be persuaded. They will argue that the basic principles of logic do not merely constitute one language game among many. Moreover, they will claim that Nietzsche begs all the critical questions—he assumes as true that which he purports to prove. By ruling out, virtually by fiat, the reality of an external world not of our making, the possibility of truths that transcend perspectives emanating from human desire, and all the rest, he immunizes himself from critical attack by mainstream philosophers and thereby trivializes his own position. His followers can always say, as I have, that others cannot criticize him (without begging the question against him) from the typical standpoints because those are the very standpoints he wishes to deny. But that, say critics, only reveals the desperation and vacuity of Nietzsche's position.

Fundamentally, critics argue that if Nietzsche was aware of the conditionality of his own position then that undercuts his persuasiveness. If Nietzsche's own themes are merely perspectival renderings emanating from Nietzsche's "will to power," as molded from his historical and social contexts, then those who oppose Nietzsche's conclusions have little antecedent reason to be swayed from their own views.

However, defenders of Nietzsche have a rejoinder. Critics assume that "persuasion" is equivalent to "rational demonstration in accord with bivalent logic." But Nietzsche's views are always tied in with ways of life. One should not be persuaded to Nietzsche's view because it is demanded by impartial reason, that itself would be un-Nietzschean. Nietzsche does not seek disciples from commonplace minds or abject hero worshipers. At bottom, he does not want his views to be mainstream for that would suggest that the herd mentality is compatible with those views. He pitches his case to the few, those of aristocratic temperament who can joyfully and eagerly welcome the realization that conflict, contingency, and instability prevail in life. Perspectives are not merely belief-structures; they reflect and affect entire ways of life. But closing themselves off from Nietzschean themes, critics reveal their preferences for stability and authority, their resistance to ambiguity and nuance, and their yearning to inhabit a black-and-white-world. Nietzscheans would advise such critics to open themselves to the possibilities of life and revel in human powers of creation.

But critics are unlikely to accept these remarks. To them, Nietzsche's self-conscious acceptance of the contingency of his own views remains problematic. Why should we think, even under Nietzsche's own broad themes, that Nietzsche's conclusions are anything more than a reflection of Nietzsche's psychology? And, if so, why would we want a life such as Nietzsche's? He was a recurrently ill, isolated, alienated writer who went insane, possibly from syphilis he contracted during one of his few sexual encounters. Perhaps he could write a good life, if one views his work charitably, but he surely did not lead one.

Defenders of Nietzsche will insist that Nietzsche intends only to undermine the absolutism of one of our second-order beliefs (one of our beliefs about our beliefs) about truths: the belief that our truths are rationally required for all people. He clearly does not hold the feckless views that "every view is as good as every other" or that "believing something to be the case is sufficient to make it the case." According to Nietzsche, we can still have strong convictions and beliefs while acknowledging the fallibility of those beliefs. This is especially the case when he recognizes that such convictions and beliefs are necessary for life and that aperspective truths are unavailable to human beings. Nietzsche is interested in the relations of power that generate our discourse of truth/falsity and what effects that discourse itself generates. So he does not try to prove his conclusions through the fixed methods of deductive logic for then he would really have a self-referential paradox: establishing broad themes of contingency, flux, and perspectivity through narrow categories of necessity, fixed meanings, and absolutism. Instead, he casts suspicion on the origins and modes of life embodied by mainstream views and he invites us to a special dance: deconstruction, reimagination, and re-creation in the service of new ways of life. Because conclusions supposedly arise from a person's motives and character, Nietzsche's perspectivism includes a psychological test: What kind of person would embrace this position or view? The answer to this question will not automatically reveal the truth or falsity of the position or view, but it will help produce the genealogical account of how the position or view was spawned.

Critics will deny that the relationship between our beliefs and our beliefs about our beliefs is as simple as Nietzscheans have suggested. Whether we believe that our beliefs about, say, justice, fairness, and equality are objectively grounded is paramount to the fervor with which we hold and express them. You need only look to the history of religious fanaticism to see this: holy wars, grand inquisitions, suicide missions, martyrdom, centuries-old feuds over allegedly sacred land, intractable policy differences, and the like. To "cast suspicion upon" our second-order beliefs has a profound influence on the way we perceive our first-order beliefs.

Perhaps, though, Nietzsche undermines our second-order belief in the absolutism of our beliefs because he wants to have a profound influence on the way we perceive our first-order beliefs. He suggests that people of greatness, those mentally and physically capable of transcending the herd mentality, will find their creative energies animated by the joyous embrace of radical contingency. Nietzsche would reject the view that a belief in the objectivity of our first-order beliefs is necessary for robust convictions. Does not Nietzsche himself demonstrate that such is not the case? Does he not have firm convictions, held fallibilistically? Can't we recognize the revisability and finitude of our beliefs, yet still express them strongly? Why think that dogmatism and absolutism must underwrite our thoughts and practices?

Moreover, Nietzsche cannot, once we understand his broad themes, advance any theory of truth as a fixed doctrine. He is more interested in painting a picture, demonstrating a dance, singing a song. We will be drawn to his aesthetics (in a broad sense), we will be repelled, or we will be indifferent. Our reactions, contrary to the understandings of mainstream analytic philosophers, will result not from differing applications of the humorless, prosaic categories of bivalent logic, but from differing temperaments and ways of life. Again, Nietzsche does not seek universal acceptance of his convictions; indeed, such acceptance would be the clearest refutation of his thoughts because it would signal their co-optation by the herd; and insofar as the categories of logic demand universal assent they falsify the fluidity and rank order of life. Thus, Nietzsche is simply not, indeed cannot be, interested in providing neat theoretical structures for his convictions. Given his broad themes, any attempt to do so would be fatal to Nietzsche's project. He knows that he cannot hope to refute mainstream philosophy by employing its own conceptual tools.

Critics will find these remarks too facile. If I disagree with Nietzsche that actually confirms his broadest themes and establishes what he presupposes: I accept mainstream philosophical argumentation so I must be temperamentally and intellectually deficient. If I point out the puzzles and problems within Nietzsche's thought then all Nietzscheans rejoice because it shows that he has succeeded in provoking the herd mentality, in unsettling its confidence, and in exposing life's paradoxes. For Nietzscheans, their leader does not have to resolve paradox and conflict. Instead, he must only raise doubts, manifest contingency, and cast suspicion on mainstream ideas. To fascinate, provoke, fragment, and deconstruct become the core of the "philosopher of the future"—the philosopher as performative artist.

The critics' comments are telling, but omit several Nietzschean aspirations. For example, Nietzsche has an overriding concern for cultural reimagination and re-creation; style is important for Nietzsche because he sees the link between the writings of the great philosophers and their lives; and he recognizes a range of motivations which correlate to the rank order of human beings. Nietzsche is wary of theories of truth because he suspects the motives and impugns the historical uses which they have served. Theories of truth have been vessels for evading responsibility for our beliefs, social practices, and personal actions. Worse, they are the prime collaborators with dogmatism in nurturing uniformity of belief.[1] Thus, they deny the rank order of life by appealing to universality, objectivity, and impersonal (or supernatural) authority. Moreover, notions of truth obscure the fluidity of the world and the "dynamical importance of ideas as vehicles for promoting and stultifying various forms of life."[2] Nietzsche treats his own ideas as experiments, as transitory, as robustly conditioned by his historical context. He understands fully that he cannot advocate that everyone should ahistorically abrogate the notion of unconditional truth.[3] The herd mentality, part of which involves wholesale acceptance of unconditional truth generated from supernatural sources, is fine for those who are (inherently?) members of the herd. What Nietzsche resists is the herd mentality's resentful and vengeful claims to universality; its hostile quest to impose its mindset on everyone forever. If the herd is successful then the result would be widespread mediocrity which would minimize the development of great individuals and cultural breakthroughs. At his core, Nietzsche is more concerned with promoting possibilities for refined ways of life than he is with abstract renderings of allegedly eternal truths.

So truth and falsity, for Nietzsche, are not dualisms, but differences of degree; different people, although all possessing the will to power, express their power in different measures of refinement which manifest their various types and specific ways of life. Nietzsche's warm embrace of radical contingency undermines the fixed categories of binary oppositions. In some sense, Nietzsche thought it was sufficient merely to admit the conditionality of his own views—to accept the contingent perspectivism of his perspectivism, to highlight the inevitability of conceptual conflict in human thought, and to underscore the experimentalism of his own conclusions. These thoughts would be amicable with, indeed they partly constitute, Nietzsche's broad themes. Nietzsche does not completely reject logic and reason. In fact his own thought, as it must, embodies patterns, a logic of deconstruction, reversal, and rehabilitation, and appreciation of the historical role of mainstream rhetoric. What he objects to is the dogmatism of first-order world views. He is not necessarily asserting that perspectivism as a second-order metatheory was absolutely true, only that it could possibly be absolutely true. Such a stance would preserve the core of his broad themes yet permit him to sidestep the paradox of self-reference.

At bottom, the trajectory of Nietzsche's thought will always appear unsatisfying to mainstream analytic philosophers. They will respond that if perspectivism as a second-order metatheory could be possibly absolutely true then why can't (some? most? all?) of the claims of particular first-order world views possibly be absolutely true? They will grant that if perspectivism is absolutely true as a second-order metatheory then the claims of first-order world views could not be absolutely true, but they would then relocate their inquiry about the vantage point from which the absolute truth of the metatheory could be made (consistent with Nietzsche's broad themes). But if Nietzscheans finesse the critics' original complaint by resorting to the mere possibility of perspectivism being absolutely true as a second-order metatheory then critics can resuscitate the possibility of the absolute truth of at least some first-order world views. Unless and until the two sides resolve the respective 'possibilities,' Nietzscheans and mainstreamers might be left with a rhetorical stalemate.

The safest position for Nietzsche is to hold that perspectivism as a second-order metatheory is the view that most merits our belief and allegiance. Nietzsche does not want us all to think and act alike, and does not desire universal acceptance of his thought. He does not want any abject disciples. In sum, we must overcome not only our selves and our cultural inheritance (to the extent possible), but also Nietzsche's own thought. The notion of self-overcoming may well be the quasi-foundational foil that binds Nietzsche's broad themes together. All philosophies and perspectives necessarily depend on presuppositions. Nietzsche's perspectivism, as a second-order metatheory, revels in the rank order of life: it denies that we can measure all people by a single scale, and it denies the neutrality of first-order perspectives.[4] Perspectivism does not claim that every view is necessarily an interpretation and thus perspectivism cannot be disproved by showing that it is possible that some views are not interpretations. Such a showing would suggest only that perspectivism is possibly false, not that perspectivism is false. Thus to disprove perspectivism one would have to show that some views are not in fact interpretations, not merely that it is possible that some views are not interpretations.[5]

But does it help Nietzsche to insist that perspectivism is actually true (first-order belief) although it may possibly be untrue (second-order belief)? What would permit Nietzsche to make such a claim? Would he merely be begging the question against critics?

Nietzscheans might respond in several ways. First, it may well be the critics of Nietzsche who beg the question by implicitly viewing perspectival interpretation as an ersatz form of understanding. Second, while perspectivism cannot compel its own acceptance under this argument that correlates well with Nietzsche's denial of dogmatism, his refusal to seek universal agreement, and his constant reminder that different interpretations of the world flow from different kinds of people. Nietzscheans should concede straightaway, in concert with Nietzsche's broad themes, that they cannot convince everyone—that is, there is no neutral argumentation method antecedently binding on all—that Nietzsche's perspectivism escapes self-referential paradox. To think otherwise is to reinstate dogmatism. All they can do is cast suspicion on the beliefs of those who insist that Nietzsche's perspectivism is clearly refuted by self-referential paradox. They can call into question the motives of critics, and undermine the genealogy and the value of the life forms partially generated by their foundational beliefs. They can also engage in immanent critique by entering the favored categories and language games of the critics and make the case that their proofs fail when judged by their own standards. They cannot, however, within the critics' preferred categories and language games prove that Nietzsche's perspectivism is untouched by self-referential paradox or that perspectivism must   be accepted.

Critics will rejoin that the laws of logical thought are not merely one set of category or language game among many. Instead, they are purely formal and necessary for rational thought. They are "neutral" in that they do not inherently recommend any particular form of life. While their origins may lie in the human need to impose order and meaning on the world, that correlates with Nietzsche's broad themes. Thus, to refer to the laws of logical thought as a language game preferred by some or as mainstream categories is misleading.

From a Nietzschean perspective, however, the laws of thought and formal logic are particular ways of carving up the world. They may be "necessary" for us but only given the people we are and the historical legacy we have inherited. While they do not, say, imply any particular moral or political structure—they aren't part of a democratic conspiracy or a communist plot—their binary and dualistic prejudices may well nurture dogmatism and thereby artificially limit possibilities. If there are numerous possible ways to categorize the world of flux then the structures of bivalent logic are themselves only one among many possibilities. Thus their claims to ahistorical necessity would be false. Even within the categories of mainstream reasoning there are multivalent logics which deny the necessity and practical viability of binary oppositions. Multivalent logics see the world as ambiguous and filled with conflicts. They take "paradoxes of self-reference [to be] half-truths. Fuzzy contradictions. A AND not-A holds but A is true only 50% and not-A is true only 50%. The paradoxes are literally half true and half false. They reside at midpoints of fuzzy cubes, equidistant from the black-and-white corners."[6] Much Eastern thought, for example, sees the world filled "with things and not-things, with roses that are both red and not red, with A AND not-A."[7] Multivalent logics hold that the proof techniques of binary logic falsify the world. More important, such logics have proved superior to binary logics in a host of practical contexts.[8] Perhaps, then, the standard Western categories of thought are not ahistorically necessary, especially because robust ways of life have been formed without them.

Still, to conclude that the laws of formal logic are presupposed in our discourse is reasonable. Also, Nietzscheans depend on these laws even to unsettle their authority and "fuzzy logics" must depend on the standard categories of thought to make their probabilistic claims.

Nietzscheans will insist that it may seem that way, but only because they need to make themselves intelligible in standard discourse to communicate with mainstreamers. Nietzsche realizes that changing the paradigms of philosophical discourse requires the positing of new criteria and new presuppositions, but he also knows he cannot escape from all elements of established paradigms. Indeed these paradigms form the context from which Nietzsche critiques and from which (at least to some extent) he will be evaluated. Perhaps Nietzsche's pattern of deconstruction, reversal, and re-creation is tacit admission of all this. However, Nietzsche's project is fundamentally practical not theoretical; it concerns action not merely reflection.[9]

The brunt of Nietzsche's suspicions is cast at bivalent logic, not all logic. For example, Nietzsche wonders, "What forces us at all to suppose that there is an essential opposition of 'true' and 'false'? Is it not sufficient to assume degrees of apparentness?" (BGE 34) Also, he retains some appreciation for even bivalent logic as a means of ordering the inherent chaos that is the cosmos. Although Nietzsche is suspicious of the way bivalent logic can lure us into accepting Platonic realism, he takes (multivalent?) logic to be a presupposition of thought and perhaps of life. Thus, Nietzsche does not wage a wholesale assault on logic as such, but, typically, only against certain effects and second-order beliefs encouraged by a particular form of logic. And, again typically, he tries to unsettle those effects and second-order beliefs because of the ersatz attitudes toward life they allegedly nurture.

There are numerous ways of trying to confront the self-referential paradox as it pertains to Nietzsche's perspectivism, of trying to undermine its imperialism, of trying to soften its effects and appeal without disproving its applicability. The force of the self-referential paradox depends on a dogmatic acceptance of bivalent logic and an interpretation of perspectivism that forces it to make the claim that every assertion bears a truth value that is perspective-specific. One might claim, on behalf of Nietzscheans, that while virtually all assertions bear truth values that are perspective-specific, a few assertions bear the same truth values in all human perspectives.[10] This version of perspectivism may evade self-referential paradox, because a statement of its own truth may be one of these few assertions that is true in all human perspectives. In fact this version of perspectivism can claim that the only assertions that are true in all human perspectives are assertions about perspectivism's own truth and whatever else Nietzsche requires as a quasi-foundation for his philosophy—his broad themes and the presuppositions required to assert his broad themes.

The benefit of this approach is that it neither reinstates absolutism nor seriously compromises Nietzsche's broad themes of radical contingency and self-overcoming. We could view the convergence of truth claims across all human perspectives as historically but not ahistorically necessary. In other words, perspectivism itself is not objectively true in the sense of being embedded in nature or of being decreed by a nonhuman legislator of truth. Instead, it could be viewed as merely historically necessary given the peoples now inhabiting the earth and the modes of life they have constructed. Such a view would permit Nietzsche to retain the fallibalism of second-order beliefs while strategizing within mainstream language games. Although I cannot claim that Nietzsche would adopt this approach, given his practical orientation that he would be troubled by the paradox of self-reference is doubtful.

The approach I have suggested, however, is not beyond criticism. It may strike critics of Nietzsche as ad hoc and a desperate attempt to exempt Nietzsche's assertions about the truth of perspectivism itself from perspectivism's own critical bite. What basis would I have for selecting a favored few across-perspectives-truths? What criteria distinguish truths that are and are not perspective-specific? The only ground appears to be Nietzsche's need to exempt some of his assertions in order to evade a self-referential paradox. Surely, need is an unsound criterion of categorization. Furthermore, critics might argue that it is not enough to claim that perspectivism itself, Nietzsche's broad themes, and the presuppositions needed to make those broad themes may be across-perspectives-truths. I would need to demonstrate in an independent fashion that they are across-perspectives-truths. The mere claimed possibility that these favored few assertions are across-perspectives-truths is insufficient to evade the lingering presence of self-referential paradox.

But I am not trying to prove that Nietzsche's views can be interpreted in a way that escapes the claws of the prized strategy of bivalent logic: the self-referential paradox. I am only trying to loosen its grip and soften its pressure. In fact to prove that perspectivism is immune from the paradox would be untrue to Nietzsche's broad themes. Accordingly, any criticisms from mainstreamers that demonstrate my inability to prove what I do not intend to prove are misguided. The self-understandings—the dogmatism and absolutism—of numerous perspectives refer to their second-order beliefs. My offering on behalf of Nietzschean perspectivism concerns first order perspectives themselves. Obviously, I would never refer to the actual self-understandings of extant perspectives as evidence for my suggested approach. Most of Nietzsche's work calls those self-understandings into question as its fundamental project.

A key distinction under my approach is that "between something being true in all [human] perspectives and something being true outside of all perspectives."[11] Nietzsche must deny the latter because it is an implication of his anti-metaphysical position: his rejection of things-in-themselves, divine legislators, inherent order in the universe, and neutral vantage points. Nietzsche, if I am correct, can accept the former because it is compatible with his broad themes. Thus, across-perspectives-truths have no special metaphysical status, even though they are true in all human perspectives. There would remain, for Nietzscheans, no extra-perspectival truths. For Nietzsche, perspectives are action-guiding, life-molding, evaluative understandings of a world of undetermined flux. The world becomes a product of perspectival interpretations.

But does my approach relegate Nietzsche to the type of dogmatism and absolutism that he otherwise disparages? I do not think so if we distinguish between dangerous dogmatism and benign dogmatism. The dangerous kind of dogmatism takes what is good for some people at some time as metaphysically mandatory for all people at all times. My approach has no such implication; it is compatible with a contingent, historical convergence of all human perspectives. This holds open the possibility of new human types and new human contexts whose perspectives would not converge with the established across-perspectives-truths. This possibility preserves and highlights Nietzsche's broad theme of self-overcoming. Thus the dogmatism of my approach is benign: it neither depends on accepting metaphysical foundations nor posits timeless truths. Nietzscheans could therefore retain their second-order belief in fallibalism.

Although Nietzsche attacks the metaphysician's search for foundational truths as revealing moral weakness and fear of contingency, he also praises intellectual rigor as a refusal to accept received opinion unquestioningly. He subscribes wholeheartedly to the critical impulses of the will to truth, but rejects its yearning for eternal, foundational grounds. His point is that the critical impulses of the will to truth undermine acceptance of the foundationalists' quest. Thus, the will to truth, when understood honestly, must resist one of its own aspirations: foundationalism.

The core of Nietzschean perspectivism is not any specific conglomerate of views and evaluations but the broad theme that numerous clusters of views and evaluations are possible and apt for different peoples. Although, for the sake of effective articulation, I have been presenting Nietzschean themes in simplified, rigid form, he understood that he could not describe, advance, and defend his views in the standard manner. I have written about Nietzsche or Nietzscheans "asserting" this or that, and thereby have suffocated Nietzsche's thought by divorcing it from his literary style and by artificially forcing it into propositional form. To that extent my articulation is an ersatz imitation of Nietzsche's thought that too often fails to highlight another one of his broad themes: He must exemplify rather than assert his views and evaluations. He must embody them and manifest to others—but only a few others—their possibilities for facilitating new modes of life. Readers must then ask themselves "What type of person do I want to become?" and "Am I able to become such a person?"[12]

Again, we must underscore a few of Nietzsche's most important broad themes: Nietzsche understands that perspectivism cannot be proved; he does not and cannot claim that all others are required by reason to embrace it; he gives psychological explanations of why some people are attracted to perspectivism while others are not; and he pitches his presentation to rare, superior types who can become legislators, not merely reflectors, of values.

Unscrupulous types, wrongly supposing themselves to be a higher breed, may wrongly try to invoke Nietzsche's work as an imprimatur for their indefensible aspirations. Indeed, history shows this can occur. But we should not conclude that the work of mainstream analytic philosophers is invulnerable to such abuse. For Nietzsche, such thinkers are masters of illusion who are likely to conceal the origins and purposes of their work, and to deny the autobiographical elements of their thoughts. But in their more sober moments they understand that even our most useful scientific theories are underdetermined by the evidence and that the evidence itself is not pure—it is "infected" by our theories; that our language cannot reflect reality but instead manifests our interests, purposes, desires, and power; that the rules of rationality themselves cannot be independently justified because they themselves determine what should count as a good reason or a sound justification. Thus what theories we prefer are mainly a function of interests and powers, and what theories prevail in a society are mainly a function of what groups have the most power to effect their wills and instantiate their interests.

All this is lost, however, and we sustain illusions by clinging to notions such as the objectivity of knowledge; the ahistorical understanding of reason and institutions; the refusal to examine the genealogy—the history—of how things, including standards of reason, became as they are; the disinclination to see power for what it is; and the inclination to mask the role of social conflict in establishing truths.

As always, however, remaining true to Nietzsche requires that we view events from multiple perspectives; that we interrogate what seem to be firm Nietzschean conclusions from the vantage point of immanent critique. Are Nietzscheans deceived about their own motives and the genealogy of their own views? Do they tacitly yearn for metaphysical certainty and transcendental standards, but when such certainty and standards cannot be independently established conclude there is only nihilism? Do they detect limitations and fragility in the mainstream criteria of logic, language, and morality then conclude hastily that radical indeterminacy and contingency are all-pervasive. At bottom, do they actually accept the polarities of either metaphysical realism (the view that numerous truths about the world are mind-independent: embedded in the universe and discoverable by human reason) or radical contingency (the view that there are many incommensurable, conflicting paradigms, theories, and life forms). If so, do these polarities exude vitality only if we share the conviction that the two alternatives define the range of possibilities? Perhaps those who share that conviction are unwitting collaborators in the same discourse, not true adversaries. Might Nietzscheans be merely closet metaphysical realists who have lost their faith?

Such questions merit and reward a close study. But we first need to distinguish Nietzsche from the run-of-the-mill apostle of radical contingency. He never stops at "either metaphysical realism or radical contingency." He exemplifies how the philosophers of the future, as legislators of values, can overcome the nihilistic moment and use radical contingency for practical advantages. Nietzsche's view can be better described as "metaphysical realism or radical contingency or recurrent deconstruction, reimagination, re-creation." Furthermore, different types of human beings will embrace different "solutions" to the problem of human life: the herd will still cling to versions of metaphysical realism; the severely alienated will wallow in passive or pathetic nihilism and be overwhelmed by radical contingency; while the higher human types will gratefully luxuriate in deconstruction, reimagination, re-creation.

We must not forget that Nietzsche does not separate theoretical and practical concerns.[13] He also underscores the connection between theoretical knowledge and practical action; how one's theoretical commitments can vivify one's life style. Nietzsche perceives the recurrent need to overcome forms of truth in the service of creating new possibilities for life. In that vein, philosophers of the future must overcome the "spirit of gravity" whose unbearable heaviness threatens to keep us rooted in familiar contexts and institutions. With regard to language, Nietzsche warns us of its inherent function to mislead: to present itself as mirroring reality while in fact it partially constitutes a way human beings have imposed meaning and order on the world of

Becoming. Because of the limitations of language, truth and reality itself must remain ineffable. As we impose seemingly fixed categories and doctrines we simplify and falsify. For Nietzsche, none of this is horrifying; it is just part of the human condition.

Nietzsche's conception of language fits well with his general understanding of theories and doctrines. Instead of asking what features in the world make a doctrine true, he asks what types of needs, interests, desires, and distribution of powers exist (or must be created) to underwrite the doctrine. Thus Nietzsche ties in theory with modes of life. And that is why he thinks we cannot distinguish thinkers from their thought. All writing is autobiographical because philosophy must be lived prior to being disseminated, it must be exemplified instead of being aridly taught. Because there are numerous human types and numerous modes of life Nietzsche refuses to subscribe to second-order dogmatism and absolutism.

For example, how much one tolerates ambiguity, how community minded or individualistic one is, what elements most fully constitute one's sense of identity, one's personal and family history—How could these not affect greatly, perhaps even determine, philosopher's acceptance or rejection of various philosophical positions that embody various images of these influences? But we cannot oversimplify all this. We must not conclude that univocal, transparent psychological profiles of authors can be easily extracted from perusing a few pieces of their work.[14] Nietzsche celebrates the multiplicity of drives that constitute human beings. Profound spirits do not deny their inner conflicts or seek solace in the homogenizing labors of mainstream analytic philosophy, which disguises then renounces the contradictions partially constituting the human condition. Instead, Nietzsche sees the quest for fixed, unambiguous doctrines, social practices, and values as decadent, as symptoms of decline.

2. Genealogical Critiques

Nietzsche casts suspicion on dominant understandings by revealing their disreputable origins and their checkered history. Genealogical critiques are designed to undermine the pretensions that received opinions are natural, inevitable, unconditional, and universal. For Nietzsche, several factors make a view's origin disreputable: It may conflict with Nietzsche's highest value, *amor fati*, a maximally affirmative attitude toward life; it may arise from inferior psychology, such as *ressentiment;* it may tend toward egalitarianism and the leveling of culture; it may reflect the interests of unworthy types of human beings; or it may blossom from a dubious perspective.

We might be tempted to conclude that Nietzsche repeatedly commits the genetic fallacy, an elementary logical error. That conclusion would be mistaken. The genetic fallacy occurs when someone tries to prove the falsity of a belief by impugning the origins of that belief (for example, the feckless character of the person who holds the belief or the deplorable conditions under which the belief was embraced). If someone argued "belief X is false because it is held by person P who is deficient / dim-witted / ill-motivated / mean-spirited / or the like" that person would be committing the genetic fallacy. Beliefs and conclusions are considered true or false independently of the character of the people who hold them or the way they came to be believed.

Nietzsche seems to commit the genetic fallacy when, for example, he argues that dominant values are promulgated by weaker human types pervaded by *ressentiment*; or when he argues that mainstream morality and religion are creations flowing from the needs of a herd mentality that characterizes the mediocre masses.

But first appearances are often deceiving. Nietzsche does not commit the genetic fallacy because he does not argue that the views of last men or the herd are false. That is, Nietzsche does not argue that the dominant ideas are false because of the type of people who hold them or how they were originally constructed. He, instead, uses his genealogical critiques to cast suspicion on certain beliefs (in contrast to trying to prove them false). He concludes that the values of the herd are unworthy of belief, at least for those who are not members of the herd. The distinction is between (a) establishing truth and falsity and (b) scrambling for what we are warranted in believing—what is reasonable to believe given the overall circumstances.

For example, if a five-year-old, who is often wrong, states that a certain scientific hypothesis is true you have much less reason to believe that hypothesis than you would if the top scientist in the USA stated the same hypothesis to you. The truth of the hypothesis is independent of who tells it to you, but your basis and warrant for believing the hypothesis does vary in the two cases presented. Only if you argued "The hypothesis must be false because the simple child believes it" would you be committing the genetic fallacy. If you concluded "I have little or no reason to believe in the hypothesis because the simple child believes it," you would not be committing the genetic fallacy. What Nietzsche does is much more like the latter than the former.

3. Crafting a Worthy Self

For Nietzsche, the paramount human task is the ongoing project of *crafting a worthy self*. He downplays the pursuit of learning for its own sake and, instead, stresses how the acquisition of knowledge should enhance life. In that vein, the best among us will represent the full process of Nietzschean becoming—recurrent deconstruction, re-imagination, and re-creation—the virtues of the active nihilist. To prepare to even approximate a higher human type, we must pass through "three metamorphoses" of discipline, defiance, and creation (Z I, "On the Three Metamorphoses"). The spirit, like a camel, flees into the desert to bear enormous burdens (the process of social construction); the spirit, like a lion, must transform itself into a master, a conqueror who releases its own freedom by destroying traditional prohibitions (the process of deconstruction of and liberation from the past); but the lion cannot create new values, so the spirit must transform itself into a child, whose playful innocence, ability to forget, and capability for creative games signals the spirit's willing its own will (the processes of re-imagination and re-creation). This cycle continues until we die or lose the human capabilities required to participate. At all stages, learning informs the process. New understandings and findings propel us forward.

The thrust of Nietzsche's thought is that we can formulate entirely new modes of evaluation that correspond to new, higher forms of life. The value of humanity is established by its highest exemplars and their creations. The higher human forms are extremely fragile and rare: self-control, mastery of inclinations, resisting obstacles, experimentation, and forging a unified character require recurrent destruction and re-creation of the self.

We can never transcend our conditionality and the lack of inherent meaning in the world of Becoming but at least a few of us can loosen the limits of contingency, experience fully the multiplicity of our spirits, forge a coherent unity from our internal conflicts, and learn to overcome ourselves and our institutions: theoretical insight can be turned to practical advantage. The episodic rhythms of the camel, the lion, and the child resonate. The process not only transforms the self, but also creates new values. Thus, Nietzsche anticipates modern existentialism in holding that human beings legislate values through their choices and actions. This process, however, is not merely one of unilateral imposition. That is, the mere desire that something be valuable is insufficient to establish its value.

4. Values

Nietzsche rejects the notion of intrinsic values, in the sense of objects that are valuable in and of themselves. For him, there are no values without valuing beings. The core of *amor fati* is that the world is most valuable to those who are most strongly drawn to it. The *measure of value* is power, understood as expressing and transforming ourselves, extending our influence, dominating our environment, and self-realization. In contrast, conscious subjective states such as pleasure, contentment, internal peace, happiness, and the like are not valuable as such. They may accompany or follow an increase in power, which remains the genuine value.

The virtues of perspectivism and genealogical critique must be connected explicitly to self-development and to support of a robust will to power. As such, examining the origins of dominant cultural understandings; viewing objects and ideas from a variety of perspectives; promoting a maximally affirmative attitude toward life; accelerating self-revision; and nurturing higher human types are crucial aspects of life.

Again, Nietzsche denies the existence of intrinsic value in the sense of value in and of itself, value that can exist without beings who evaluate. Unsurprisingly, for Nietzsche, power—understood as the activity of extending one's influence through more extensive overcoming and mastering—is the measure of value. We must distinguish Nietzsche's position from abject subjectivism that holds that a person's feeling or judgment that something is valuable is sufficient to establish that object's value and from metaphysical objectivism that accepts mind-independent value (WP 647, 707). For Nietzsche, the basis for positive values and for negative disvalues is the inner power to attract or to repel. The more attracting power an object or goal embodies the greater is its value. Thus, value is a relation between an object and an evaluating being. Thus, values are structured by who we are, what constitutes our nature and our socialized selves. Nietzsche is uninterested in trying to universalize values or to posit unconditional values because he explicitly ties particular values to types of persons. Only those who are roughly akin to Nietzsche will be drawn to his values; others will, quite appropriately from Nietzsche's own broad themes, be repelled by his values.

Typically, the attainment of an object or a goal will realize value, a proportionate increase of power, commensurate with the intensity of the inner power that attracted the person to that object or goal. In those instances where the power of a person is adversely influenced by the attainment of an object or goal no such proportionate increase of power occurs. Nietzsche's highest value is *amor fati*, a maximally affirmative attitude toward life, because that approach represents the greatest attainment of power. Everything valuable should energize life by increasing the power that draws evaluating beings toward objects and goals or should enhance life by creating new objects or goals that increase the possibilities toward which evaluating beings can be strongly attracted. When life is either energized or enhanced, value itself increases. The higher values, for Nietzsche, will be those that maximize and refine one's power, while creating new goals or objects that energize or enhance life (WP 354).

Nietzsche's philosophy is complex and challenging because it is structured within his general themes of recurrent flux, internal conflict, and perspectivism. His most important revelations include the death of God, the genealogy of the master and slave moralities, the need to go beyond conventional notions of good and evil, the hypothesis of eternal recurrence, the interplay between philosophy and psychology, the connections of literary style and rhetoric, and his tragic view of life.

5. Nietzsche's Glad Tidings

In perhaps his most famous parable, Nietzsche announces the death of God (GS 125; See also GS 108 and 343; Z IV, "Retired"; Z IV, "The Ugliest-Man"). The "death of God" parable consists of several messages. The news is spread in the market place—the center of commerce, the focus of modern life, and the symbol of the dominant culture. The bearer of the news is a madman because such a denial of God's efficacy in a Europe dominated by Christian religion would strike the masses as deranged. Moreover, the madman, already stigmatized as an aberration within society, with his lantern is the bearer of special insight. The news itself is not a banal assertion of atheism but rather an observation of historical trajectory: the notion of God either is or will soon be unworthy of belief even if the masses are currently unaware that cultural conditions no longer support fervent religious belief and practice. The development of science and technology spawns explanations that were previously supplied only by robust belief in God, his powers, and his Grand Design. Faith in God in earlier decades had energized everyday life, but that conviction was weakening and was rapidly transforming into merely a series of institutional religious routines and rituals animated more by habit than by fervent passion. The dramatic, poetic conclusion that we have wiped "away the entire horizon" underscores Nietzsche's contention that without zealous religious belief and practice our standards of truth, foundations of meaning, and understanding of transcendent redemption evaporate: without God the world of Being collapses, only the world of Becoming which precludes inherent meaning remains. We have all "murdered" God in the sense that we constitute a culture in which integrity, intellectual cleanliness, and pursuit of truth undermine continued religious belief. The "scientific conscience," which in its quest for objectivity, absolute truth, and universal application is a sublimated form of the "Christian conscience," fuels the death of God. Thus, with typical irony, Nietzsche claims that God was "murdered" by the very Christian morality that originally needed to invoke Him (GS 357).

The death of God extinguishes the source of foundational meaning and engenders the specter of nihilism. "Nihilism" is the condition of the spirit which occurs after we recognize that the highest values have devalued themselves. With the further recognition that there are no foundations for inherent meaning, values seem arbitrary, goals lack purpose, and horizons of understanding dry up. How shall we reconstruct ourselves without God? What new myths will be necessary? Must we become our own gods?

Nietzsche is concerned with the links between the conditions and fulfillment of culture and a tragic view of life. For Nietzsche, recognizing "the death of God" forces human beings to acknowledge the lack of objective foundations and justifications for their most important truth claims about meaning, value, and purpose. This introduces the "nihilistic moment" or stage when conclusions about these crucial dimensions of human life are up for grabs. Nietzsche cannot guarantee that human beings will respond energetically to the possibilities open in the nihilistic moment. For him, the loss of a secure foundation for our dearest substantive beliefs suggests that we must ultimately choose under conditions of radical uncertainty. Human reason cannot redeem our predicament. Some of us will shrink back in horror. We will resign ourselves to bitterness and self-pity, and conclude that all is lost ("pathetic nihilism"). Some of us will refuse to relinquish the fantasy of a transcendent world and blissful afterlife ("passive nihilism"; Z II, "The Soothsayer"). Others of us will accept cosmic meaninglessness and use it as a point of departure for grand creativity ("active nihilism"). Having "killed" God by developing science and technology, and by creating the social conditions that provide compelling explanations for natural phenomena that in previous ages were explainable only by reference to God, we must now come to grips with the aftershock of our cultural accomplishment (GM I 12, II 24; GS 108, 283, 343, 382; WP 585).

Nietzsche did not anticipate an even more virulent form of nihilism. Deconstructive nihilists rage against the existing social order without any re-creative vision. They glisten with the worst attributes of obstreperous two-year-old children: an inflated sense of entitlement leavened by a deficient understanding of civilized life. Deconstructive nihilists are empowered by the nihilistic moment, but cannot transcend this stage because they lack the creativity required to re-imagine and re-make their social contexts. Instead, they invoke "nihilism" as an excuse to ineffectually advance their narrow self-interest.

Nietzsche is an unapologetic active nihilist. Embracing cosmic meaninglessness as the springboard to creative possibilities; reveling in radical contingency; relishing the human condition fully while recognizing its tragic dimensions; re-creating the self; and rejoicing in liberation from imposed values and meanings are at the heart of active nihilism. Active nihilism places paramount value on this life and this world.

The difference between pathetic, passive and active nihilism can be illustrated by the ancient Myth of Sisyphus.[15] Condemned by the gods to push a huge rock to the top of a hill from which it fell down the other side, to be pushed again to the top from which it fell again, and so on forever, Sisyphus was doomed to futile, pointless, unrewarded labor. His immortality was part of his punishment. His consciousness of the futility of his project was his tragedy. Sisyphus's life is representative of human life: repetitious, meaningless, pointless toil that adds up to nothing in the end. The myth portrays the eternal human struggle and indestructible human spirit. Although Sisyphus is not mortal, that deepens and does not redeem the absurdity of his life. While human life bears more variety than Sisyphus's life, the matter is only one of small degree. While some human beings take solace in producing and raising children, reproduction can be viewed as more of the same: adding zeros to zeros.

When faced with Sisyphus's sentence, a pathetic nihilist would metaphorically skulk off into a corner, curl up into the fetal position, and cry for relief. A passive nihilist would counsel Sisyphus to withdraw from his task of endlessly pushing the boulder up a hill, and, failing that possibility, to detach himself from the task as he performs it. Nietzsche would advise Sisyphus to affirm his fate, to desire nothing more than to do what he is fated to do eternally, to luxuriate in the immediate texture of what he does, to confer, through attitude and will, meaning on an inherently meaningless task.

Pathetic and passive nihilists fail to see that value and meaning need not be permanent to be real; that process renders fulfillments independently of attaining goals; that the attainments of great effort and creation do not instantaneously produce emptiness; and that suffering is not inherently negative but can be transfigured for creative advantage.

To what state do passive nihilists aspire? Do they secretly yearn for a condition of never-ending bliss? Does freedom from suffering require that we want nothing more? Many would find such a life deadening. A life devoid of new projects, adventures, journeys, and goals lacks creativity: bland contentment replaces vigorous thought and action. Perhaps suffering is produced not by the process of seeking fulfillment of new desires but by the taming of our desire-creating mechanism. Having unfulfilled desires need not be painful; it is often exhilarating. We imagine rewarding new situations and pursue them vigorously. We find fulfillments in the process and, often, in achieving the goal. Our insatiability ensures that we continue to imagine and pursue rewarding projects, rather than being limited to contemplating earlier fulfillments. Whether the new desires we create produce overall suffering depends on what they are and how we pursue them, not solely on their presence.

Recognizing this, Nietzsche embraces an active nihilism grounded in the criterion of power: exertion, struggle and suffering are at the core of overcoming obstacles, and it is only through overcoming obstacles that human beings experience, truly feel, their power. For those courageous enough to reject cheerfully that conviction, the death of God promises creative opportunities. An active nihilism can rejuvenate the will to power, not by returning to a historically obsolete pre-Christian, Homeric morality, but through celebration of contingency and the creation of new values. The best of us must become our own gods.

6. Master and Slave Moralities

Nietzsche's specific genealogical account invokes the images of master and slave moralities. The master morality defines "good" in terms of men's character, not their actions. Under this view, "good" equates to worldly success: achieving one's goals of conquest, fame, wealth, and adventure; and embodying pride, strength, passion, and guiltless joy. Nietzsche relishes the master morality's limit- breaking activities and robust nobility. Moreover, the master morality prefigures some of Nietzsche's broad themes: the need to transcend present contexts and create values out of the abundance of one's life and strengths; the desire to creatively use passion; the joyful affirmation of this world; the manifestation of self-possession; the lack of repressed hostility; and the production and honoring of higher human types.

The master morality, which for Nietzsche symbolizes the Greeks of the Homeric age, did not perceive itself as unconditional or universal. This morality did not prescribe how others (nonmasters) should conduct their lives and understood explicitly that its evaluations pertained only to a certain type of human. In that vein, masters sought friends and adversaries only from members of their own rank. Nietzsche approves of recognizing the rank order of human types and of applying different evaluations appropriate to the various types of human beings.

The master morality was dominant and ruled over slaves. These slaves, however, developed their own version of morality. Slave morality reflected and sustained what was beneficial for the masses or herd of men. The slave morality's notion of "good" applied to the actions and intentions of men, instead of their dispositions and characters. Because the herd is inherently mediocre its values celebrate sympathy, kindness, and general benevolence: virtues that serve the weak and aspire to widespread equality. The values of masters—such as power, self-assertion, and world success—are retranslated in slave morality as vices. While the masters were essentially indifferent to slaves, viewing them as different human types, slaves bear *ressentiment*—a sense of hostility directed at that which one identifies as the cause of one's frustration—toward the masters. In effect, the slaves blame the masters for the frustration that overwhelms them.

Prior to the slave revolt in morality which led to the end of the domination of master morality, the "bad conscience" emerged. When human beings become enthralled with society, civilization, and peace, their instincts are not discharged externally, but are instead internalized. This process culminates in self-hate and self-destruction (GM II, 16, 17-19). The bad conscience, although at first blush the facilitator of repression and internal turmoil, can be used creatively by the excellent few to control, sublimate, and integrate their multiple drives.

In contrast to masters who act on their emotions and then forget their past grievances against others, slaves repress their hostile feelings because of their fears which stem from their relative powerlessness. For Nietzsche, forgetting exhibits strength because it opens the way to self-overcoming and re-creation (GM II, 1). *Ressentiment* is bottled-up hatred, bitterness and aggression caused by repressing one's hostile feelings. Although masters are the source of the slaves' hostile feelings, slaves are afraid to confront their superiors. Accordingly, the slaves' intense humiliation and hostility are internalized. These hostile feelings, however, are eventually expressed in cunning fashion: they produce the slave morality whose cleverest trick is the revaluation of master morality.

> The slave revolt in morality begins when *ressentiment* itself becomes creative and gives birth to values: the *ressentiment* of natures that are denied the true reaction, that of deeds, and compensate themselves with

an imaginary revenge. While every noble morality develops from a triumphant affirmation of itself, slave morality from the outset says No to . . . what is 'different' . . . and this No is its creative deed. This inversion of the value-positing eye—this need to direct one's view outward instead of back to oneself—is of the essence of *ressentiment* (GM I, 10).

Accordingly, the pursuit of sex, power, overt aggression, and conquest become refashioned as immoralities, while chastity, humility, obedience, and meekness become the cornerstones of "morality." Slave morality also extols the unconditionality and universality of its own perspective and attempts to undermine the character advantages and superiority of masters by labeling them "evil." These strategies are indispensable to the success of the slave revolt: unless slaves could universalize their values their leveling efforts would be unsuccessful and slaves would still be vulnerable to the greater powers of masters.

Slave morality, then, is fundamentally reactive and fueled by fear and hostility. To solidify its powers of revaluation, slave morality appealed to a transcendent world ruled by a supernatural being. Thus, the triumph of equality, deprecation of this world, and celebration of fixed values in the West were begun by the Jews and refined by Christianity (BGE 195; GM I, 7 and 8).

Christianity has been the most calamitous kind of arrogance yet. Men, not high and hard enough to have any right to try to form man as artists; men, not strong and farsighted enough to let the foreground law of thousandfold failure and ruin prevail, though it cost them sublime self-conquest; men, not noble enough to see the abysmally different order of rank . . . between man and man—such men have so far held sway over the fate of Europe, with their 'equal before God,' until finally a smaller, almost ridiculous type, a herd animal . . . has been bred (BGE 62).

Invoking the imperatives of a supreme being solidified several themes of slave morality: the equality of all humans despite their obvious factual differences; the vision of this world as an inferior copy of a transcendent world; the assurance that a final judgment of all human actions will constitute perfect justice; and the full meaning and consequences of the terms "guilt," "personal responsibility and moral autonomy," and "good and evil."

A series of dualisms underwrite these themes of slave morality. The herd privileged the soul over the body; reason (carefully circumscribed by religious authority) over the passions; and the transcendent world over this world. In this fashion, according to Nietzsche, the slaves' *ressentiment* culminates in revenge: the revaluation of the masters' judgments. Thus, slaves reduce the importance of robustly living this life for "the meek will inherit the earth"; they minimize the pursuit of worldly success for "it is easier for a camel to pass through the eye of a needle than for a rich man to enter heaven"; they elevate pity and sympathy, sentiments permitting herd members to wallow in their weakness, to virtues; and they deny currency to factual human differences in deference to the virtues of modesty, deference, and humility. In this insidious manner, and especially through the connivance of the priestly class and its invocation of a supposedly omnipotent God, people of excellence become unwittingly collaborators in undermining the social conditions under which they had flourished.

For Nietzsche, the slave morality, particularly its glorification of pity and sympathy, encourages a life of minimal exertion and avoidance of risk. Nietzsche judges moralities, cultures and people in part by the way they confront suffering and the tragic dimensions of life. The robust life requires self-mastery through confronting obstacles, overcoming suffering, and affirming tragedies. Greatness and excellence require creative confrontation with suffering and pain: surmounting obstacles is the core of the will to power.

Instead of reveling in the adventure that is life, however, the slave morality aspires to eliminate pain and to nurture limited vulnerability and few demands: the "good" person is merely one who assiduously avoids proscribed actions. Worse, the celebration of pity and sympathy stem from weakness and timidity: "Pity . . . is a weakness, like every losing of oneself through a harmful affect. It increases the amount of suffering in the world . . . Supposing it was dominant even for a single day, mankind would immediately perish of it" (D 134). The noble human being may well help the unfortunate, but not as expression of pity. Instead, the noble man, who is invariably severe with himself in terms of expectations and the bearing of burdens, acts from his "excess of power" and is proud that "he is not made for pity (BGE 260).

Nietzsche identifies three dubious metaphysical assumptions about human beings that underwrite slave morality: that human beings embody a free will that permits independent moral choice; that human motives and intentions for action can be discerned and evaluated comparatively; and that human beings are morally equal. These three assumptions lead to further conclusions about the institutions of morality: individuals are responsible for their actions; they deserve to be either rewarded for good actions or punished for evil actions; and the application of moral principles must be universal.

Nietzsche resists the three metaphysical assumptions and the conclusions they generate. First, he denies the notion of free will as a wrongful reification of cause and effect, as mistaking conventional fictions for metaphysical explanations, as positing an underlying substance called "will" which can be free or determined (TI, "The Four Great Errors," 7; BGE 17, 21 and 213; D 148; WP 484). For Nietzsche, just as there are no things-in-themselves there are no substantial selves. We are merely our passions, past experiences, drives, instincts, and other dispositions which language seduces us into attributing to the individual subject. Each human being embodies similar basic drives whose intensity varies from person to person.

Second, Nietzsche questions our ability to discern and evaluate motives and intentions for acting. He is convinced that human intentions are merely signs or symptoms that require further interpretation. Much that lies psychologically beneath conscious intentions and motives is crucial to understanding human action (BGE 32; GS 335; D 119, 129; WP 291, 294, 492).

Third, Nietzsche holds adamantly that values serve particular interests at particular times, that humans have strikingly different interests, and that universalizing moral judgments of the slave mentality under such circumstances itself promotes the interests of the herd. The slave morality takes itself to be more than it is. In its pretenses to unconditionality and universality, the slave morality camouflages how it privileges the interests of the masses and marginalizes the interests of potential noble human beings (BGE 221, 43).

Finally, the three metaphysical assumptions about human beings that support slave morality betray a misunderstanding of the complexity of the world of Becoming. These assumptions posit a dualistic world of good/evil, altruism/egoism, love/hate, and so on, which wrongly denies the interdependences between the posited elements. Oppositional dualisms trouble Nietzsche primarily because they renege on life's complexity. They fail to appreciate the interdependences of our motives and the genealogy of our practices: how morality flows from immorality, selflessness emerges from selfishness, truth blossoms from illusion, and good from evil. For Nietzsche everything valuable once depended on a seemingly opposed value (GS 19, 21, 121; BGE 2, 229; GM I, 8).

Furthermore, Nietzsche resists the conviction that certain actions or beliefs are inherently good or bad. Context and perspective are required for evaluation. Thus, human beings endow drives, activities, and beliefs with value according to the group interests that emerge victorious in social struggle. Human beings have always done this, although the will to objectification has often led them for strategic reasons to present their values as transcendent.

Despite his occasional disclaimers to having preferences as between the two moralities, that Nietzsche prefers master morality to slave morality is clear. In his view, the slave morality embodies numerous deficiencies. First, its origins are unworthy: *ressentiment* of the superiority of nobles and vengeful commitment to reorder values. Second, it embraces suspicious metaphysical assumptions: belief in a supreme being, the fixed duality of good and evil, and the existence of a transcendent world. Third, it produces harmful consequences: it nurtures a pernicious egalitarianism, devalues our world in deference to the world beyond, privileges social conformity, and suffocates human creativity. Fourth, its substance is unworthy: it celebrates pity, limits human possibilities, and champions submission to external authority. Finally, it is grounded in dubious second-order beliefs: the advocates of slave morality are steeped in universalism, dogmatism, and absolutism. For Nietzsche, the worst aspect of slave morality is its failure to restrict its convictions and imperatives to members of the herd. By extending its reach to everyone, slave morality contaminates social life and deflates numerous glorious expressions of the will to power.

But, as usual, simple statements such as this one are too crude to capture Nietzsche's full evaluation. Nietzsche accepts slave morality as appropriate for the herd. He is upset only by the slave morality's pretensions to dogmatism and universalism which deny the rank order among human beings and undermine social conditions necessary for excellence. Thus it is not the existence or even the content of slave morality that triggers Nietzsche's concern, only the scope of its application and its metaphysical underpinnings. Moreover, the master morality consists of unrefined, unsublimated passions which too often lead to brutality instead of higher culture. We cannot and should not return to the simple Homeric warrior ethic. Finally, Nietzsche recognizes that the slave morality introduces a cleverness, cunning, and mendacity to human beings that was lacking in the crude master morality (GM I, 6, 10).

Nietzsche's critique of the herd morality is genealogical—it impugns the content and pretensions of that moral code by providing a historical account of how it arose from unworthy motives. A critic might well object that as a matter of historical reconstruction Nietzsche's genealogical account of conventional morality is utterly unpersuasive. The appeal to gods generously predated the heroic Homeric age and arose from numerous motivations, such as fear of the unknown and insecurity in the face of human mortality; the desire to arrive at an explanation for events that were not humanly created; and a variety of other psychological needs including the hope of immortality, a yearning for an ultimate culmination that would render human life purposive and meaningful, the desire to connect to enduring value, and the urge to depict the cosmos as rational and just. Moreover, if Nietzsche's genealogical account is historically accurate the so-called nobles were collectively dim-witted as they surrendered their alleged superiority when confronted by the herd's far-fetched fable. Finally, how does Nietzsche escape his context in a way that permits him to see what others cannot? How can Nietzsche consistently assume that his account is superior to other possible accounts given his broad theme that data underdetermine theory?

Perhaps the most plausible response to such objections centers on a wider understanding of Nietzsche's philosophical motives. Nietzsche's main aim is, as always, the undermining of dogmatism. By showing how social practices emerge from power struggles, he unsettles the conviction that our practices and values are embedded in the rationality of nature. Recognizing the perspectival character of values and practices also promotes our reimagining and re-creating them. In order to remain loyal to his broad themes, Nietzsche cannot claim his genealogical accounts are pure, dispassionate descriptions. His own aristocratic commitments, psychological understandings, and personal interests intrude freely, as they must. As do all explanatory accounts, Nietzsche's presents itself as accurate history while masking its own mythological and psychological origins. This is mainly the result of the limitations of our language and categories of logic. Nietzsche cannot claim that he escapes his context; instead he nourishes the subversive seeds contained therein. Given his commitments to his broad themes, he cannot claim that his genealogical account is the only available interpretation of the "data" or that it emerges from an impartial vantage point. His account must be self-consciously partial and a product of his own will to power.

A critic may well wonder on what ground Nietzsche can claim superiority for his account given that he offers an admittedly biased genealogy of the origins of dominant morality, an account that he hopes will resuscitate aristocratic fervor.

Nietzsche knows that he cannot undermine dogmatism directly, by meeting it on its own logical grounds and by using its own criteria of acceptable argument. Those grounds and criteria presuppose dogmatism so any attempt to employ them directly to undermine dogmatism will ultimately reinstate the "necessity" of dogmatism. That is precisely how charges of self-referential paradox gain their currency. Instead, Nietzsche must chip away at dogmatism indirectly: through self-consciously partial genealogical accounts, by demonstrating dogmatism's unprovable presuppositions, by appealing to different pictures of life, by dancing a different dance.

What Nietzsche does is show the poverty of the fact-value distinction. As corollaries of perspectives and power relationships, values cannot inhabit a logical category separate from facts. If Nietzsche's genealogical account is successful it will not establish a new, fixed understanding of the origins of our dominant values, but will, instead, stimulate the creative interpretive and practical activities of others. Once again genealogy returns to and substantiates the power of Nietzsche's broad themes.

Still, critics might insist, What about the character Thrasymachus in Plato's Republic? He anticipated Nietzsche's position on the relations between value and power, but provided a much different account of the origins of conventional morality. Thrasymachus claimed that our notions of justice were established by the strongest in the society, by those able to exert their will because of their social position and overall power. They set the terms of existence because they had the might to do so and, after time, those terms became codified in concepts of "justice" and "right." Nietzsche advances a different view: justice is in the interests of the weakest elements in society, the herd. Here we have two different "genealogies" of morality advanced by two figures who agree broadly on the connections between value and power.

Perhaps, however, Nietzsche and Thrasymachus are less different than first imagined. For Nietzsche the highest human types are also the most fragile. They are strongest in the sense of physical, mental, and spiritual creativity, but it does not follow that they are more likely than the herd to be preserved. On the contrary, they are more likely to perish in explosive self-annihilations (TI, "Skirmishes in a War with the Age," 44).

So which is truly stronger, the herd or the nobility? The answer must be typically Nietzschean: there is no stronger as such, only a stronger in relation to specified criteria. In regard to creative genius and cultural excellence the nobility is stronger, in regard to numbers and survival instincts the herd is stronger. Moreover, if Nietzsche is correct, the herd supplements its strength by invoking supernatural authority and the promise of eternal happiness—if you toe the herd's line! Thus it is reasonable to see some convergence between Nietzsche and Thrasymachus: "justice" is in the interests of the strongest. But what Nietzsche and Thrasymachus take to be the criterion of "strongest" differs. From a Nietzschean perspective, Thrasymachus failed to understand how those with social power—at least in the ages of democracy, socialism, communism, and the major religions—have already been deeply infected with herd mentality. Alternately, one can read Thrasymachus as tolling Homeric themes, as recalling a time when leaders set the terms of existence in accord with master morality because they ruled prior to the ages of our mainstream religions and politics. Under either interpretation, Nietzsche and Thrasymachus have much in common. At least, no necessary contradiction exists between their two genealogical accounts of conventional morality.

In that vein, we can invoke another character in a Platonic dialogue, Callicles in the *Gorgias* (480 a-522e). Callicles is a tough, aspiring politician—a man of action much like the historical Pericles. He argues that morality is merely a matter of social convention, not the felicitous correspondence of reason to the imperatives of nature. He insists that the truth of nature is that the stronger, physically and mentally, profits, while the weaker suffers. But the weaker, understood collectively, invent morality to constrain the stronger. They invent words and notions such as "dishonorable" and "unjust" to shame the stronger into submission. While nature rewards the more powerful, conventional morality benefits the weaker. Callicles' account precedes Nietzsche's by over twenty-one centuries. We can assume that Nietzsche was familiar with Plato's work; thus, to conclude that Nietzsche was influenced by the *Gorgias* is reasonable. This conclusion effaces the originality of Nietzsche's account of morality, but also underscores my earlier point regarding the lack of a necessary contradiction between the understandings of Nietzsche and Thrasymachus. In the *Gorgias*, Socrates responds that if weak men band together they are collectively stronger than a few powerful men, making the collectivity the superior force. Accordingly, what we accept as the criterion of the stronger is crucial in these debates.

Nietzsche stresses that judging and evaluating is a central focus of human life. Valuing one thing over another is critical even though our conclusions are not grounded in transcendent, objective considerations (GM II, 8; BGE 9). In his view, the minions of conventional morality claim that their normative conclusions embody universal, unconditional authority because of their dubious psychology. As always, Nietzsche links what people believe to what types of people they are. Those who cling to the fantasies that conventional (herd) morality arises from transcendent, objective imperatives that issue universal, unconditional prescriptions do so because they are uncomfortable with ambiguity, too timid to cope with complexity, and too devoted to order and security (BGE 31, 59; GS 5). In short, they are weak, needy people who require firm structure to cope with the vicissitudes of life. Lacking a robust sense of self and the courage to recognize the rank-ordering of life, these apostles of egalitarianism seek solace in applying the same moral code to everyone (BGE 221). Nietzsche insists that judging and evaluating require discrimination not sameness: we must conclude one thing or person is better or more valuable than others. To do this, requires a society that is rank-ordered and that encourages a "pathos of distance," whereby higher human types fully recognize their superiority to the masses (BGE 257; GM I, 2). The egalitarianism of conventional morality resists these requirements. Furthermore, Nietzsche evaluates people on the basis of what they find valuable because judgments about comparative worth reveal human psychology; they are the data from which Nietzsche draws his psychological conclusions about what type of person someone is and where they rank in his hierarchy.

Nietzschean norms gain their authority from being self-imposed. Once they are in place they govern a person's desire and preferences of the moment. We must often resist the impulses at hand in order to fulfill our more profound commitments and convictions. For Nietzsche, freedom is an achievement, not a given. To win freedom, people must distance themselves from much of their early and ongoing socialization. Freedom, then, is not license to do whatever one currently proposes, but involves perceiving, reflecting, and legislating enduring burdens upon the self. Licentious deeds are arbitrary in that they cannot form a coherent whole. Legislating norms and earning freedom are connected to leading a certain kind of life, not to abstract formulations of allegedly universal prescriptions or gratifying immediate whims. The nihilistic moment depicted in Nietzsche's death of god narrative (GS 125) depicts the trajectory of human beings becoming aware that the normative standards they have taken to be objective and transcendent are merely contestable, cultural creations. Upon coming to this realization, human beings must either "become their own gods" and invent new, more life-affirming norms; or inauthentically crawl back to the discredited conviction that the established standards are transcendentally warranted; or simply withdraw from vigorous participation in life. The process of devising self-imposed norms is a project of self-discovery and self-creation. We are in part the values we embody. Attaining freedom involves the ongoing enterprise of creating meaning, value, and significance in one's life in accord with self-imposed restraints. We begin from a situated context that requires extensive revision.

Given his own broad themes, Nietzsche's aristocratic conception of morality has no greater objective warrant than any other version of morality. They are all on the same footing in this sense: none arises from transcendent, objective authority; all flow from different perspectives, none of which reflects the view from an Archimedean point. Nietzsche might claim that his conception of morality has epistemic privilege because it is the product of viewing the world from multiple perspectives—which is his thin version of objectivity. But such an assertion would be self-serving and difficult to sustain. How can we be sure that Nietzsche has viewed the world from multiple perspectives? More important, how can we be sure that even if Nietzsche did so that the resulting product benefited from that process?

At bottom, Nietzsche does not claim that his conception of morality will win wide support. In fact, if it did win wide support that would supply evidence of its unacceptability for Nietzsche: that which the masses embrace must have suspicious origins and dubious implications. Nietzsche pitches his conception to only a few; to the "right types" of people; to those aristocrats who meet Nietzsche's psychological test of eternal recurrence and who embrace the values of *amor fati*. In a clever but circular way, a reader's response to Nietzsche's philosophy and conception of morality is taken as additional data from which Nietzsche would draw psychological conclusions about the type of person the reader is and where in the rank order of human beings that person belongs. From Nietzsche's (self-serving?) perspective to reject his philosophy and moral conception is to reveal your own weakness, timidity, and, possibly, *ressentiment*. To dismiss Nietzsche is to surrender to the dwarf within you and to reveal your last-man proclivities.

But why would supposed aristocrats be drawn to Nietzsche's philosophy and to his conception of morality? We must conclude that they would not accept Nietzsche's philosophy and conception of morality because of the demands of reason, for Nietzsche cannot persuasively claim epistemic privilege for his views given his own broad themes. Those drawn to Nietzsche's normative conclusions must do based on their passions, sense of evaluative taste, and, probably, because they see themselves (rightly or wrongly) as people of potential greatness. For such people, Nietzsche's philosophy and conception of morality are avenues for unleashing their presumed greatness. Unfettered from the chains of conventional morality and egalitarian sensibilities, they judge that their higher human potentials can be actualized. Perhaps they, like Nietzsche, will open themselves to the possibilities of loving life and fate unconditionally and affirming the question posed by eternal recurrence. As such, a reader's predispositions, temperament, and psychology are the important dimensions that will lead them to or distance them from Nietzsche's philosophy and moral conception—at least from the vantage point of Nietzsche's own broad themes: "Moral evaluation is an exegesis, a way of interpreting. The exegesis itself is a symptom of certain physiological conditions, likewise of a particular spiritual level of prevalent judgments: Who interprets? Our affects" (WP 254).

Some support for Nietzsche's assumption that people will be attracted to or repelled by his philosophy and moral conception based on their passions, evaluative tastes, and temperament can be gleaned from contemporary research in the social sciences. In that vein, Jonathan Haidt argues that moral reasoning and moral arguments are "mostly post hoc constructions made up on the fly, crafted to advance one or more strategic objectives."[16] Intuitions flowing from what Nietzsche would call passions, evaluative tastes, and temperament lead us to accept or reject normative conclusions; we later offer moral theory and arguments to justify our choices. Our normative reasoning, then, is done in service of our moral emotions and evaluative tastes: "the intuition launched the reasoning, but the intuition did not depend on the success or failure of the reasoning."[17] Our emotions and evaluative tastes in turn may be shaped importantly by evolution. As such, moral reasoning and argument is advanced for purposes of persuasion: "We do moral reasoning not to reconstruct the actual reasons why we *ourselves* came to a judgment; we reason to find the best possible reasons why *somebody else ought to join us* in our judgment."[18]

The contrast is not between reason and non-reason. As the Stoics contended centuries ago, our intuitions, emotions, and evaluative tastes all contain a quantum of reason. They are different cognitive forms involving different levels of self-awareness. We are fully conscious of our moral arguments and theory, not so of our intuitions, emotions, and evaluative tastes. In accord with Nietzsche's claims about fate and predispositions, Haidt concludes that "genetics explains between a third and a half of the variability among people on their political attitudes."[19] Who we are in terms of basic genetic wiring, then, greatly influences the normative views we embrace. Furthermore, Haidt's findings support Nietzsche's views about unconditional, universal morality: "Beware of anyone who insists that there is one true morality for all people, times, and places—particularly if that morality is founded upon a single moral foundation. Human societies are complex; their needs and challenges are variable."[20]

Mainstream philosophers will be unmoved. They have long recognized the difference between the context of discovery—how we arrive at certain positions—and the context of justification—how we defend those positions. Also, they will point out that our efforts of justification, contra Haidt, do play a strong role in correcting our intuitions. That is, our intuitions, evaluative tastes, and emotions are not fixed, but are open to revision often generated by our attempts at justification and those of others.

Still, contemporary social science research does provide some support for Nietzsche's method of understanding the circumscribed nature of his project: in effect, he is preaching to the choir—those antecedently inclined to celebrate his philosophy based on their genetic make-up, evaluative tastes, passions, and temperament. By stressing the link between adopting a philosophy and embodying a particular psychology Nietzsche underscores that message. Furthermore, the entire Nietzschean enterprise is designed to loosen the limits imposed by Platonic-Christian invocations of a world of Being and promises of permanent fulfillment, and instead open human life to more possibilities in the world of Becoming. Part of that project is liberation from the seeming external imperatives of universal, unconditional, moral truths that, if Nietzsche is correct, are no more than masked human inventions. The overall test of a perspective or a judgment, says Nietzsche is pragmatic; "The question is to what extent [a judgment] is life-promoting, life-preserving, species-preserving, perhaps even species-cultivating" (BGE 4). The answer determines the usefulness, not the alleged objective truth of a perspective or judgment. But if objective moral truth is unavailable to us, Nietzsche might well ask, "Then, what else is left?"

7. Going Beyond Good and Evil

To transvalue values—to overturn the dominant values of the status quo and to create new values—requires changing a person's or a society's self-conception or their vision of the world. Thus, for Nietzsche, "going beyond good and evil" requires a new conception of what constitutes the higher human types and a revised vision of the nature of our world. Accordingly, his philosophy, as ever, has practical aspirations: the creation of new values in service of his reimagined self-conception—one based on the primacy of a robust will to power, the importance of struggle and overcoming, and the project of ongoing adventure and risk—and a reformulated vision of the world—as radically contingent, inherently meaningless, and open to seemingly infinite possibilities.

As always, Nietzsche centers on cultivating individual excellence. The overman is superior because he embodies *amor fati* to the fullest. He exudes maximum love and enthusiasm for this life, while understanding its tragic dimensions. Whereas Plato was drawn to the unchanging, the eternal, and the formulaic, Nietzsche is attracted to the contingent, the re-created, and the constantly transformative. Nietzsche cannot provide deeper, rational arguments in support of the value of *amor fati*. A maximally affirmative attitude toward life is his "primitive," his basic value. Instead, Nietzsche presents his vision of higher human types and displays his picture of the world: The world is most valuable to those who are most strongly attracted to it and higher human types are distinguished by the inner power that draws them to the world. For Nietzsche, as always, the will to power is the psychological motivation for human action.

To understand the directions Nietzsche prefigures for those strong enough to undertake them, I will review the aspects of conventional morality that he resists. The unpalatable elements of slave morality embody suspicious origins, contents, metaphysical presuppositions, effects, and second-order beliefs. The origins reside in *ressentiment* and reaction; the contents consist of its evaluation of particular actions, of glorifying pity, of downplaying earthly success and life, of submitting to external authority, of imposing a false equality; the metaphysical presuppositions include belief in a supernatural being, free will, independent moral choice, the transparency and accessibility of human motives and intentions, and the fixed opposition of good and evil; the negative effects include leveling all human beings to the standards of the herd, postponing gratification, marginalizing nobility, stifling human creativity, deflating human instincts and passions, viewing contentment and tame happiness as primary goods, and sanctifying social conformity; the pernicious second-order beliefs are the universalism, dogmatism, and absolutism required to sustain the entire program.

To conclude that any form of morality which embodies such elements would repel Nietzsche is reasonable. Although he will be indifferent to slave moralities as such, their harmful second-order beliefs and negative effects upon culture and standards of excellence ultimately prevent their coexistence with higher forms of life: by their very nature they cannot restrict their tenets and convictions to the herd. Thus slave moralities devalue cultural health, higher forms of life, and numerous expressions of power.

Accordingly, Nietzsche's attacks on morality are criticisms of the undesirable elements outlined above rather than efforts to alter all present evaluations of right and wrong actions. In fact Nietzsche says that:

> I also deny immorality: not that countless people *feel* themselves to be immoral, but that there is any true reason so to feel. It goes without saying that I do not deny—unless I am a fool—that many actions called immoral ought to be avoided and resisted, or that many called moral ought to be done and encouraged—but I think that the one should be encouraged and the other avoided *for other reasons than hitherto* (D 103).

Nietzsche does not prescribe the end of all evaluation; on the contrary, the imposition of meaning, order, and value on a world of Becoming is a paramount creative activity. To "go beyond good and evil" involves, among other things, recognizing truth as perspectival, refusing to submit to notions of equality, understanding suffering as necessary for creative greatness, and honoring the rank order among human beings (BGE 4, 44, 56, 260). Moreover, the transvaluation of slave moralities requires robust self-affirmation and joyous overcoming of passive and pathetic nihilisms. The suspicious origins, contents, metaphysical presuppositions, effects, and second-order beliefs of slave moralities must be rejected, at least by higher human types, in the service of cultural health, refined life forms, and intense expressions of the will to power.

Nietzsche suspects that the more we venerate the transcendent Judeo-Christian world, the less we regard ourselves. Part of the "ascetic" mindset is a lingering sense of the inferiority of this world and its creatures when judged against the imagined perfection of the other world. Although the nihilistic moment—during which the death of God is seen as the termination of all foundational meaning and fixed interpretive horizons—generates immediate chaos and social breakdown, it also offers fruitful possibilities for personal and cultural reimagination and re-creation. Also, to go beyond good and evil requires affirmation of this world and everything in it: its transitoriness, one's own mortality, the tragedy and suffering that partly constitute life, the interdependence of posited dualisms, and the radical conditionality of relationships and institutions. Great character and healthy self-regard animate the transvaluation of slave moralities (BGE 260, 287; GM I, 10, and WP 876).

The thrust of Nietzsche's thought is that we can formulate entirely new modes of evaluation that correspond to new, higher forms of life. The value of humanity is established by its highest exemplars and their creations. The higher human forms are extremely fragile and rare: self-control, mastery of inclinations, resisting obstacles, experimentation, and forging a unified character require recurrent destruction (and re-creation) of self (GM III, 27).

We can never transcend our conditionality and the lack of inherent meaning in the world of Becoming but at least a few of us can loosen the limits of contingency, experience fully the multiplicity of our spirits, forge a coherent unity from our internal conflicts, and learn to overcome ourselves and our institutions: theoretical insight can be turned to practical advantage.

Nietzsche's call to go beyond good and evil includes some disturbing corollaries: his use of warrior rhetoric and military imagery, as well as his apparent willingness to sacrifice and exploit members of the "herd" in service of his preferred "aristocrats." This side of Nietzsche will strike most contemporary readers as repulsive: its content is redolent with the stench of "might makes right"; it does not appreciate the real human cost of such irresponsible talk; it oozes danger in a juvenile way. Moreover, coming from a man such as Nietzsche it reeks of fantasy—a fatuous overcompensation for his own sense of physical inadequacy. For example, Nietzsche claims that a robust aristocracy perceives accurately that it is the meaning and justification of the species and accepts unsqueamishly that those of lesser rank are properly used as instruments for its benefit (BGE 258); that the essential character of life is exploitation and overpowering of that which is weaker (BGE 259); that the goal of humanity lies only in its highest exemplars (UM, "On the uses and disadvantages of history for life," 9); that every strengthening of human beings requires a new type of enslavement (GS 377); that "blond beasts of prey," comprising a "master race" conquer others and a state thereby arises (GM II, 17); and that higher cultures begin when "men of prey who were still in possession of unbroken strength of will and lust for power, hurled themselves upon weaker, more civilized, more peaceful races" (BGE 257).

Apologists for Nietzsche will respond generally by cautioning against taking Nietzsche's rhetoric too seriously and too literally. In several of the examples cited, Nietzsche is merely reporting and not automatically endorsing a sequence of events. A more refined interpretation of his position would recognize three aspects of the warrior imagery. First, the military metaphors pertain most directly to a person's internal struggles with conflicting impulses and multiple drives. To overcome one's self, to forge a unity and dramatic character out of inherent chaos requires confrontation and conquest. But the most important parts of the process occur *within* a person and do not involve physically subduing others. Second, the confrontations and conquests are spiritual "wars" even when undertaken on a cultural level: they are battles over ideals and visions of the good life; they are not military campaigns or true warfare. Third, we should not forget Nietzsche's stylistic preoccupations: to provoke, to gain attention, to stir controversy, to exaggerate self-consciously, to provide vivid imagery. These stylistic aims are more easily fulfilled through warrior rhetoric than through unadorned prose.

In short, Nietzsche does not herald barbaric displays of dominance over others, but, instead, cherishes sublimated passions that generate high cultures. The spiritualization of raging power, as illustrated by great artists and philosophers, is the culmination of Nietzsche's active nihilism. Although Nietzsche favorably mentions several military figures such as Napoleon and Caesar in his work, he does so in recognition of their vigorous will to power not because he considers them his model of cultural refinement. The process of personal and cultural deconstruction, reimagination, and re-creation is the journey toward excellence; while pursuit of crude, physical power over others demonstrates lack of creative imagination and immersion in facticity.

If we examine more closely some of the cited passages we will see that Nietzsche is only recounting how states and cultures arose historically. He isn't advocating a new age of "blond beasts." He stresses the barbaric aspects of the beginnings of the state to disarm the sentimentality of liberal ideologues who romanticize innate human goodness. And it is obvious that "blond beast" bears no particular racial connotation and probably refers to unrefined animal passion such as embodied by lions.[21] Nietzsche explicitly ties the blond beast imagery to a host of historical peoples, such as "the Roman, Arabian, Germanic, Japanese nobility, the Homeric heroes, the Scandinavian Vikings" who searched avidly for victory (GM I, 11).

Furthermore, in other passages Nietzsche stresses the connection between his warrior rhetoric, military imagery, and the internal conflicts that higher human beings confront. For example, he celebrates the need for the strongest human beings to be hard with themselves and the "joy of self-conquest" that often results, as well as the duty of higher human types to treat the mediocre masses tenderly (AC 57); he emphasizes the need to sublimate crude, cruel impulses in service of higher culture (BGE 229); and the need to give style to one's character by confronting and ordering multiple, conflicting drives in service of rising above revenge against others (GS 290).

Still, critics will charge that we should so conveniently overlook Nietzsche's willingness to sacrifice, even enslave, the masses for the benefit of aristocratic notions of "higher culture" and the times when Nietzsche's warrior rhetoric cannot plausibly be taken as hyperbole. He talks about "universal military service with real wars" as a remedy of modernity (WP 126); about how military developments happily affirm the "barbarian and wild beast in each of us" (WP 127); and he often talks about how war is necessary for the state, how a just war sanctifies any cause, how it trains men for freedom, and nurtures strength (See, e.g., TI and Z).

But Nietzsche is never a toady of state purposes. He opposes the major political forms with which he is familiar: democracy, communism, socialism, fascism. Historically, war and the state have joined together as naturally as pasta and olive oil. But when Nietzsche celebrates war he does so only because it vivifies the will to power: struggle, passion, an antidote to the indolence of last men. Nietzsche uses warrior rhetoric in part because of his admiration of Homeric heroes and their (unrefined) will to power. But he is clear that barbaric struggle is not the goal of active nihilists. Nietzsche does not endorse war and cruelty as such. War, however, is better than the insipid peace of last men because war indicates vigorous will to power that, if refined, could animate cultural greatness; while peace among the indolent indicates a muted will to power that ensures cultural mediocrity.

The goal, if there is one, is peace among the strong whose spiritualized will to power no longer requires war: "And perhaps the great day will come when a people, distinguished by wars and victories and by the highest development of a military order and intelligence, and accustomed to make the heaviest sacrifices for these things, will exclaim of its own free will, 'We break the sword,' and will smash its entire military establishment down to its lowest foundations" (WS 284).

In sum, at times Nietzsche seems to glorify military warfare and on other occasions he merely uses warrior images as metaphors for internal personal struggles. Both the effort to portray him as an idolater of armed conflict and as a humanistic wordsmith must account for the other side of Nietzsche's philosophy.

8. Eternal Recurrence

Nietzsche writes that the "fundamental conception" of *Thus Spoke Zarathustra* is "the idea of the eternal recurrence, this highest formula of affirmation that is at all attainable." (EH, "Thus Spoke Zarathustra," 1).

The eternal recurrence holds that events in the world comprise a cyclical eternity: whatever is occurring will recur again and is a return of itself; it has all occurred before and will occur again, in exactly the same way each cycle, eternally. There is no beginning, no end, and no middle of the history of our world.

In another of his eloquent fables, Nietzsche describes the eternal recurrence as a proposition put forth by a demon: How would you react if you were informed that you will live your life repeatedly in the exact sequence in which you are living it now? Nothing could be edited out and everything great and small will return. Would you be elated and yearn fervently for this "eternal confirmation and seal"? Or would you "gnash your teeth and curse the demon" who related the news? (GS 341).

Whether the eternal recurrence should be interpreted as a cosmological doctrine, a tentative hypothesis, a moral imperative, a psychological test, a reaffirmation of the death of God, or an attempt at secular redemption from the nihilistic moment is unclear.

In his *Nachlass*, Nietzsche, at least, toys with the eternal recurrence as a cosmological doctrine.[22] Taken as a cosmological doctrine, eternal recurrence is problematic for a host of reasons.[23] Most strikingly, eternal recurrence as a cosmological doctrine is unverifiable because we cannot distinguish one cycle of power configurations from another which is a duplicate. Without the ability to distinguish cycles it is impossible to empirically verify the thesis of eternal recurrence, or even the belief that there are two cycles to compare.

Understanding eternal recurrence as a moral imperative also raises grave difficulties. One possibility is that Nietzsche is advising his audience to perform a certain action if and only if we can will that it becomes a universal act (in the sense of being performed by everyone under the same relevant circumstances) for eternity. But this is certainly not to what Nietzsche aspires. He denies the universality of moral judgments as misguided dogmatism that nurtures mediocrity. A second possibility is that Nietzsche intends a more specific normative message: perform a certain act if and only if you can will that you will perform X for eternity. But this interpretation confronts the obstacle that Nietzsche never ponders the moral quality of specific acts. While he is concerned with one's style, character, and manifestation of will to power, he never analyzes the inherent or even instrumental value of particular moral actions. In part this is due to his desire to distance himself from Platonic-Judeo-Christian morality and in part to his veneration of the order of human rank: one cannot assess the quality of specific actions, moral or otherwise, in the abstract but only in relation to particular types of people at particular times.

A third way to view eternal recurrence as a moral imperative is to focus on an entire life rather than specific acts. Because any universalized formulation will run afoul of Nietzsche's insistence on rank order and specific evaluations, the most plausible rendering would be along these lines: lead only that life that you can will you would live eternally. This rendering does not depend on a Kantian notion of willing—in terms of logically consistent actions and choices—but, instead, on one's subjective acceptance of the magnitude (or insignificance) of leading this life an infinite number of times. As such, it retains a secular version of the Christian appeal to the eternal because it makes infinity a component of evaluation. Whereas Christians rely on the alleged imperatives of eternity in a transcendent world, this version of eternal recurrence relies on the alleged imperatives of eternity in this world. One may well ask: If this life lived once has a certain value how does the prospect of this life lived an infinite number of times change the value of that life now? While an advocate could argue that from the vantage point of eternity the value or disvalue of the life is magnified infinitely, why should that necessarily affect evaluation from my vantage point now? Why should acting as if eternal recurrence were true have any significant impact on my decisions?

One might rejoin that the value of certain actions is dependent on the number of times they occur. For example, climbing Mt. Everest was a monumental event when it was first done, but if hundreds of thousands of people did it annually the significance of the climb would evaporate. But this rejoinder does not help. It could be used to show that no action would bear significance because of uniqueness from the vantage point of eternity because all actions, if eternal recurrence is true or we act as if it is true, would have infinite occurrences. Or it could be used to show that all actions bear the same significance within a cycle of power configurations as they would if eternal recurrence was false.

Moreover, if eternal recurrence is true as a cosmological doctrine—if everything that is occurring has and will occur again—how can I possibly not comply with the "imperatives" of the moral interpretation of eternal recurrence? The moral interpretation's imperatives would be illusory because whatever life I "choose" is what has come before and what will come later; or, more precisely, what is eternally.

In fact, to view eternal recurrence as a moral hypothesis or as issuing moral imperatives is probably a mistake. Nietzsche was not concerned with moral evaluations as such. He directs his attention, instead, to Greek notions of goodness as personal excellence: achievement, intelligence, creative power, superior capacities, and deriving the merit of actions only from the actor's character. Clearly, one can embody this notion of personal excellence without exemplifying the goodness commanded by conventional morality. Furthermore, Nietzsche explicitly renounces the connection between moral rules and human action even when that connection claims to be person-specific (TI, "Morality as Anti-Nature," 6).

Eternal recurrence is probably viewed best as a psychological test: one's reaction to the thought of eternal recurrence is evidence of one's place in the order of human rank. Eternal recurrence underscores the lack of inherent cosmic meaning and purpose and challenges us to respond positively: to accept our lives in their entireties and to fashion them in such a way that we luxuriate in our time on earth without the distractions of revenge and *ressentiment*. Nietzsche captures this response in his call for *amor fati* (love of fate): "I do not want in the least that anything should become different than it is; I myself do not want to become different (EH, "Why I Am So Clever," 9). My formula for greatness in a human being is *amor fati*: that one wants nothing to be different . . . not in all eternity. Not merely bear what is necessary . . . but love it" (EH, "Why I Am So Clever,"10).

The acceptance of everything is paramount for Nietzsche because he thinks that if my life were different in any way it would no longer be my life but the life of a different person. Moreover, he also thinks that events in the world are closely interrelated such that to want things to be different is a denial of this world and one's self. Accordingly, eternal recurrence interpreted as a psychological test highlights several Nietzschean themes: become who you are (by fully embracing all events in your life); celebrate this life and this world (by not deferring robust living in hopes of transcendent salvation); and avoid revenge and *ressentiment* (by affirming fate and understanding that the past is unalterable). Eternal recurrence eliminates the possibility of another life, either here or in a transcendent world. Although recognizing that we are in fact mortal, higher types can impress the form of eternity upon their lives by fashioning lives they can embrace joyfully in their entireties. To want nothing in one's life or in the world to be different in any way is the mark of higher human types.

For Nietzsche, the mark of lower human types is their need to edit out the pain, tragedy, and hardship in their lives. The desire for a life without struggle, suffering, distinction, and failure is the invariable sign of last men. Last men will "throw themselves down and gnash their teeth and curse the demon" who brings the message of eternal recurrence: their hopes for transcendent salvation have been dashed, their *ressentiment* of superior types has been rendered pointless, their (largely unconscious) transvaluation of master values has been devalued, and their irredeemable weakness and inadequacy have been unmasked.

Higher human types, at first, will wince at the abysmal thought of the eternal return of the petty, the ugly, and the small. But upon fully understanding the interrelatedness of all events, the circularity of time, and the pointlessness of revenge, they will answer the demon: "You are a god and never have I heard anything more divine." At birth we all find ourselves in unchosen social contexts. Celebrants of *amor fati* will distinguish themselves by the quality of their performance—their confrontations with obstacles and suffering; their ability to forge a unified style out of their inherent multiplicity; their recurring self-creations and self-overcomings; their ability to luxuriate in the immediacy of life; their understanding of life as a sequence of aesthetically self-fulfilling moments.

Unlike eastern religions that seek detachment from the suffering of this world through minimizing desire and maximizing transcendence, and western stoics who moderate passion as a means of coping with both the tragedies and triumphs of life, Nietzsche's eternal recurrence glorifies life in all its tragic dimensions. Moreover, eternal recurrence excludes every goal and purpose outside the eternal circularity of all things. Thus, one must affirm life without the invocation of linear goals.

The thought of eternal recurrence, however, invites numerous questions: Why and how are events in the world and within a life so closely interrelated that the slightest alteration has significant consequences? Why should the demon's message of eternal recurrence by itself cause any "gnashing of teeth" or proclamations of "divinity"? Couldn't members of the lowly herd sincerely shout, "*Amor fati!*" once they understand eternal recurrence metaphorically? How can Nietzsche, the acolyte of "Becoming," rely coherently on the notion of eternity, the paradigm of "Being," as the ballast for affirming life? Does Nietzsche's reliance on eternity betray the vestiges of herd morality within his soul? Would not eternal recurrence cultivate a passivity or resignation, responses antithetical to Nietzschean self-overcoming, in the hearts of believers?

Taken as a cosmological doctrine, eternal recurrence is simply poor science and unsound reasoning. Taken as a moral doctrine it seems vacuous in that it amounts to only a reification of subjective whim: what a particular person happens to affirm. Taken as a psychological test, eternal recurrence also seems empty, at least at first blush. Why should the mere thought of eternal recurrence cause me to "gnash my teeth" or to rejoice? Why should it have any effect on what I do and how I act *now*? If I experience the same life an infinite number of times then during each cycle I would be unaware of previous cycles—because if I were aware of upcoming or could recall previous cycles then each subsequent life cycle would be different from the others. Thus, eternal recurrence must imply that I am unaware of the past and unable to anticipate the future. If so, I would feel no anxiety at upcoming events, could take no steps to avoid previous errors, nor foretell in any way my coming fate. The "eternality" of the events would have no bearing on "me" because I would experience myself as living the events only once. If Sisyphus knows that he is eternally doomed to push the boulder up the hill only to have it fall down that is much different from his being unaware that he is doomed to that fate for a finite number of years. In the former case, he could genuinely anticipate and experience the eternality of his fate, while in the latter case appeals to eternality are purely hypothetical. Taken as a psychological doctrine, eternal recurrence seems to be a bogeyman; it raises a pseudo-terrifying specter.

Perhaps we should view eternal recurrence as a combination of cosmological doctrine and psychological test if the doctrine is to embody any content.[24] If eternal recurrence is viewed merely as fable or myth it amounts to a question in a parlor game: What if you were to live this life eternally? The answer could well be that nobody cares. Unless I can entertain that I (and not merely someone substantially similar to me) in fact will live this life eternally the question of eternal recurrence lacks a point. In that case, whatever answer I give to the "what if" question will be tainted by my understanding of the inquiry as purely hypothetical. What if I were 7-feet tall, would I be a great basketball player? What if I were female instead of male, would I be recognized as a great artist? Such questions can be interesting and can elicit imaginative responses, but they suffer from their purely hypothetical natures:

they neither engage our identities nor pose any significant practical problems. That is why one might conclude that eternal recurrence must retain a cosmological flavor if it is to serve as a serious psychological test.

Nietzscheans might rejoin that they can accept "retaining a cosmological flavor" in at least one sense: It is true that for eternal recurrence to gain vivid hold we must entertain a vantage point outside of our current cycle and imagine it returning again and again. But in fact, eternal recurrence is not a doctrine at all. At best, it is a hypothesis which underscores some of Nietzsche's broad themes about life: the importance of the moment; the futility of revenge and *ressentiment*; the need to affirm life as a whole; the lack of inherent and ultimate cosmic meaning; the essential unity of joy and despair; and the need to embrace all events in your life because they constitute who you are. In fact eternal recurrence may not even be a hypothesis; instead, it may be a metaphor for self-overcoming in the face of cosmic purposelessness: the pursuit of recurring, transitory goals where there is no Goal; the celebration of a graceful dance, raucous laughter, and stirring performance where there is no final End.

For example, if we affirm the totality of life as it is—*amor fati*!—then attitudes of revenge and *ressentiment* are futile and self-defeating. Those negative attitudes seek to right the perceived wrongs of the past, in effect to change the past. But eternal recurrence undermines such hopes because it suggests a circular, not linear, notion of time. The acceptance of eternal recurrence not only eliminates the possibility of the transcendent world of Being, but also manifests the poverty of Platonic-Judeo-Christian metaphysics: free will, immortal souls, infinite redemption, the justification of punishment, the will to equality, and so on.[25]

In eternal recurrence the past and future meld together into an infinite moment. If everything recurs then events of the future are merely events of a more distant past. Thus, the present is highlighted as every part of life is bound together in eternal flux.[26] Eternal recurrence contrasts with the linear trajectory of progressivism and evolution, it underscores the death of God, it affirms the creative unity of all things and events, and it invites higher types to overcome the lack of cosmic meaning by life-affirming destruction, reimagination, and re-creation.

On this interpretation, eternal recurrence does not merely nurture fatalism and passivity; it is not simply a call for resignation in the face of eternal monotony or a stoical acceptance of the status quo. Or more precisely, only lower human types will evince such a reaction. Overcome by the spirit of gravity, lacking the exuberance to affirm life in the face of cosmic meaninglessness, and clinging to the shadows of gods and transcendent redemption, last men will wallow in comforting, life-denying illusions and hinder their own self-overcomings. Just as the burdens of Sisyphus would annihilate lower types, the thought of eternal recurrence can lead to passive nihilism at its worst.

Higher human types, though, will see eternal recurrence as an opportunity to rebel and become who they are by creatively willing their fate: by embracing the entirety of life as self-overcoming in the world of Becoming. Remember, if Sisyphus has the desire to roll his boulder up the hill and then watch it roll back down eternally his fate would not be meaningless. Such a desire creates meaning where none antecedently existed and Sisyphus would thereby become who he was. Fortunately, higher types are in a much better position than Sisyphus, even with his imagined desire: higher types contemplating eternal recurrence can still revel in the process of self-overcoming which Sisyphus cannot.

However, Nietzscheans should not invoke "self-overcoming" as a talismanic incantation that remedies all philosophical ills. Why is self-overcoming anything more than a symptom of discontent, insecurity, and desperation? Is it not only the wearing of different masks, the playing of different roles, perhaps the strained thespianism of those lacking a sense of self? Self-overcoming may well conjure the image of reptiles that regularly shed their skins.

Of course, Nietzsche denies that there is one best kind of life for all human beings. Thus, we must all discharge the burden of forging our own lives. Nietzsche also denies the presence of a substantive self-lingering beneath appearances. We are our "masks." So he thinks higher human types should aspire to be the most interesting series of masks they can create. To accept a particular mask or role as definitive of who you are during a lifetime is to truncate artificially the multiplicity you embody and to accept the life-denying, illusory world of Being. To live beyond yourself in self-creation is to forge a complex, subtle character that is worthy of "strutting its hour upon the stage" many times, even eternally.

Brushing these matters aside for the moment, the deeper question remains: Can eternal recurrence truly serve as a psychological test that distinguishes higher from lower human types? Nietzsche's affirmative answer can be summarized thusly: Eternal recurrence and attitude of *amor fati* do not merely permit but demand active response. First, at the very least, human beings have the freedom to order their interior life, their responses, to the thought of eternal recurrence. While lower human types would adopt passive or pathetic nihilism, higher human types will embrace the entirety of life and view the lack of inherent cosmic meaning and infinite redemption as liberation from external authority. Nature cannot control our attitudes toward events in the world. To become who you are, to self-overcome, and to destroy, reimagine, and re-create require an active nihilism that elevates the present into a fated eternity. Embracing eternal recurrence rejoices in the return, not the abnegation, of our own wills.[27] Higher human types will recognize that passive nihilism or fatalism rests on the life-denying illusion that the "individual" is separate from the world. On the contrary, the thought of eternal recurrence underscores the individual's complete immersion in the world of Becoming: cosmic fate is not external to us, it partially constitutes us. Moreover, instead of inputting a crude determinism to the acceptance of eternal recurrence, we can view acceptance as a free act: the immediate moment, the present, affirming and characterizing its own return and that of every other "moment." By visualizing the present moment in terms of eternity, Nietzsche challenges us to embrace the ceaseless world of Becoming in which eternity does not freeze our choices but, instead, fulfills the present with endless possibility.[28]

Thus, the eternal recurrence, in typical Nietzschean fashion, bears ambiguous tidings. For those clinging to the influences of religion and conventional morality which have historically sought to marginalize the self, the thought of eternal recurrence will lead to despair and self-abandonment. For those higher types who can will the return of even the small, ugly, and petty, the thought of eternal recurrence facilitates self-mastery. In affirming eternal recurrence we are willing the flux of life and acknowledging the unity of opposites. What is eternal is the inherent flux and chaos of the world of Becoming. Affirmation leads to our willing creatively what we had previously muddled through unconsciously. We become who we are through this affirmation: by altering our attitude we take responsibility (although not in the Christian sense) for the people we are.[29]

Despite the plausibility of this account, doubts remain. For critics, Nietzsche's talk of eternity, willing the world, self-overcoming, and transcendence is redolent with the fragrance of secular redemption: religion for those who have lost their faith but retained their need. Furthermore, there is a hollow "this is the best of all possible worlds" aura surrounding eternal recurrence interpreted as a psychological test. How can rational, sensitive people affirm the horrors of slavery, genocide, the subjugation of women, and intractable racial and ethnic strife?

Nietzscheans might rejoin that when we take responsibility for ourselves, by willing eternal recurrence and by becoming who we are, we are also willing and creating the world. Given Nietzsche's conviction that the world lacks inherent meaning, purpose, and order, we must become as gods: imposing order on chaos, creating meaning. This gigantic responsibility, along with the necessity of willing the return of the ugly, petty, and small, and directly facing cosmic meaninglessness, creates the "great weight" that lies upon our actions (GS 341). The choices of active versus passive nihilism are transformed into human alternatives: to be finite gods or to self-annihilate. Moreover, because these alternatives form a unity (as do all "opposites") the choices are not as clear-cut as we have been imagining them.

Furthermore, the texture and shadings of Nietzschean transcendence, eternality, and world creation are much different from religious versions. The focus is on this world, the premises are cosmic meaninglessness and a tragic view of life, the eternality is recurrent flux, and the transcendence is the process of destruction, reimagination, and re-creation. In sum, Nietzschean redemption is nothing more than a response to the lack of religious redemption, a message of affirmation to nudge away the nihilistic moment: there are no cosmic congratulations but higher human types, who embody the proper attitudes, do not need any.

As for this being the best of all possible worlds: Nietzsche understands suffering and the horrors of existence. (Remember this is a man whose final moment of sanity was squandered trying to protect a horse who was being flogged.) But given the unity of opposites and the interrelatedness of events and things in the world, we cannot edit life to fit our preconceptions. To affirm life is to affirm the entirety of the cosmos: we must love the whole.

Perhaps the major problem for eternal recurrence as a psychological test of greatness is that it is unclear whether all and only higher human types will affirm the hypothesis. For example, could not a last man, largely satisfied with the indolent life he is leading, desire that he live that life in all its dimensions over and over again? Given that last men live the longest, are often happy (when judged on hedonistic grounds), and endure the least stress, Nietzsche provides no reason why they must judge their lives to be unsatisfactory. The alleged test of eternal recurrence may well be nothing more than an exercise in subjective judgment: Are you so satisfied with your life that you can rejoice at the thought that you would live it precisely as you have lived it innumerable times in the future? If so, Nietzsche may not glean the results that he desires. The possibility that some last men could embrace eternal recurrence suggests that being a higher human type is not a necessary condition for celebrating the possibility of living an infinite number of the same life. Thus, that *only* higher human types will affirm the hypothesis of eternal recurrence is false.

Furthermore, might a higher human type reject the hypothesis of eternal recurrence? For example, a higher human being who relishes the values of innovation, originality, and even uniqueness might shudder at living precisely the same life innumerable times. The first iteration of such a life might well be viewed as glorious—from the imaginary standpoint of an ideal observer evaluating that life—but future iterations of that life could be viewed as simply more of the same. Whatever luster and panache the first iteration of that life exuded may well seem passé when the same life is lived over and over again. If so, then being a higher human type may not be a sufficient condition for celebrating the possibility of living an infinite number of the same life. Thus, that *all* higher human types will affirm the hypothesis of eternal recurrence may be false. If all this is true, then the hypothesis of eternal recurrence will not automatically generate the results that Nietzsche supposes and it will prove a feckless tool for distinguishing higher from lower human types.

Nietzsche might argue that last men who affirm the test of eternal recurrence are victims of self-deception: they have failed to see their lives for what they are. If last men would evaluate their lives accurately they would shrink back in horror at the thought of those lives being repeated infinitely. But, surely, if last men could evaluate their lives accurately they would not be last men. Instead, they would possess the insight to perceive the poverty of their existence and they would neither experience nor invent happiness. If Nietzsche resorts to an objective standard—what the value of the lives of last men and higher human types are in fact—instead of a subjective standard—the value that last men and higher human types take their lives to embody—he has little more than a question-begging hypothesis: higher human types should affirm and last men should resist eternal recurrence regardless of how they actually respond. But such a hypothesis cannot serve as a test for determining who is a higher human type and who is a last man. For subjective affirmation or rejection would no longer be dispositive in distinguishing the two types of human beings.

Finally, there is a problem with simultaneously embracing eternal recurrence and embodying a maximally affirmative attitude toward life. To rest affirmation of *amor fati* on feelings of gratitude is misguided. Lacking an antecedent notion of what, if anything, is genetically and culturally due to us from parents, formative environment, and the world, we can in every case fantasize about what we might have been and be resentful of being shortchanged and deprived, rather than grateful for who and what we are. If preoccupied by the gap between our real and fantasized selves, we are likely to blame the imagined discrepancy on others or the human condition itself. No matter who we are we can always imagine a better life than the one we enjoy. Moreover, if Nietzscheans claim that to imagine a better, or even different, life is to imagine a different person they may tacitly be accepting the notion of a substantive self. Unless one clings truculently to the peculiar doctrine that all events equally constitute who I am, it is possible to affirm who I am and to affirm the world while desiring to edit out certain past events. The notion that people cannot separate their lives into discrete moments that can be evaluated independently, and cannot affirm most aspects of their lives while editing out a few discomforting episodes may well strike us as unreasonable. Gratitude, then, must be our response once we have affirmed eternal recurrence and embraced *amor fati*. But sentiments of gratitude cannot be the basis upon which we decide to affirm eternal recurrence and love fate.

To deepen the paradox of eternal recurrence and *amor fati* and to refine our understandings of both ideas we must focus on Nietzsche's connecting notion of loving life.

Nietzsche's invocation of *amor fati* requires more than merely enduring what is necessary—tolerating and accepting things as they are and have been—but also the proper emotional disposition (EH, "Why I Am So Clever," 10). Those capable of doing so should *love* fate. To love something goes beyond tolerating, accepting, or even valuing that something. We can value an object without loving it. For example, I value the qualities and overall character of numerous people, most of whom I do not love. But how is one to love the banal or horrifying or devastating events that partially constitute fate? To answer this question, we must first examine the nature of love and then analyze how Nietzsche might apply that emotion to events.

To love something implies that we either perceive (rightly or wrongly) value in that object or that we bestow value upon that object through our love. We either love something because we think it is valuable or that something is valuable because we love it. Thus, to love something implies that we value that something, either because we perceive its antecedent worth or confer value upon it through our love. But perceiving the value in horrifying historical events is difficult. Major atrocities such as the holocaust, calculated genocides, atomic warfare, and the wholesale slaughter of innocent people seem paradigms of events that lack value. Also, should we love these events, for whatever strange reasons, that our affection would confer value on them is far from obvious. More likely, our love for them would call into question our own judgment and capability for evaluating. If loving fate requires loving historical atrocities something seems to have gone wrong. After all, fate is not designed antecedently to facilitate our interests or advance our fulfillment. We are under its domain and cannot alter its course. Thus, the purpose of our love is obscure: regardless of whether I love, despise, or am indifferent to fate nothing about it changes. So why should anyone adopt *amor fati* as his or her highest value?

Nietzsche suggests that people of the proper spirit are to "make things beautiful" and to "see as beautiful what is necessary in things" (GS 276). They are to bestow value on even horrifying historical events through their love for them; they are to love them agapically. Merely perceiving antecedent value in events would not be sufficient for loving them because we can value objects but not love them. Also, we cannot love objects merely by an act of will. For example, after accurately perceiving the value of other people and even after judging that I should love them because of that value I may still not love them. An act of will alone cannot generate love grounded in the perceived merit of another person. Part of the mystery of erotic love consists in the circumstances under which it arises. We can perceive accurately that Jones has more of what we value than does Smith but still love Smith and not Jones even though we would prefer to love Jones. Part of the process of erotic love transcends our acts of volition.

Are we to love even horrifying events as individual occurrences or because they are part of a general sequence of life? That is, are we to love and bestow value upon each particular historical event or are we to love and bestow value upon the entire sequence of events? On the second interpretation, horrifying events are to be loved because of their connection to life as a whole. Perhaps on this account, we could rationalize that historical atrocities play a role in what we conclude is an overall "beautiful" process. Even if an atrocity is not itself beautiful we would confer love and thereby value upon it because of its part in the overall scheme. On the first interpretation, horrifying events are to be loved as such; we would bestow love and thereby value upon them without reference to their interrelatedness to the overall scheme.

Although the first interpretation is the more difficult to accept, it may well describe Nietzsche's position (EH, "Why I Am So Clever," 10; WP 1041).

If this is correct, then we are to love agapically all events that constitute fate, even those that are initially horrifying. By loving in this fashion we will see as beautiful and bestow value upon that which was initially judged to be ugly, base, and irredeemable. But is not such a project peculiar? Why should we love such events? Even if we concluded that we should love them how would our love arise? The problems deepen when Nietzsche unveils eternal recurrence: we should not only love fate but fervently desire its infinite reiterations.

Agapic love is grounded more in the nature of the lover than in the nature of its object. Because love, whether erotic or agapic, does not arise from volition alone we cannot will *amor fati*. Instead, we must be open to it; cultivate a character compatible with it; act in ways that facilitate it; but we cannot guarantee its arrival. Nietzsche on several occasions claims to have attained *amor fati* as part of his nature (EH, "Why I Am So Clever," 9, 10; EH, "The Case of Wagner," 4; NCW, Epilogue, 1; WP 1041). In fact in most of the passages in which he extols *amor fati* as his highest value he does so by way of self-revelation: he informs readers how the world and fate appear to a person, Nietzsche himself, who has attained the highest value. Nietzsche, ever the self-promoter, is luxuriating in his accomplishment while admitting that his attainment is only partially attributable to his will. Agapic love, then, is an achievement of the spirit aided by some sort of fortuity and a manifestation of a certain type of nature. From the vantage point of *amor fati*, what are typically judged to be horrifying events are no longer experienced as such. Furthermore, attaining the vantage point of *amor fati* deepens as well as reveals the nature and character of the person who has ascended to it. The process by which a person rises to this perspective must be specific to each person who attains it.

For Nietzsche, the two possibilities are his thought of eternal recurrence—"this highest formula of affirmation that is at all attainable" (EH, "Thus Spoke Zarathustra," 1)—and his transformation of his own suffering to practical advantage. Instead of being a genuine test of greatness, the thought of eternal return may be Nietzsche's revelatory moment that he has attained *amor fati*. On this reading, eternal recurrence cannot separate higher human types from last men on the basis of whether a person is satisfied with his or her life. I have already argued that being a higher human type is not necessary and probably not sufficient for desiring that one's life be repeated. Instead, the thought of eternal recurrence can separate those who have attained *amor fati*—those who can will infinite reiterations of everything in life, not just in their life—from those who have not. Nietzsche *experiences* the thought of eternal recurrence as a "tremendous moment" (GS 341) and as an insatiable yearning for eternity (BGE 56) and as a "love" (EH, "Why I Am So Clever," 10). Nietzsche is overwhelmed because his life will never be the same again (pun intended). He lives thereafter basking in the experience of this revelatory moment. Nietzsche is now conscious of what he has attained: the value of *amor fati*. As all love, however, the value and experience must be won anew. Love typically fades when it is taken for granted. As are all human emotions, love is fragile and must be renewed and sustained. As this is not merely a function of individual volition, the continued presence of *amor fati* is ever at risk.

Still, even if correct, this account explains when Nietzsche came to understand he had attained *amor fati*, how that experience deepened his commitment to that value, and why that realization was personally transformative. But we need more to explain why Nietzsche attained *amor fati*. What was it in his life that turned him in that direction; that made him receptive to the mindset conducive to embracing *amor fati*; that opened his heart and soul to loving everything in life?

The unilluminating answer would be everything that comprised his life—all events, all of his associations, and all of his reactions to them. But we need something more specific. The obvious choice may well be his recurrent suffering. Physically ill throughout his life, disappointed in his relationships, frustrated in his efforts at personal love, Nietzsche endured uncommonly intense suffering: "*great* suffering—do you not know that only this discipline has created all enhancements of man so far?" (BGE 225) Opening ourselves to the possibility of being hurt and heightened vulnerability to disappointment are prerequisites for attaining the highest Nietzschean values and for warding off the "dwarf" within us all that reacts to setbacks with self-pity, recrimination, and *ressentiment*. Artfully managing suffering—turning it to practical advantage—positively transforms the self: "What does not kill me makes me stronger" (TI, "Maxims and Arrows," 8).

Based on his own experiences with intense, ongoing suffering, Nietzsche reveals that such pain can nurture our character. Through our responses to adversity we can develop strength, courage, and the resolve to resist the dwarf within us. More strikingly, we can develop the disposition to love fate and life agapically and thereby realize the value of *amor fati*. We can understand fully the tragic dimensions of life yet commit ourselves to bestow value on them through our love of them: "True, we love life, not because we are used to living but because we are used to loving. There is always some madness in love. But there is also always some reason in madness" (Z I, "On Reading and Writing"). Crucial to this process is the spirit of gratitude. To love fate and life is to be grateful for every moment: "To preserve an equilibrium and composure in the face of life and even a sense of gratitude toward it" (HAH II, "Preface," 5). Accordingly, while it is true that Nietzsche's embrace of *amor fati* does not alter the world it alters his perception of and approach to the world and events constituting it. Anticipating Jean-Paul Sartre, Nietzsche understands *amor fati* as Sartre would later understand the emotions: as conduits to magically transform and empower ourselves.

But, again, no method or 12-step plan or act of volition can guarantee that we will attain the wholesale affirmation that defines *amor fati*. Nor can we ensure that our love of fate and life will persist even after we have attained it. We can only do what we can to open ourselves to love's possibilities, sculpt ourselves in ways that actualize our higher human potentials, and cultivate the art of turning adversity to practical advantage.

If my interpretation is sound, that explains why affirming eternal recurrence distinguishes higher human types from last men. First, we should not view that affirmation as merely registering a person's satisfaction with his or her own life such that he or she would want to live that life in all its dimensions an infinite number of times. As I have argued, being a higher human type is not necessary for that affirmation and may not be sufficient for it. Second, we should understand eternal recurrence as bonded tightly to the value of *amor fati*: a person embracing a maximally affirming attitude toward life must be grateful for and love unconditionally all the events that constitute fate and life. Third, such a loving extension of the self requires enduring intense, recurrent suffering; positively transforming the self; making oneself radically vulnerable; and discovering that one's volition and loving disposition have coalesced and attained *amor fati* even though that result could never have been guaranteed. Nietzsche is convinced that only a higher human type can endure and embrace such a process.

For Nietzsche, artfully transforming suffering to practical advantage, luxuriating in the world of Becoming, enthusiastically engaging the process of recurrent deconstruction, reimagination, re-creation, and recognizing that permanent fulfillment is impossible are necessary for maximally affirming life. His hypothesis of eternal recurrence underscores some of those themes. Under that thought experiment, eternal life is impossible; instead, we imagine that our finite life is repeated an infinite number of times.

To affirm eternal recurrence is, then, not merely to register satisfaction with your life whatever values that life happens to include. For Nietzsche, affirming eternal recurrence must involve embracing certain values and rejecting others. If the thought experiment that is eternal recurrence eliminates the possibility of eternal life then those under the spell of Platonic-Christian metaphysics cannot affirm the hypothesis even if they are quite satisfied with the life they are leading because one of their main aspirations would be quelled: the desire for eternal bliss. If the possibility of finite life repeated an infinite number of times defines eternal recurrence then all values and hopes related to the world of Being—such as the quest for permanence and the preference for the unchanging and fixed—wither away. This may well be Nietzsche's message, the connection between adopting a certain set of values—those of becoming, process, impermanence, and creativity—as necessary for affirming the hypothesis, that energized his joy.

Still, why should we esteem and love horrifying events that did not directly harm us and those whom we know but did cruelly slaughter millions of innocent human beings? Why should we bestow value upon the holocaust, countless efforts at genocide across the globe, wars of stark aggression, and the like? If we do so, does that mark us as higher human types or does it stigmatize us as heartless, sadistic beasts? Assuming that Nietzsche cannot view such atrocities as the masses serving the deserving interests of their betters, we should be hard-pressed to love such events unconditionally, much less to will their return.

One possibility is that Nietzsche's autographical report of the experience of attaining *amor fati* is purely personal. On this interpretation, eternal recurrence and *amor fati* are proper responses to what happens to me, but not automatically proper responses to what happens to others. Thus, I could bay "*amor fati*" at the moon, but still regret horrifying events that resulted in the slaughter of millions of innocent people. On this account, loving my own life need not imply that I love the fate and life of others. The problem with this solution is that it collapses back into understanding affirming eternal recurrence as merely registering satisfaction with one's own life. As I have sketched, such a rendering of eternal recurrence will not serve Nietzsche's purpose of distinguishing last men from higher human types; eternal recurrence would merely test whether people are subjectively satisfied with their lives such that they could will infinite reiterations of it. Accordingly, on this account, eternal recurrence is not the love of fate and life, but only the love of my fate and my life. Nietzsche's intent in raising the hypothesis of eternal recurrence goes beyond the personal. He is enamored with all life and fate not merely what happened to befall him.

Another possibility is that Nietzsche carves a distinction between affirming the return of everything and wholeheartedly embracing the return of everything. Thus, on this view, we might affirm fate and life as they are, but prefer that a different chronology of events would take place that would edit out the most horrifying, seemingly senseless events and replace them with benign or beneficial happenings. This possibility reinstates the global affirmation of eternal recurrence—its affirmation of all fate and life, not just my own—but permits an aversion to the most horrifying historical events. The problem here is that the account severs eternal recurrence from the value of *amor fati*. Nietzsche reports that he *loves* fate and life, and wills its endless reiterations; he does not relate that he merely *affirms* everything. He is able to confer value upon events that are inherently valueless through this unconditional love. That this could include a preference that certain events be different is deeply problematic.

Can we love and affirm fate and life unconditionally yet prefer that some events were different? One possibility is parental unconditional love. Some parents love their children unconditionally; could affirm infinite reiterations of their children through time; but nevertheless prefer that their children were more intelligent, neater, more considerate, and the like. Even if their children never change—even if they remain obtuse, sloppy, and insensitive—the parents will steadfastly love them because their affection is not grounded in perceptions of their children's excellences. Presumably, parental agapic love confers additional value upon children even where these scions are deeply flawed. Perhaps Nietzsche's affirmation of eternal recurrence and experience of *amor fati* can follow a similar path.

But two considerations should serve as a caution. First, Nietzsche is clear that editing out painful or even horrifying events is unacceptable: "there will be nothing new in [the next life cycle] . . . everything in the same series and sequence" (GS 341). To even *prefer* that some events be edited from fate and life seems to renege on the joyful affirmation central to *amor fati* and eternal recurrence. Second, bestowing unconditional love on flawed children whom you spawned, for whom you are responsible, and with whom you share an inexorable biological bond is one thing; conferring unconditional love upon the most repulsive and devastating events in history is quite another. The animating force of parental agapic love is much easier to identify than any supposed energizing impulse to bestow value upon occurrences such as the holocaust.

Of course, on any account of affirming and loving all fate and life we must include our revulsion to the most horrifying events in history. If I was nauseated by the holocaust when it occurred, if I revolted against it and provided aid to those who were assaulted and threatened by it, then affirming eternal recurrence implies that I must also love and affirm my resistance. Paradoxically, then, attaining the value of *amor fati* and affirming eternal recurrence requires, among other things, that I love unconditionally and thereby bestow value on both the most horrifying events in history *and* my fervent opposition to those events when they occurred. I must love these horrifying events and my resistance to them when viewing them from the vantage point that is outside my life, but resist these horrifying events vigorously when living my life. (But what if I was an enthusiastic agent of evil? What if I was one of the perpetrators of a horrifying historical event? What if my only regret was that my deeds were detected and thwarted?) As such, the paradox of conferring value on horrifying events through unconditional love may be impossible to untangle.

A further question remains: Why should we aspire to sign on to the arduous task of opening ourselves to the possibilities offered by *amor fati* and eternal recurrence? We cannot alter fate or life. Yes, we can transform the self, but do those changes elevate our spirits tangibly? Again, Nietzsche speaks to us as one who has (temporarily?) attained a maximally affirmative attitude toward life and fate. The experience of realizing *amor fati* is itself inherently fulfilling for Nietzsche. He writes joyfully, virtually enraptured, as he experiences the psychological state to which he has risen. His will to power glistens as he realizes his accomplishment. Also, he alludes to instrumental benefits: no obstacle will seem too daunting for a person in love with fate and life; the petty responses of self-pity, recrimination, and *ressentiment* will wither before the grandeur of unconditional love; the higher human potentials that were actualized along the way may be further refined and strengthened; a person in love with fate and life will more readily cast his or her enthusiasms and energies into the world and thereby live intensely and fully; and the value of *amor fati* invigorates the practice of personal deconstruction, reimagination, re-creation.

Do the (tentative) results justify the journey? Readers of Nietzsche must judge that for themselves. He can only report his own experiences. Furthermore, because acts of volition cannot by themselves ensure that we will be able to love fate and life unconditionally, the entire Nietzschean process seems, well, quasi-religious. Those embarking on the Nietzschean journey must take a prodigious leap of faith. Nietzsche would have it no other way.

9. Philosophy and Psychology

Nietzsche is unique among philosophers in inviting readers to examine his psychology and life while exploring his writings. Although he does not issue this invitation straightforwardly, it is surely a consequence of what he says about the connections between literary style, philosophical content, and autobiography.

First, he tells us that philosophical writings are intimately connected with personal confessions, even if involuntarily: "Every great philosophy [has been] the personal confession of its author and a kind of involuntary and unconscious memoir" (BGE 6) and "most of the conscious thinking of a philosopher is secretly guided and forced into certain channels by his instincts" (BGE 3).

Second, Nietzsche cautions us about the self-deluded poses of objectivity and purely rational discovery that philosophers too often strike: "[Philosophers] all pose as if they had discovered and reached their opinions through the self-development of a cold, pure, divinely unconcerned dialectic . . . while at bottom it is an assumption, a hunch, indeed a kind of 'inspiration'—most often a desire of the heart that has been filtered and made abstract—that they defend with reasons they have sought after the fact" (BGE 5).

The poses of objectivity and purely rational discovery also generate methodological weaknesses: they obscure the order of rank in deference to a reassuring egalitarianism; they aspire to a universal human being as a common standard; they too easily degenerate into ahistoricism and abstraction; and they disguise the underlying origins of one's thought. Instead, readers should investigate the life influences on a writer—the instincts, drives, passions, and experiences that constitute a writer's psychological base.

Third, a writer's philosophical writings transfigure his internal condition into spiritual form. Intense suffering is especially useful for those strong enough to channel it for artistic advantage (GS "Preface," 3).

Taken together, these three elements of Nietzsche's thought do not merely invite readers to examine Nietzsche's own psychology; they insist that readers who shun this task are misguided from the outset (EH, "Why I Am So Clever," 9). He also recognizes, immodestly as usual, that he is at once a decadent, in the sense of declining life, and a beginning, in the sense of ascending life (EH, "Why I Am So Wise," 1). Nietzsche even explains his solitude and celibacy. He must sublimate much of his sociable and sexual energy in service of artistic expression (GM III, 8).

For Nietzsche, then, the philosophical is the personal: his writings chronicle, often explicitly, his struggles with the human condition and mirror his interior life. He thus denies, contrary to the self-understandings of most philosophers, any clear distinction between philosophically significant and merely autobiographical literature.

Those who accept Nietzsche's view on this matter will understand that robust philosophical critique cannot consist merely of systematic analysis of abstract propositions in terms of truth, logical implications, and soundness of argument. Indeed, if Nietzsche is correct, systematic analysis of this sort will obscure more than it reveals. To even understand a thinker's work concretely an interpreter must attend to the psychological base, historical context, and internal struggles that define the author. Moreover, we must regard carefully the tone, diction, voice, and language in which the author's thought is expressed.[30] Nietzsche applies these principles when dissecting the life, teachings, and psychology of Jesus.

Accordingly, interpretation and critique become more complex and difficult. If readers have not shared an author's relevant experiences or historical context, or if they lack reliable access to an author's psychological base, they cannot fully understand and fairly critique that author's work. Such readers could perform only the arid dissections of systematic analysis or (mis)interpret the author's work in accord with their own psychological base, historical context, and internal struggles.

Nietzsche recognizes explicitly that reporting his spiritual struggles, creating art, and critiquing mainstream philosophy are merely pale images of his vivid, lived experiences (BGE 296). Although philosophical writing cannot capture the vivacity of lived experience, it can nevertheless serve multiple purposes: sharing the products of one's thoughts and experiences, even if in ersatz form; externalizing one's thoughts in order to open paths for new experiments and experiences; and creating literature as a form of personal therapy.[31]

The connection between philosophy and psychology includes aspects of language that govern argument. Call these aspects of language "rhetorical strategies" or "modes of thought" or "dialectical categories." If we track philosophical argument we will detect these dialectical categories employed in different degrees by the participants. They will be most deeply engaged when they both speak from the same category or from similar categories. The participants in the argument will experience their deepest mutual frustrations and gravest sense of incommensurability when they speak from dissimilar categories.[32]

The first rhetorical strategy is the *analytic*. This is the strategy of classical logic and argumentation: deductive, inductive, analogical, and practical. The validity and soundness of argument are adjudicated by universal laws of reason, while intellectual inconsistency, ignorance, and falsity are understood as the primary adversaries of truth. The analytic strategy has much confidence in theoretical explanations and (often) justifications of established social doctrines and practices. This strategy self-consciously embodies a second-order dogmatic belief: certain truth-claims pertain to all human beings in all contexts at all times; at least some of these claims are discoverable by human reason; and once discovered and validated, some of these claims are fixed and final and can thus serve as epistemological foundations.

Although Nietzscheans distrust this strategy deeply they must still at times use it to articulate and to defend their own convictions. At those times, Nietzscheans run their greatest risks. They sound a bit like dogmatists themselves, their thoughts seem fixed and doctrinal, their avowed fluidity and radical contingency are (momentarily) arrested. The use of parables and aphorisms as forms of expression ameliorates but cannot escape this problem.

The second rhetorical is the *intuitive*. Participants in normative and epistemological debate when pressed thoroughly must resort to "primitives": self-evident principles, undefended axioms, or allegedly universal practices as the foundations of their theories. These are appeals to intuitions which, at bottom, rest on the authority of tradition, faith, or social conventions. Such appeals cannot interrogate their own starting points but, instead, accept the facticity or givenness of established methodologies, privileged texts, and institutional practices. This rhetorical strategy need not be grounded in a special faculty of the intellect called "intuition," but, instead, use the term to cover a hodgepodge of dimly understood ways through which we arrive at world views, as well as conclusions on narrower matters. These ways typically have a deep social genesis and can include psychological conversions and gestalt switches.

The third rhetorical strategy is the *pragmatic*. This strategy typically celebrates community and conversation and is skeptical of totalizing schemes and critiques. It often attacks the analytic rhetorical strategy for its dualism and proclivity to freeze fluid distinctions into inflexible polarities. The pragmatic strategy champions the flux and pluralism of social life and opposes the projects of foundationalists. Furthermore, the pragmatic strategy privileges fallibilism and marginalizes the solitary reasoner as well as ideal reasoning situations.

Surely the notions of pluralism, fallibilism, fluidity, anti-systematization, and anti-foundationalism are amicable to Nietzsche's thought. And that is why some commentators conclude that Nietzsche was a pragmatist. Nietzsche was, of course, interested in ideas and perspectives as instruments for achieving various purposes. But, clearly, Nietzsche did not subscribe to the pragmatic theory of truth: a propositional is true if and only if it is useful or works in some sense. The term "pragmatist" has so many related meanings in the literature that even savvy commentators sometimes get confused.

Also, that Nietzsche did not fully accept the pragmatic rhetorical strategy is clear. He would suspect that "community" and "conversation" could easily degenerate into the herd mentality. Nietzsche, however, would embrace community and conversation among higher human types as prerequisites for higher cultures. Also, he would have more appreciation for solitary reasoners, at least those of the proper type, than the pragmatic strategy suggests. Unsurprisingly, Nietzsche did not employ only one of these rhetorical strategies; he employed all of them to different degrees. As always, Nietzsche's broad themes of multiplicity of drives, conflicting passions, and plurality of perspectives prevail.

The fourth rhetoric strategy is the *substructuralist*. This strategy posits nonrational, often total, explanations for choices of social practices, perspectives, and settled doctrine. The substructural strategy does not take the claims of reason at face value. Instead, it highlights experience and practice, while devaluing the primacy of reason. Here are a few examples of substructural strategies: Marx's reliance on contradictions among the forces and relations of production as the engine of social change; Weber's understanding of bureaucratic organization; Freud's reliance on the unconscious; and Nietzsche's reliance on the will to power. Recall Marx's claim that the economic base gives rise to an ideological superstructure that serves to legitimate the base from which it arose. Here we can see the core of a substructuralist strategy: a critique of capitalist arrangements as a viciously circular process (of legitimation) which mirrors underlying reality (actual economic conditions) in a false fashion (as ideology which unconsciously masks its own origins and presents itself as independent justification).

The fifth and most notorious rhetorical strategy is the *deconstructive*. This strategy seems closely connected with style. It often deliberately offends and irritates mainstream sensibilities as it strives to advance the "unpresentable" in the "presentation" itself. The deconstructive strategy often seems to be deliberately mocking the pretensions of other strategies while advocating an "anything goes" form. It opposes all totalizing ambitions and purposefully breaks the rules of ordinary discourse. The deconstructive strategy rejects the quest for a universal audience and common ground and, instead, celebrates the irony of difference, discontinuity, and disjuncture.

We can discern some use of deconstruction in Nietzsche's literary styles, in his joy at irony, in his rejection of a universal audience, and in his glee at pushing over tottering mainstream structures. Perhaps we can now account for those critics who wrongly see Nietzsche as an apostle of anarchistic nihilism (the view that the lack of inherent cosmic meaning implies that human beings are free from all rules and ideals—all is permitted and we are limited only by our physical and mental deficiencies): they have been lured to this view by their preoccupation with his use of the deconstructive rhetorical strategy and by their failure to attend sufficiently to his frequent uses of the other strategies.

What are the lessons we can derive from this catalog of five rhetorical strategies? First, although it is possible for incommensurability to arise between participants speaking in the same rhetorical strategy and for engagement to occur between participants using different strategies, typically incommensurability arises when speakers are using significantly different strategies.

Second, speakers shift among the different strategies. Rarely does any theorist speak systematically from only one rhetorical strategy. Perhaps those who speak from within the analytic strategy come closest to achieving complete consistency because that strategy is clearly dominant. But even from those speaking predominantly from within the analytic strategy, we will almost always find invocations of the intuitive and pragmatic modes.

This may account for the impasses between Nietzscheans and analytic philosophers. For example, analytics often assume that in order for Nietzscheans to advance valid claims, they must project the same kinds of interpretive and theoretical presupposition as those projected by analytics. If a Nietzschean is trying to assert (or exemplify) substructural claims, the force of her position will be obscured by an analytic philosopher's reformulation of those claims as analytic, a reformulation which itself depends on an intuitive strategy. An analytic philosopher's assumption that all valid claims flow from the analytic is itself an implicit reliance on an intuitive commitment which privileges that philosopher's own intellectual sources.

We must be careful to remind ourselves that we are not doing anything illicit, or illogical, or even undesirable as we shift among rhetorical strategies. To different degrees we all tend to use whatever cognitive and rhetorical tools are available to address the problem at hand. Rhetorical shifts constitute a clash of paradigms of discourse which may itself be healthy and progressive. There is an irony in all this: the extent and degree of rhetorical shifting often results in more immediate incommensurability, but also long-term testing and progress of discourse as the various rhetorical modes refine themselves. Nietzscheans will quickly remind us that we will never reach the point of everlasting equilibrium, where rhetorical shifting ceases and discourse stabilizes once and forever. But this observation should not alarm: because of audience fragmentation it is highly unlikely that any system of discourse can guarantee communicative transparency. Another Nietzschean gloss on this sketch of rhetorical strategies is apparent. Perhaps we can reconceive theoretical debates as the relentless, often incommensurable competition of rhetorical strategies. That would fit well with Nietzsche's broad themes!

Still, the analytic mode is unquestionably the dominant strategy of discourse, in philosophy and generally. It often successfully domesticates and assimilates the apparent insights of the other strategies. Is this the case because the analytic mode is a socially necessary hygienic that mediates the dissonance in our life and language? Or does the analytic mode remain supreme by co-opting and reformulating the potentially unsettling effects of the other strategies? Our answer may well depend on how we intuitively privilege certain of these rhetorical strategies over others, the particular rank ordering to which we subscribe.

While rhetorical strategies, of themselves, may not seem to have any necessary political implications, they do have a few tenuous contingent connections. Political centrists will most frequently employ analytic and pragmatic strategies; conservatives will most frequently employ intuitive and analytic strategies; leftists will most frequently employ substructural, and deconstructive strategies. These are generalities which admit of significant variation.

10. Style and Rhetoric

Nietzsche embraces a variety of literary styles and a multiplicity of critical perspectives. Aphorisms, metaphors, poetry, calculated hyperboles, genealogical critiques, and personal invectives coalesce uneasily in his work. Some of the resulting literary tensions, which exacerbate the problems of clear interpretation, arise from Nietzsche's purposeful verbal equivocations or readers' failure to attend carefully to different contexts; others reflect Nietzsche's understanding of the complexity of reality which requires the use of multiple perspectives; others exemplify some of Nietzsche's broad themes such as the inescapability of inner conflict, the connection between writing and life, the denial of absolutism, and the importance of self-overcoming in a world of flux.

That Nietzsche's choices of style are not random is clear. He employs literary styles as strategies: as ways, alternately, to provoke readers to examine their most settled convictions, to underscore the indeterminacy and tragedy of life, to highlight his aversion to dogmatism, to chronicle his spiritual struggles, to undermine his own convictions, and to glorify rank order. Although he could assert these ideas in the typical style of straightforward, didactic, philosophical discourse, to do so would renege on his understanding of the connections between form, content, and personal psychology.[33]

Nietzsche's styles exemplify, rather than merely report, his philosophy by embodying the motifs closest to Nietzsche's soul. Thus he writes in ways that resist univocal interpretation, that are not intended for a universal audience, that demonstrate the lack of fixed meaning in a world of Becoming, that sometimes indulge in self-congratulations only to later enjoy self-parody, and that present views in the strongest terms while simultaneously unmasking the pretensions of dogmatism.

He knowingly confronts and basks in a paradox of prose: to the extent we accept unconditionally Nietzsche's own conclusions we mock his antidogmatism, call for self-overcoming, and commitment to rank order. The world of Becoming and the differences among humans demand that Nietzsche's views cannot win universal, absolute allegiance. Not that such allegiance was ever a genuine possibility.

Nietzsche, unlike mainstream philosophers, does not try to mask his partiality and partisanship. His views, including his notion of "will to power," arise from his will to power. His "perspectivism" emerges from his perspective (or, more precisely, his multiple perspectives). His bluster and self-aggrandizing prose burst forth from his aristocratic understanding of human beings. His reversals and self-parodies demonstrate self-overcoming in a world of flux. His (sometimes strained) attempts to self-justify his life manifest the attitude of *amor fati*. In sum, rarely does literary style track content as closely as it does in Nietzsche's work.

In that vein, Nietzsche relishes the oxymoronic character of his writings: "immoral morality," "illusory truth," "irrational rationality," "dogmatic nondogmatism," "irreligious religion," "ungodly gods," and the like. Under his broad themes, there cannot be one uniquely correct interpretation of Nietzsche's own work. There is no essence of Nietzsche to discover. Readers must creatively interpret Nietzsche from their perspectives, in accord with their wills to power, for their purposes, in their contexts. If Nietzsche is correct, dominant conventional interpretations of his work will arise from victories won in social struggle: institutional power—whether governmental, academic, literary, or other media—will solidify interpretations that fulfill its purposes, but the work remains inherently contestable. There are no fixed renderings, no final serenities, no unshakeable discoveries. The good news: we can rejoice in our freedom, search for our insights, and test Nietzsche's thought by our lives. The bad news: attempts to present Nietzsche's work to others, including the instant effort, are doomed to trivialize, to (over)simplify, and to (mis)interpret. Readers must grapple with Nietzsche's thought directly, not learn of him through intermediaries. We must confront Nietzsche's modes of address and challenges of transformation on a personal and passionate, not merely abstract and rational, level.

Still, critics will object by invoking one of Nietzsche's recurring themes: philosophical content and style are autobiographical. Judged by his own criterion, Nietzsche led a shallow life. Writing a robust life is not living one. He gives credence to those who talk about ivory tower intellectuals, the very "scholarly oxen" he otherwise disparaged. In fact his life did not even rise to *that* level. He left academe to pursue even deeper solitude and refuge from the world. The tally of his life is meager: no wives; chastity or near chastity; no children; a few friends who always seem to lurk in the distance; disappointments in his major emotional commitments (for example, Wagner, Ree, Salome); ambiguous relations—mostly negative—with his mother, sister, and aunts; physical debilities throughout; every excursion away from his writing produced yet another physical humiliation; at a relatively early age he goes insane; later he is exploited by his own sister—including being occasionally dressed in white robes and put on display for gawkers; and his work is subsequently expropriated in service of Nazi propaganda. Neither his autobiographical life (the chronicle of events he authored through his agency) nor his biographical life (the sum of his autobiographical life, other events he participated in but did not author, and posthumous occurrences) inspires emulation. In fact, the best part of Nietzsche's biographical life probably begins in the 1960s—six decades after his death—when his work is rehabilitated in the Anglo-American philosophical community and spreads beyond.

Nietzscheans will respond by rejecting the assumption that intellectual activity, particularly writing, is not living life, but is only chronicling life. The major part of Nietzsche's life was his work. It was not separate from life, it was life.[34] Nietzsche wages war in the life of the interior: he battles demons, overcomes illness, gives style to his life, creates himself as a literary figure, and records his triumphs in his writings. Granted, outsiders are denied direct access to his life of the interior—after all, it is his life—but we get images and indirect understanding from Nietzsche's work. Nietzsche squarely faces the human condition but renounces pessimism and passive nihilism. He is a Sisyphus who refuses yield. He joyfully embraces the world, he is grateful for his life, he lives his philosophy: self-overcoming, grand creation, cheerful demeanor, a courageous warrior waging battles that he knows resist final victories. For Nietzsche to enter the world of commerce, pursuit of worldly success, or profound heterosexual relationships would have been to retreat from his interior life. He needed to sublimate his sexual and competitive energies in the service of great art. He led a grand life, but it is simply not the typical life to which most of us aspire. In fact most of us are incapable of replicating Nietzsche's life: we lack the self-knowledge, the strength of character, and the remarkable spirit needed to cast aside revenge and *ressentiment*. How many of us could attain Nietzsche's joy given his physical suffering? Nietzsche led a glorious life of the interior that, for him, far exceeded the models of existence most of us hold dear.

Critics are unlikely to embrace this interpretation of Nietzsche's life. Instead, they will argue that the "will to power" is Nietzsche's desperate attempt to understand his own impotence in the world; the affirmation of "eternal recurrence" punctuated with squeals of "*amor fati*!" is a feeble effort to rationalize his illnesses and awkward personal relationships—what I cannot succeed in I will feign acceptance of; and the overman is an adolescent fantasy which, even if a mere thought-experiment, manifests Nietzsche's thinly-concealed dissatisfaction with human beings and the world. Nietzsche craved worldly success deeply and resented it when it was not forthcoming. His disdain of the masses as constitutive of herd mentality is nothing less than an indictment of those whom he believes have been too dense to honor him. He sees himself as a higher type who, like Zarathustra, is too glorious to be appreciated by the dwarfs, oxen, spiders, and clowns who populate the earth.

To continue: He subconsciously blamed himself for his father's early death; he both feared and secretly needed women; he struck out, in writing, against all those he was too weak to strike out against physically. He retreated to "the life of the interior" because he was incapable of winning a high place in the world of everyday life. He battled with quill and paper, a warrior of the mind who waged bloodless skirmishes whose outcomes were fixed from the outset by their creator. Like many intellectuals, he vented his frustrations with words written in isolation instead of confronting his enemies directly. He used philosophy to act out the resentments, reconciliations, and emotions he could not express in person. Nietzsche's final irony is that, despite his pitiless excoriation of the irrelevance of mainstream philosophers, he chose the abstractness of intellectual activity over the concreteness of robust interpersonal relations. Nietzsche's final tragedy is that in affirming life through philosophical legerdemain he denied himself life in its only meaningful form.

Nietzscheans will insist that Nietzsche's writings are not a *substitute* for life, they are his recordings of his life. True, his autobiographical reports are stale when compared to the experiences themselves, but they do nevertheless partially constitute his life. Where Nietzsche and his critics differ is on the value of literary creation: he believes that the spiritualization and sublimation of competitive and sexual passions in the service of great art is a worthy tradeoff, at least for him; critics believe that more commonplace pursuits, such as family and immersion in the daily activity of the external world, should not be ignored even if doing so decreases the prospects that one will create great art. While this judgment may well be sound—for most of us—for Nietzsche, it rings hollow. When observers deny that Nietzsche's life was truly robust, perhaps they are revealing their own dogmatism.

Nietzsche's internal struggles were neither contrived nor self-created. His struggles are our struggles: the search for meaning and value in an inherently meaningless and valueless cosmos. There is nothing abstract about these struggles and Nietzsche could not have made them abstract even if he had wanted to. These struggles define the core of the human condition; they are as concrete as life itself. Nietzsche was not living his life through written words; he was purging himself of the stale thoughts that dimly or falsely chronicle his life experiences. Nietzsche's writing was obviously a part of his life; it consumed so much of his time and thought that parts of his books are second-order writings about his writings. Clearly, we should separate "life" from "writing." So we should, for precision's sake, talk about his non-writing experiences and his writing experiences as constitutive of his life. His writing experiences often report on the non-writing experiences of his life: his inner battles with fundamental intellectual and physical conflicts, his search for meaning and value. Nietzsche was an artist of a certain sort: graced with high energy, astounding intellect, and fragile mental and physical constitution.

Neither his life nor his writing will appeal to everyone; in fact, they will appeal only to a few. He understands and underscores this.

Nietzsche's writings reflect, to the extent possible, the complexity and multivalence of life. While we may strive to embrace joyfully all the features of life, we should not deceive ourselves about the human condition: in the absence of ultimate meaning and value, human existence is inherently problematic. The "solutions," if any, that we adopt cannot purge themselves of the enigmas that are life. Nietzsche's writings explicitly retain their enigmatic flavor both to celebrate his broad themes (for example, radical contingency, flux, perspectivism) and to mirror the mysteries of life itself. For Nietzsche we *are* our masks, there is no clear separation between an authentic self and apparent self. Indeed, for Nietzsche there is no substantive self at all.

If there is a measure of fantasy and wish-fulfillment in his work that just shows that Nietzsche was human. Still, we can gain much from grappling with his work and asking the paramount questions about meaning, truth, value, motives, and origins he poses. Nietzsche is convinced that there is no neutral, Archimedean point from which to assess truth claims. But he is neither a subjectivist nor a cultural relativist regarding truth. Nietzsche holds that all of our truth-seeking goes beyond ourselves in that we are not merely surveying our current internal state to determine what is "true" once and forever. Remember, for Nietzsche "truth" itself is in flux and our language is inadequate to resolve the paradoxes of our experiences. Nietzsche relishes experiential paradoxes and is convinced they cannot be resolved, at least not in the sense most people demand. There is no firmer ground we can access, no different light to use as background, no penetrating vision we can invoke to "resolve" these paradoxes in this, or any other, context. We are condemned to our cognitive and spiritual struggles.

In general, Nietzsche's literary styles distance him from the dominant form of analytic philosophy; underscore his perspectivism; trumpet his experimentalism; declare his partiality, and report his biases. Although Nietzsche understands that the limitations of our language and rhetorical strategies force him at times to sound like a dogmatist, his use of a variety of literary forms unsettles that dogmatic tone.

Specifically, each of the literary forms has its particular purposes.[35] Aphorisms are fragments that resist the type of fixed philosophical systems that repel Nietzsche. They exemplify Nietzsche's goal of re-asking the enduring questions of human existence in full knowledge that these questions refuse final answers. Aphorisms generally contain no deductive arguments and when joined together do not necessarily form a consistent whole. Thus they celebrate, at least when Nietzsche employs them, discontinuity and liberation from fixed meaning. Hyperbole attracts attention, reveals new connections, provokes response, and cultivates self-parody.[36] Metaphors may illustrate Nietzsche's aristocratic commitments. He does not write for everyone and seemingly judges the rank of readers by their ability to discern the subtlety of his broad themes in his literary forms. Interpretation of metaphors can be a badge of membership: aristocrats recognize each other by their similar interpretations; the masses are excluded by their dissimilar interpretations or abject puzzlement. Metaphors, like aphorisms, recognize their own conditionality and thus elude final, univocal interpretations.

Genealogy, as we have seen, raises suspicions about the origins and partiality of dominant social practices and institutions. In so doing, genealogy forces us to confront the value-ladenness of our views and demands that we exit from the false shelter of abstract reasoning. Logical argument too often embodies an ahistoricism that permits us to forget the class interests and modes of life underwriting our institutions. Genealogy does not pretend to be a substitute for logical proof, but, instead, an antidote for narrowness and blindness. Accordingly, Nietzsche's polemics, including his ad hominem attacks, are self-consciously provocative.[37]

11. Tragic View of Life

Nietzsche is concerned with the links between the conditions and fulfillment of culture and a tragic view of life. Nietzsche's tragic view of life was influenced significantly by Arthur Schopenhauer who was in turn influenced significantly by Buddhist thought.

Schopenhauer's pessimistic outlook can be summarized thusly: human life is beset with universal, unavoidable suffering which precludes robust fulfillment of basic needs and wants. Life itself, not merely mortality and fear of death, is what renders human existence problematic. Although our world of appearance pertains us the illusion of individuation, Reality, as thing-in-itself, is a primal unity without individual parts. Our notions of space, time, and causality are functions of the way the human mind actively shapes and organizes sensory material, they have no independent existence as substances of categories of Reality.

We are aware of ourselves as self-moving and active, as direct expressors of wills. Schopenhauer took this inner consciousness to be basic and irreducible. What we will and what we do are one phenomena viewed from the different vantage points of inner consciousness and body, respectively. He extended his notion of will, seeing it as definitive of the fundamental character of the universe, in order to undermine those who insisted on the underlying rationality and morality of the cosmos.[38]

Schopenhauer tries to reorient philosophy away from the dominant rationalism of his day to greater emphasis on unconscious, biological forces. He rejected such ideas, prevalent among Hegelians, as the inevitability of human progress and the perfectibility of man. Instead, Schopenhauer concludes that human beings are condemned to a life of torment and misery, punctuated by diversions and respites.

Striving is the basic nature of the will, but there is no finished project that can end striving. Because striving is incapable of final serenity, we oscillate between the lack of fulfillment we feel when not achieving temporary goals and the sense of letdown and boredom we feel when we attain them. Schopenhauer concludes, along with the Buddhists, that we minimize our attachments to and withdraw as much as possible from this life.

Although Nietzsche tries to distance himself from Schopenhauer, that his own views on suffering, the pervasiveness of will, the lack of final resolutions, the role of strife, and the contingency of individuation all owe much to Schopenhauer's work is clear. Still, Nietzsche manages to distance himself from Schopenhauer's pessimistic conclusions. Whereas Schopenhauer counsels withdrawal or detachment from the petty tasks of human life and extols the temporary escapism provided by contemplating music, art and philosophy, Nietzsche advises human beings to affirm their lives maximally by desiring nothing more than to do what we are fated to do eternally. Thus, we should luxuriate in the immediate texture of what we do, thereby conferring—through attitude and will—meaning on a series of inherently meaningless tasks.

Whereas Schopenhauer tacitly accepts the criteria of hedonism and permanence, Nietzsche embraces the criterion of power: exertion, struggle and suffering are at the core of overcoming obstacles, and it is only through overcoming obstacles that humans experience, truly feel, their power. Higher human types joyfully embrace the values of power, while last men and utilitarian philosophers extol the values of hedonism: "Man does *not* strive for pleasure; only the Englishman does" (TI, "Maxims and Arrows," 12).

Nietzsche's tragic view of life understands fully the inevitability of human suffering, the flux that is the world, the Sisyphus-like character of daily life. Yet it is in one's response to tragedy that one manifests either heroism or herd mentality. We cannot rationalize or justify the inherent meaningless of our suffering. We cannot transcend our vulnerability and journey to fixed security. We are contingent, mortal beings and will remain so.

But we are free to create ourselves: we bear no antecedent duties to external authority, we are under the yoke of no preestablished goals. We need not recoil squeamishly from the horrors of existence, instead, we can rejoice in a passionate life of perpetual self-overcoming. And there is always art to validate our creativity and laughter to ease our pain and soften our pretensions: "This crown of him who laughs, this rose-wreath crown: I myself have put on this crown, I myself have pronounced my laughter holy" (Z IV, "On the Higher Man," 18).

Nietzsche does not issue a series of concrete proposals for how to live, nor does he unveil ten new commandments for philosophers of the future. But his work is much different from the dreary, logic-crunching of mainstream academic philosophy. He forces us to confront the paramount questions of human existence, invites us to live—and not merely contemplate—our answers, and challenges us to take responsibility for the persons we are becoming. Nietzsche was deeply appreciative of the Homeric Greeks capability to affirm life while recognizing its tragic dimensions. In his early writings, Nietzsche celebrates aesthetic principles which he associates with two Greek gods, Dionysus and Apollo.

Dionysus symbolizes the stream of life, the overcoming of obstacles, and the crushing of barriers. As further expressed in lyric poetry, tragedy, and music, the Dionysian impulse embraces life joyfully and irreverently. The Dionysian impulse breaks down form, dissolves individuation, and strives for unification with the underlying primal unity. The Dionysian mocks the distinction between appearance and reality: "Under the charm of the Dionysian not only is the union between man and man reaffirmed, but nature which has become alienated, hostile, or subjugated, celebrates once more her reconciliation with her lost son, man" (BT 1).

Apollo symbolizes light, measure, restraint, and beauty. As further expressed in sculpture, painting, epic, and myth, the Apollinian impulse orders and shapes the world of Becoming: "We might say of Apollo that in him the unshaken faith in this *principium* [*individuationis*] and the calm repose of the man wrapped up in it receive their most sublime expression . . . through whose gestures and eyes all the joy and wisdom of 'illusion,' together with its beauty, speak to us" (BT 1). Through concepts and classifications, the Apollinian impulse elevates the world of appearances into reality.

The tensions between the Dionysian, as embodying tragic passion, and the Apollinian, as embodying Socratic reason, are a macrocosm of the antagonisms within human beings. In his early writings, the two impulses appear as metaphysical principles of nature. The Apollinian can serve as the completion or the antithesis of the Dionysian. If Apollinian impulses predominate for too long, however, "rigidity and coldness" solidify (BT 9).

In Nietzsche's later work, the duality between Dionysus and Apollo as aesthetic principles disappears as Nietzsche more thoroughly disavows "metaphysical comforts" (BT 17, 18) that make life bearable—including the synthesis of Apollinian and Dionysian impulses—and more clearly affirms eternal recurrence: "Saying Yes to life even in its strangest and hardest problems, the will to life rejoicing over its own inexhaustibility even in the very sacrifice of its highest types . . . Not in order to be liberated from terror and pity, not in order to purge *oneself* of a dangerous affect by its vehement discharge . . . but in order to be oneself the eternal joy of becoming, beyond all terror and pity—that joy which included even joy in destroying" (TI, "What I Owe to the Ancients," 5).

The Dionysian hero in *The Birth of Tragedy* is the tragic artist as exemplified by Richard Wagner. There Nietzsche views Dionysian art—lyric poetry, tragedy, dance, and music—as a source of transcendent insight. In his later writings, however, Nietzsche abandons his overly sanguine view of the fine arts as a source of special insight and philosophers-of-the-future assume the mantle of Dionysian genius. Just as Wagner's flagrant Christianity, anti-Semitism, and nationalism eventually repel Nietzsche, so, too, the metaphysical consolations of the tragic artist lose some of their appeal.

Dionysus, thus, remains in a transformed role: as symbolic of the indestructibility of life itself, as affirmer of eternal recurrence, as symbolic of the greatest human exemplars, and as the enhancer of life through creative strife. Whether or not Dionysus-transformed is a union of the Dionysus and Apollo impulses of *The Birth of Tragedy* is a matter of scholarly dispute. Walter Kaufmann, for example, argues that the Dionysus of the early writings was conceived as a "flood of passion to which the Apollinian principle of individuation might give form."[39] In Nietzsche's later writings, Kaufmann claims, he abrogates his metaphysical dualism and Dionysus represents sublimated passion, discipline, and self-integration.[40] Bruce Detwiler, however, emphasizes that in *The Birth of Tragedy* Nietzsche is under the influence of a cosmology he later repudiates: "the cosmology of *The Birth of Tragedy* invokes a distinction between the everyday world of mere appearance and a truer, more essential reality upon which mere appearance depends. Beneath the apparent world in which we all live . . . there lies a 'truly existent primordial unity,' also described as the 'world will,' which perpetually brings the world of appearance into being and then lets it pass away again.[41]

Detwiler argues that to view Dionysus as merely a deity of formless frenzy is a mistake : "On the metaphysical level Dionysus also appears to represent primal creativity."[42] By refusing to view Dionysus and Apollo as starkly opposed in Nietzsche's early writings, Detwiler draws the contrast between the early and late Dionysian heroes differently from Kaufmann: "In the *Birth* Dionysian man joins his god by obliterating himself, whereas in the final period Dionysian man experiences his own divinity by obliterating self-consciousness and by going under, reuniting with the primal ground of his being."[43] Whereas Kaufmann celebrates the "rational self-mastery" of Dionysus-transformed, Detwiler underscores "intoxication owing to increased strength": "In the Dionysian life affirmer the dominant creative drive is a kind of spiritualized sexual impulse to create the world in his own image. For the organism as a whole, to become more beautiful is to become more perfectly sublimated, to harmonize desire."[44]

The images of Dionysus and Apollo, in any event, prefigure numerous persistent Nietzschean themes: the mutual exclusivity between genuine creativity and conscious reflection; the human need to deconstruct, reimagine, and re-create; the inherent conflicting impulses within humans; the need to affirm life while embracing its tragic dimensions; and the value of self-overcoming.

12. Jesus and Nietzsche

In general terms of morality, Jesus and Nietzsche are similar: both take a virtue ethics approach which prizes inner motives and intentions; both are reluctant—Nietzsche even more so than Jesus—to issue particular judgments about specific cases. They seem to agree that nurturing the proper dispositions of character and becoming a certain type of person will facilitate making the appropriate normative choices. Both Jesus and Nietzsche resist formalistic and mechanical application of supposed normative laws to specific cases. They are most concerned with providing guidance on who we should be rather than insisting on what we must do on particular occasions.

Beyond his general agreement, the teachings of Jesus and Nietzsche vary strikingly. In terms of epistemology, whereas Jesus extols the Archimedean point of the Ideal Observer, God, Nietzsche celebrates perspectivism; whereas Jesus invokes the universal and unconditional, Nietzsche privileges the particular and contingent. Regarding normative judgments, whereas Jesus grounds his teaching in what is common among human beings—their supposed spark of divinity and shared membership in the human community—Nietzsche insists that contingent factual differences among human beings establishe a rank order that bears existential implications. Whereas Jesus is firmly convinced that we should embrace a radical egalitarianism, and extend unconditional love and concern to everyone, especially to those with special needs, Nietzsche unsqueamishly champions an aristocratic attitude that recognizes the rank order of human beings.

Regarding the best approach to living our lives, whereas Jesus warns us against pursuing material accumulation and worldly fame, Nietzsche cheers the grand striver who continuously aspires to overcome and surpass his present self-understanding. Whereas Jesus advises humility and self-abnegation before God, Nietzsche professes that a deserved self-pride is our reward for successfully negotiating the recurring cycles of deconstruction, reimagination, and re-creation in the service of new ways of life. Whereas Jesus prizes a robust communitarianism, Nietzsche exalts a hearty individualism. All of these themes are vividly displayed in the differences between the human paradigms the two thinkers sketch: Jesus depicts the ardent unconditional lover, while Nietzsche portrays the grand striver brandishing a stalwart will to power.

Three

FUNDAMENTAL UNDERSTANDINGS OF HUMAN BEINGS: UNCONDITIONAL LOVE AND THE WILL TO POWER

Jesus advances unconditional love as the highest human fulfillment, while Nietzsche concludes that the will to power is the fundamental drive of living things. To understand the differences in these two concepts is to begin to appreciate the stunning disparity between Jesus' ideal human being and Nietzsche's overman.

1. The Power of Unconditional Love

In the parable of the prodigal son (Luke 15: 11-32), the younger of two sons asks his father for his inheritance.[1] By his request, the prodigal son reveals several moral deficiencies. His request demonstrates conclusively that he undervalues his relationship with his father; that he is unconcerned about his future responsibility to help care for his aging father; that he is avaricious and is overly concerned with material accumulation; and that he yearns to cast aside highly respected agricultural work and to leave his family, underscoring his feckless values and broken relationships. That the younger son did not consult with his older brother prior to lodging his inheritance claim shows additional disrespect for family relations. Most important, leaving the family land signals a significant change of identity; the prodigal son seeks to distance himself from his family and his past, and to remake his self-image.

His conduct after receiving the early inheritance only compounds his depravity: he squanders his money with "riotous living." The prodigal son scampers off to a "far country," presumably Gentile. He exhausts his money foolishly on "riotous living," the nature of which our imaginations can speculate. Then a great famine strikes the land—to ancient minds perhaps symbolic of divine retribution—and the prodigal son becomes a field hand who cares for the swine owned by a citizen (undoubtedly a Gentile) of the forsaken country. The prodigal son is reduced to collaborating in his own shame. To an ancient Jew, few labors would have been considered more despicable than caring for swine. The Old Testament stigmatized swine as unclean; eating and even touching swine were proscribed.

Formerly a privileged offspring of a respected patriarch, the prodigal son is reduced to lusting after "the husks that the swine did eat" and to desperation as "no man gave unto him." The prodigal son has relinquished his manhood, and shamed himself and his family.

The prodigal son eventually "came to himself" and decides to go home and throw himself on his father's tender mercies. To what does "came to himself" translate? Does the prodigal son simply evaluate the situation, understand that his options have evaporated, regret his infelicitous handling of his money, and decide to pursue his only genuine possibility? If so, then the prodigal son is not remorseful for his sins, but regrets only that he squandered his funds unwisely and now strives to make the best of his deplorable situation.

Or does "came to himself" signify that the prodigal son now actualizes the better angels of his nature? He now realizes the goodness that has always lay within him, but that only now does it arise from his deprivation: having nothing left to lose, the prodigal senses a newly-won freedom from the bondage of material possessions and comes to terms with his "true self."

Or does "came to himself" dispense with the baggage of finding one's true self and connote, instead, the prodigal son's sincere repentance? After all, he vows that he will confess his sins against both heaven and his father. But which sins? Is he repenting only his foolishness in wasting his money which has led to his shame of family and self? Or is he thoroughly remorseful for having asked prematurely for his inheritance and all that that request signified about his values and relationships?

These possibilities are all plausible but contestable. The prodigal, however, does recognize that his past actions disqualify him from calling himself his father's son. He will ask only to become a hired servant. While the prodigal may well have been fully remorseful at the moment he "came to himself," he had certainly attained that state after luxuriating in his father's bountiful welcome upon his return home. The only difference is whether he achieved full remorse independently or whether his partial repentance blossomed into full remorse upon his father's gracious acceptance of his return. The point of the parable disappears if we suppose that the prodigal son acted only strategically when he "came to himself" and that he remained only a rational calculator of his interests upon his return.

So the prodigal son decides to return. While still "great far off," his father spots him and runs to him. In fact, a dignified patriarch with flowing robes would almost certainly not run after anything. Such action was considered beneath such a man. Of course, the father in our parable is not an ordinary man. That he would run, once again, highlights his uncommon love of and generosity toward his son. More strikingly, that the father saw the prodigal while he was still "great far off" symbolizes the patriarch's ongoing concern and vigilant aspiration that his wayward son would return. If and when that moment occurred—if he who was lost could be found—the father would be well-prepared.

The father's unconditional love of his son, again, resonates: he "fell on his neck and kissed him." He does not issue recriminations; he does not scold his son for his malfeasance; and he does not seek explanations. When his son blurts out, "Father, I have sinned against heaven, and in thy sight, and am no more worthy to be called thy son," the father does not respond directly to the assertion. Instead, he instructs servants to fetch a robe, ring, and shoes, and prepare a feast. By his words and actions, the father demonstrates his forgiveness of and visceral reconciliation with his son.

For his part, if he was not fully remorseful upon undertaking his return home, the prodigal is now totally cognizant that his underlying sin "against heaven" and his father was his fracturing of their relationship. The son could not have sapped his father's love for him. His father's love was unconditional and thus even if it was unrequited it would persist. But through his earlier actions, the prodigal had destroyed or revealed the already-decrepit state of their relationship. Unlike love which can be merely one-sided but nevertheless genuine, relationships by definition require more than one participating party. A person cannot maintain an unrequited relationship.

That the father's kiss and embrace of his son symbolize reconciliation is beyond dispute; it takes at least two parties to reconcile and repair a relationship. We can safely conclude that either the father had recognized that his son had wronged him and all was now forgiven or the father never acknowledged that his son had wronged him so there was nothing lingering to forgive. Notice that in either case the prodigal son has no reason to offer to become one of his father's hired servants, and he does not. That the father is prepared to accept him fully and reinstate complete family privileges is transparent from the father's actions and from his instructions to his servants to gather a robe, ring, and shoes for the returning prodigal and to prepare a feast. The father's unconditional love, reflecting God's limitless grace and expansive compassion for human beings, transcends contractual boundaries. Forgiveness and reconciliation resist the constraints of arms-length bargaining.

By doing the extraordinary and rushing out to meet his returning son, the father sends a message to his society: I bear only joy at my son's return. By having his servants slay the fatted calf and prepare a feast, the father invites some members of the community to participate in that joy. We must assume that people outside the immediate family attended the celebration as this was customary when a calf was slaughtered. The prodigal son's fractured relations with his community must also be repaired. In any case, I cannot overemphasis that the father's reactions to the return of his son, like his embodiment of unconditional love, are not typical of patriarchs of his time and place. He may well represent the divine spirit tending to the fallibilities of the human flock.

In all of this the stress is on personal transformation and redemption: "For this my son was dead, and is alive again; he was lost, and is found." Once the prodigal son leaves his father's home and the wider community he was in effect morally and spiritually dead. Stunningly, he "came to himself" and was reborn. Nurtured by the unconditional love and graciousness of his father, we must conclude that the prodigal son will now maximize what has hitherto lain dormant within him. He will grow into a worthy member of family and community, who evinces high moral and spiritual values. The son has always had the potential to attain this end, but for whatever reasons needed to undergo a certain painful process in order to actualize his highest attributes.

But what are we to conclude about the elder son? Although he was not consulted by his younger brother prior to the initial request for an early inheritance, he, too, received his share: "And he divided unto them his living." The older son has remained within the family and wider community and it may seem that his relationships are intact. But first impressions, like destitute relatives and sales overtures from telemarketers, are not always what they seem.

First, the older son had an obligation to broker peace between his father and the younger son. He either ignored that obligation or failed miserably in his efforts. Instead, he accepts his share of the early inheritance. Second, his reaction to the feast demonstrates the frailty of his family relations. The older son resents the attention lavished on his younger brother, is angry at his father for his generosity to the prodigal, and refuses to participate in the feast. In fact, the older son would have been expected not only to attend the feast but to discharge certain ceremonial duties. Third, when his father pleads with the older son to share in the festivities—an entreaty that should have been unnecessary—the older son is churlish. He complains that he was never given even a measly baby goat to celebrate with his friends, yet the father now has the prized fatted calf slain to celebrate the return of a son who has squandered his money with "harlots" (How does the older son know this? Is he only projecting his own subconscious desires?). The older son does not recognize that his father, under conventional understandings, might well have rebuked him severely for not attending the feast and for not discharging his family duties. Fourth, the older son reveals the spirit in which he has contributed in the past to the family: "these many years do I serve thee." He has regarded his relationship with his father as one of servant to master. He has neither recognized nor accepted his father's unconditional love. Fifth, the older son has a formalistic, narrow understanding of morality. He claims never to have transgressed a commandment and he assumes that doing no harm is equivalent to attaining moral goodness. In short, he recognizes the stringency of negative moral duties, but ignores the importance of positive moral duties. To conclude that the older son is insecure, obsessed with his place in the family hierarchy, self-absorbed, and even mean-spirited is undeniable.

Indeed, the older son is obtuse and radically misunderstands the nature of unconditional love. Such love is not finite, not a commodity to be divided among its claimants like so many slices of a delicious pie. When allotting food, supply often cannot fulfill demand. But the economics of unconditional love are different. Unlike a coveted pie, where unconditional love resides its supply can always fulfill demand: the father does not love the older son less because he now exuberantly welcomes back the prodigal son. The father loves both of his sons equally and unconditionally; he makes that clear to the resentful young man: "Son, thou art ever with me, and all that I have is thine." Moreover, the father makes clear to his older son what should have been stunningly obvious to him all along: "It was meet that we should make merry, and be glad: for this thy brother was dead, and is alive again; and was lost, and is found." The family celebrates exuberantly when one of its own is transformed and redeemed; what was fractured has been healed. Will the older son "come to himself," repair his own broken familial relationships, and bask in his father's grace and generosity? The parable ends without suggesting the answer. What is most important is that the older son has been invited to join the congregation of those rejoicing. Whether he will participate with a full heart and open mind remains a pressing question. We can only hope that he will "come to himself."

The two sons bear resemblances: "One is lawless without the law, and the other lawless within the law. Both rebel. Both break the father's heart. Both end up in a far country, one physically, the other spiritually. The same unexpected love is demonstrated in humiliation to each. For both this love is crucial if servants are to become sons."[2] In both cases, we wonder how such an evidently special father could have sired and raised such ungrateful and insensitive scions. Both sons are lost in the sense that their family relations are inadequate: the older son feels like a servant, while the younger son, prior to his return, valued his father's material goods more than he treasured his father.

The parable of the prodigal son glistens with numerous lessons: sinners can and should repent their transgressions, and seek personal transformation and redemption; participants and third parties should facilitate and rejoice in the redemption of others; where unconditional love resides, forgiveness of transgressions is warmly available when penitents are willing to embrace it; just as the historical Jesus associated with undesirables such as tax collectors (who typically collaborated with Roman oppressors and skimmed profits from overcharging their compatriots), lepers (in violation of purity laws), and prostitutes, we, too, should not simply write off those who are stigmatized as incorrigible; and to be a full member of family and community requires much more than the proper bloodline and geographic position—a proper understanding of salutary relationships is required as is the appropriate disposition of heart and soul.

Still, questions linger. From a divine perspective, the notion of unconditional love may resonant. But can human beings genuinely love others unconditionally? If so, what is the object of such a love? If human beings can love others unconditionally is such affection limited to parent-child relationships?

2. The Paradoxes of Agapic Love

In the parable, the father's love of his sons seems to be agapic.[3] If a person loves another person agapically then the beloved person's characteristics, properties, and actions are irrelevant to the lover's affection. The beloved person's perceived value as determined by individuating attributes would simply not be the ground or object of the love. On this conception, the lover loves the beloved person unconditionally. The love would be unwavering: even if the beloved person is ungrateful, even if the beloved person does not love in return, even if the lover has perceived the beloved person's personal qualities inaccurately, the lover would still love the beloved person. As such, agapic love aspires to surmount all obstacles and persist through all vicissitudes. Regardless of how the character of the beloved person changes, the lover's amorous regard remains constant. The lover desires the best for the beloved even if acting on those desires results in her self-denial. Instead, agapic love creates value in the beloved person: by dint of his love, the father bestows value upon the prodigal son and offers the same to the older brother.

However, agapic love is more easily described than experienced. The genesis of the concept is Biblical. God presumably loves all of God's creations agapically. Even if some human beings stray from the moral law repeatedly in the vilest fashions, God loves the sinner while despising her sins. God's act of creation and ongoing affection bestow value upon us. Beyond resolute divine affection, parents often seemingly love their children agapically. Despite the disappointing actions or unworthy character development of their offspring, many parents remain thoroughly loving.

Still, the paradox of agapic love is undeniable: on the one hand, the object of agapic love is supposedly a distinct individual, not merely a set of properties. The father in the parable loves the prodigal son and the older brother; he does not love everyone or, as far as we know, anyone else agapically. But, on the other hand, if a person's properties are irrelevant how can we distinguish one person from another? Stripped of all constitutive and accidental properties, what remains of a person? And if we are all the same once we are divested of our individuating properties then why love this person instead of that person? How is the prodigal son genuinely the object of his father's love if none of the son's properties are relevant to the father's love?

This paradox arises even in the case of God, who presumably loves all of God's human creations equally regardless of their individuating properties or moral worth. God's love is not discriminatory or partial. God may love human beings not for their individuating characteristics, but for their participation in a general humanity. Thus, Neera Kapur Badhwar observes that

> Agape can, consistently be unconditional in the sense of being independent of the individual's *personal* nature and worth—of that which distinguishes him from other persons—but not of his *human* nature and worth—of that which distinguishes him from non-humans. Agape also, in other words, must be of the individual for what he is, even though only qua *human being*, and not qua *person* . . . But what is the evidence for this common humanity, this equal potential for worth or virtue that we

all, supposedly, share? There seems to be no *empirical* evidence . . . the only way to sustain belief in a universal potential for goodness is by means of a transcendental metaphysics of the person (in the religious version, the idea of man as created in the image of God).[4]

However, according to religious doctrine, that God apagically loves the spark of the divine embodied by every human being is unlikely. That would transform an agapic love into an egocentric self-love: God would love that aspect of every human being that reflects God's own image. Again, we must ask: Exactly what is it that God loves agapically?

Some thinkers argue that agapic love excludes all self-love and all desire to obtain something for the lover. Thus, Andres Nygren argues that

> God does not love in order to obtain any advantage thereby, but quite simply because it is His nature to love—with a love that seeks, not to get, but to give. This means, in other words, that no teleological explanation or motivation of His love can be entertained . . . God does not love that which is already worthy of love, but on the contrary, that which in itself has no worth acquires worth just by becoming the object of God's love. Agape has nothing to do with the kind of love that depends on the recognition of a valuable quality in its object; Agape does not recognize value, but creates it.[5]

On this view, agapic love has no external grounds, but, instead, flows from the internal nature of the lover. Moreover, the agapic lover seeks nothing from the bestowal of love. Finally, God is not responding to the common humanity of human beings—their potential for worth, value, or virtue—or to the spark of the divine they presumably embody. Instead, God's agapic love is selfless, spontaneous, unmotivated by factors external to God's nature, indifferent to the value or potential for value of God's beloved creatures, and independent of desire and longing.

Although acute in several respects, Nygren's portrayal deepens the mystery of agapic love. If God must love agapicially because of God's basic nature does that suggest that God's love is not freely bestowed? If God's love is utterly unmotivated by any external considerations must that imply that God's love is independent from all desire?

For example, why cannot God freely bestow agapic love upon human beings because he desires to create value thereby? Why cannot God have other-directed desires such that God wishes to elevate human beings—enhance their worth and value—through God's love? On such a view, God's agapic love is motivated, but by reasons still internal to God's nature. That is, God would not be recognizing or responding to the antecedent, external condition of human beings, but God would be choosing to enhance the value of God's own creations.

Oddly, although Nygren emphatically concludes that God's agapic love is spontaneous and unmotivated, he later describes agape as the initiator of fellowship with God:

> In the relations between God and man the initiative in establishing the fellowship lies with Divine Agape . . . all the other ways by which man seeks to enter into fellowship with God are futile. This is above all true of the righteous man's way of meritorious conduct, but it is no less true of the sinner's way of repentance and amendment . . . God must Himself come to meet man and offer him His fellowship. There is thus no way for man to come to God, but only a way for God to come to man: the way of Divine forgiveness, Divine love.[6]

I will not consider at this time whether Nygren has described accurately the *only* way that human beings can attain fellowship with God. But he has identified a possible internal motivation of God's agapic love: to offer fellowship to human beings. Presumably, God desires that human beings accept this fellowship and God is pleased (or satisfied or fulfilled or gratified) when they do. If so, Nygren's previous explanation of agapic love—as completely free from desire, seeking no end, and indifferent to the potentials of the beloved—must be adjusted.

Perhaps we can conclude that God's agapic love flows from God's desire to elevate the worth of his human creations—either by offering fellowship or bestowing value directly by means of love; that God further desires that human beings will make the most of God's love; that God benefits in some way when that occurs, either by being gratified or pleased or the like; that whatever benefits God garners from extending love are not God's prime reason for loving; that God's love toward all human beings remains unconditional, even if his offer of fellowship is repudiated by some individuals; that while God's love is not motivated by external factors, we can identify possible internal motivations; and that God's agapic love is thus bestowed for the sake of human beings.

Such an understanding of agapic love drains some its mystery while remaining faithful to its widely-accepted basic contours. That God benefits in some way when human beings accept God's offer of love does not imply that God's love is egocentric, acquisitive, or fundamentally selfish. On the contrary, a God lacking other-directed desires would be a strange breed. (Perhaps such a God would be akin to an Epicurean deity utterly indifferent to and unaware of the external world.) That God aspires to the mutual good of fellowship with his human creations does not dilute the glory of agape, but, instead, enhances our understanding of the phenomenon. Moreover, "selfishness" connotes ignoring the interests of others when one ought not to do so—a notion completely inappropriate in this context. That a moral agent, divine or human, gains fulfillment or gratification from advancing the interests of others counts in the agent's favor; it is not a factor that degrades the quality of the action or the actor. Would it not be bizarre to aid other people in important ways yet remain utterly indifferent to the success of your deeds? Morally deficient people typically lack other-directed desires, while those of us who embody and act on such desires are more likely to fulfill our moral obligations.

Moreover, my revised understanding of agape retains the basic dimensions of the phenomenon: unconditionality, constancy, creation of value in the beloved, arising from the nature of the lover, not directed to only those deemed antecedently deserving, not derived from the perceived antecedent worth of the beloved, and not motivated by acquisitive, egocentric concerns. By stripping the concept of agape of its more mysterious elements, we render this type of love more accessible and compelling.

If we understand the Christian notion of agapic love in this way, it strays from the dominant understanding of Jesus' time. Conventional Jewish wisdom of Jesus' day was that God loved righteous worshippers, but did not love the unrighteous, the sinner, or the heathen. As always, Jesus' radical message conflicts with standard rule-book interpretations of religious and moral law. Just as Jesus consorted freely with prostitutes, tax collectors, and those deemed unclean—in opposition to the received wisdom of his culture— his interpretation of the love commandment, both in terms of divine and neighborly relations, rings a revolutionary chord.

3. Parental Agape

But how, if at all, does agape relate to human affection? Nygren believes that human agape arises from divine agape. On this view, God's love empowers people to love even their seemingly unlovable neighbors. The object of such love must be the spark of the divine that even our enemies embody.

Of course, this view leaves unexplained how someone who has not self-consciously embraced God's love could nevertheless love agapically. Although God supposedly loves all his human creatures equally, that not all of us accept that love is clear. Many (most?) human beings easily resist the call to "pass on this love" to neighbors. Thus, those who do respond positively to God's love and who do pass on that love even to "enemies" must bring something to the love relationship with God that others do not.

The most likely place to begin our inquiry into human agape is with parental love. I would argue that if parental love can be agapic, it need not be viewed as the simple passage of God's love from parents to children. Given that even nonbelievers and otherwise disreputable parents have the possibility of bestowing such love, we cannot persuasively account for the phenomenon by invoking Nygren's view of why some human beings can love their supposed enemies.

But the paradoxes of agapic love, again, arise in the case of parents. If some parents love their children agapically then the children's constitutive attributes, character development, choices, and deeds, are irrelevant to sustaining that love. What, then, is the basis of and what is the object of such a love?

I would argue that if parental agapic love is possible—and I think that it is—such affection bears both similarities to and differences from divine apagic love. For example, if parents love their children agapically, unlike God, they can still differentiate them from all others whom they do not love agapically: Angelo and Vittoria are *my* children; I helped create them; we are in the world together, we share one flesh; in a certain metaphysical sense, we are not fully separate and distinct. Such parents begin with affectionate feelings toward their offspring. These feelings reflect their sense of agency in the act of procreation, their visceral acceptance of the parent-child bond, and their place in an ongoing generational chain that widens their subjectivity. Such feelings and the phenomena that underwrite them cause parents to believe that their children are inherently and objectively valuable independently of their children's choices, deeds, and future development. Thus, in parental agapic love, at least one property of the beloved does seem relevant: "that this is my child" distinguishes the person whom the parents love agapically from the numerous other human beings that the parents do not love unconditionally. This enduring *relational* property, then, belies the tradition that insists that agapic love is *completely* devoid of attention to the properties of the beloved.

Yes, it is true that such parental love is neither completely selfless nor independent of desire. We are concerned with the quality of our existence as individuals in a sense that is fundamental and different from our concern with the quality of the existence of other individuals. If I am correct, the metaphysical connection that some parents recognize with their children extends that preference from self to progeny. Moreover, the phenomenon of parental agapic love is thereby not experienced as merely a bestowal from self to "other." Again, parents and children with the requisite metaphysical connections are not fully separate and distinct. Understood in this fashion, parental agapic love cannot be selfless. Nor is such love free of desire: the procreative process typically originates in desire and the yearning to deepen metaphysical bonds often continues as children grow. Because the parent-child bond in such cases precludes the members from being fully united and fully distinct, agapic love is also underwritten partly from other-directed desires.

Obviously, not all parents embody the feelings described for their children or bestow the agapic love depicted. I am trying to capture the phenomenology of parental agapic love as it occurs in our world. I do insist that parental agapic love does sometimes happen. To what extent and how frequently is contestable. Consider a case that I will present as a hypothetical but which I am certain has actually occurred: Parents conceive, bear, and raise their child to young adulthood. To other people, the child embodies little if any social value. He is rude, obtuse, rebellious, surly, and a sociopath. Draw the details as starkly as you prefer. Yet his parents, although heart-broken by his choices and actions, love their child agapically. Finally, the child decides to perform the ultimate treachery. He loads a shotgun and murders his father in front of his mother. He then turns to his mother and prepares to shoot her. With her final gasp, the mother whispers, "I love you," to her despicable son. With the mother's death agapic love expires.

My understanding of parental agapic love in our world can help explicate the parable of the prodigal son. The father's metaphysical connection to both his sons animates his agapic love for both: "All that I have is thine." Both of his sons acted imprudently, selfishly, and, most importantly, in utter ignorance of their father's love for them. Or, perhaps, worse: they may have been aware of their father's affection for them but, nevertheless, declined the invitation to reciprocate. Had either son, at any point, have chosen to slay their father we must assume that the patriarch's final words to his murderer would have been, "I love you."

Taken at the human level instead of the allegorical divine level, the father in the parable of the prodigal son loves both of his sons unconditionally. From the earlier discussion, I take this to be a bestowal of affection often found in our world today. Although elements of the parable would have been viewed suspiciously from the vantage point of dominant parental practice during Jesus' time, in our own time it may conjure warm memories of parents whose love overlooked our shortcomings and transgressions for the sake of the family unit. The reality of agapic parental love must be heeded. Taken at the divine level, the parable reminds us that repentance and forgiveness remain genuine possibilities; that God loves us unconditionally and seeks our fellowship; and that a resolute will and open heart ensure that personal transformation is always possible.

Of course, the parable may well be best understood as an allegory of God's love for God's human creations. Surely, Jesus was uninterested in sentimentalizing family relations in his world. Thus, the historical Jesus might well be completely indifferent to my analysis of contemporary parental agapic love. In fact, Jesus might regard parental agapic love as an obstacle to the universal benevolence that captured his interpretation of the love commandment: to the extent that parents love their children agapically they are less likely to allocate their resources impartially and more likely to circumscribe their circle of concern. Thus, my analysis of parental agapic love should be taken as a way to understand a worldly phenomenon, not automatically as the message Jesus intended to send by way of the parable of the prodigal son.

The parable of the prodigal son, then, offers us a glimpse of the unconditional love God presumably bestows upon human beings. Moreover, the story energizes our efforts to repent our transgressions, forgive those who have repented, and rejoice in the positive transformation of the human spirit. The parable reminds us that we have the power to change: where there is life there is hope. Finally, the tale can be interpreted on the human level as a glorious example of parental agape, a narrative of a parent whose affection for his children overwhelmed all resistance and recognized no limits. The deeper challenge will be to extend unconditional love to mere acquaintances, strangers and even enemies where enduring relational properties are absent.

4. The Will to Power

For Nietzsche, the fundamental drive of all living things is the will to power: the impulse to dominate one's environment and extend one's influence. In human beings the will to power sometimes manifests itself as brute force, but more frequently requires creativity, boldness, and innovation. Nietzsche claims that the typical catalog of human desires—for love, friendship, respect, procreation, biological nourishment, competitive glory, and the like—are all manifestations of the will to power. Accordingly, underlying the greatest altruistic and cultural values such as justice, truth, beauty, self-sacrifice, and art is the natural impulse to command and dominate.

Clearly, the will to power does not depend on the presence of a free or any will. All living things possess a will to power although many do not have "minds." Furthermore, even for human beings the will to power is not grounded on the power of volitions to act as causes for various effects. The will to power is a "primitive" for Nietzsche: it is life and life is a complex struggle within and outside the human psyche. The will to power is the name Nietzsche gives to the recurring struggle among closely interrelated entities in the world. Power does not mean anything when taken abstractly; instead, it requires the mutual resistance of linked, living things. More subtly, will to power underwrites the struggles among the multiple drives we embody. These multiple drives, as well as the impulse for self-overcoming, are merely different manifestations of the same instinctual drive. Sublimation, self-perfection, and self-overcoming within the individual, and influence, domination, and command over others and the world, all fall under the rubric of will to power. Moreover, the will to power connotes a process, not a fixed entity, which has growth, expansion, and accumulation at its core.

The philosophical subtext of Nietzsche's invocation of will to power is clear: our forms of knowledge, morality, truth, logic, and religion—all the alleged foundations of our institutions and theoretical enterprises—are the consequences of power struggles which themselves lack rational justification. While these alleged foundations present themselves as neutral exemplars of the persuasiveness of better rational arguments, undeniable metaphysical grounding, and glimpses of a natural order embedded in the universe, they are in fact nothing more than the effects of the will to power.

A crude reading associates the will to power with the drive for self-preservation. But Nietzsche claims that self-preservation is only one of the *effects* of the will to power, not its defining aim. Nietzsche calls higher types more fragile, more likely to squander their abundant passions in acts of self-overcoming than herd members who are concerned narrowly with species survival. Expanding one's influence and discharging one's strength often jeopardize self-preservation.

Another crude reading concludes that Nietzsche wholeheartedly endorses all manifestations of the will to power. On a trivial level that may be true: he insists that higher human types will joyfully embrace all of life and refuse to edit out unpleasant aspects from their lives. But on a practical level Nietzsche distinguishes life-affirming from life-denying manifestations of the will to power; refined from decadent wills to power; and vital from effete quantities of will to power. The will to power manifests itself in philosophers' attempts to create the world in their own image; in every attempt of overcoming; in every valuation; in every vengeful and resentful act of the herd; in every physical confrontation, including war; in every artistic creation; in every attempt to control and command through religion, politics, and military force; in every invocation of love and friendship; in every act of charity and self-sacrifice; in every attempt to procreate; in every egalitarian reform; in every aristocratic reaction; in every human act, including Nietzsche's own invocation of the will to power itself. Although all living things possess will to power, they differ in the quantity and quality of manifestations. Thus, acknowledgment of will to power and the joyous affirmation of life does not preclude the continued evaluation that itself is part of the will to power. As the basic, natural drive of life, the will to power embodies conflicting drives with self-destructive inclinations.

Nietzsche argues that the will to power is not fulfilled unless it confronts struggle, resistance, and opposition. Pursuing power, in the sense of increasing influence and strength, requires intentionally and actually finding obstacles to overcome. Indeed, the will to power is a will to the precise activity of struggling with and overcoming obstacles. Because suffering and pain attend the experience of such struggle, a robust will to power must desire suffering (BGE 225, 228). The resulting paradox is that the fulfillment of the will to power—the overcoming of resistance—results in dissatisfaction as the struggle has (temporarily) concluded. The will to power actually requires obstacles to the satisfaction of its specific desires because beyond specific desires, the will to power has a more fundamental desire to struggle with and overcome obstacles. In sum, the will to power deeply desires resistance to the satisfaction of its own specific first-order desires.

Accordingly, the will to power cannot embrace final serenity or permanent fulfillment. The satisfaction of one specific desire brings both fulfillment, a feeling of increased strength and influence, and dissatisfaction, as resistance has been overcome and is no longer present. Only endless striving and continual conquests fuel a robust will to power. Nietzsche, then, embraces the criterion of power: exertion, struggle and suffering are at the core of overcoming obstacles, and human beings experience and truly feel their power only through overcoming obstacles.

Nietzsche's notion of will to power suggests several questions: If the will to power manifests itself in every human activity does it retain any discrete meaning? Is Nietzsche wrongly reducing the activities of all living things to only one source, thereby reneging on the complexity of life? Does he yet again confront a self-referential paradox: his notion of "will to power," according to his own beliefs, emerges from his will to power? Is the use of "power" misleading? Does it slyly trade on the conventional meaning of "power" for its panache while distancing itself from that meaning once its stylized usages are unpacked?

At times, Nietzsche suggests that the will to power is not only the fundamental but the *only* drive of life. He expresses this view most forcefully in his *Nachlass*: "*This world is the will to power— and nothing besides*! And you yourselves are also this will to power—and nothing besides! (WP 1067; See also, Z I, "On the Thousand and One Goals"; Z II, "On Self-Overcoming"; Z II, "On Redemption"; BGE 13, 36, 259; GS 349; GM II, 12). As such, one might be tempted to conclude that for Nietzsche human beings can strive only for power; that power is the sole motivating force in the world; and power is thus the only goal that can and is desired. On this reading, Nietzsche would open himself to the charge that he mistakenly reduces the complexity of human psychology and life to only one overly broad concept and that concept itself thereby lacks determinate meaning. Is it not plausible to believe that human beings are sometimes motivated by impulses other than the desire to grow and extend their influence? Must other possible motivations such as the pursuit of pleasure or happiness or intimacy be reducible always to an extension of power?

A more charitable reading of Nietzsche would distance him from such a severe interpretation. Elsewhere, he seems to recognize that while the will to power is fundamental to human life, it is not the only drive, desire, or motivating force in life. Thus, he claims that "[W]here the will to power is lacking there is decline. It is my contention that all the supreme values of mankind *lack* this will" (AC 6); that the will to power may decline (AC 17); that liberal political institutions "undermine the will to power" (TI IX, 38); that "In the great economy of the whole, the terrible aspects of reality (in affects, in desires, in the will to power) are to an incalculable degree more necessary than the form of petty happiness which people call 'goodness'" (EH, "Why I am a Destiny," 4). Accordingly, if the will to power can be lacking or in decline or undermined or found alongside other affects and desires then the will to power cannot be the sole explanation of all human action.

The charitable reading of Nietzsche is contestable. Perhaps when he refers to a lack or decline or undermining of the will to power he is not automatically admitting other human affects and drives but only making a value judgment. That is, a will to power that is lacking or in decline or undermined is one that pursues inferior values, that reneges on *amor fati*, and that expends its energies on trivial pursuits or egalitarian projects. The "supreme values of mankind"—which presumably reflect the pernicious influence of herd morality—lack the type of robust will to power that Nietzsche appreciates but may nonetheless be the effects of (an effete) will to power and nothing else. Liberal political institutions may "undermine the will to power" in the sense that they aspire to an egalitarianism that Nietzsche disdains; they thereby incline the will to power toward inferior goals. Perhaps in the passages cited Nietzsche retains his view that all affects and desires arise from the will to power but is only reiterating his conviction that not all wills to power are equally robust and not all manifestations of the will to power are equally valuable.

The most convincing argument that the will to power is not the only drive or motivating force animating human life is the understanding of it that I sketched earlier. The will to power is (a) a second-order drive to have and fulfill first-order desires and (b) to confront and overcome resistance in fulfilling first-order desires. When resistance is overcome and a first-order desire is fulfilled, the will to power is initially satisfied but soon frustrated because it lacks a first-order desire and resistance to its fulfillment. Thus, the will to power requires ongoing first-order desires and resistance to their fulfillment.[7] These first-order desires—for example, to compete in sports, master a musical instrument, drink in order to quench thirst, eat in order to relieve hunger, and the like—do not arise from the will to power. That is, the will to power itself does not determine which particular first-order desires we will pursue. Drives and impulses other than the will to power must provide the first-order desires that animate the will to power's activity. Thus, the will to power cannot be the only drive or impulse embodied by human beings. The desire for power alone cannot by itself provide the necessary determinate first-order desires.

The robustness of various wills to power can be evaluated based on the significance of the obstacles they are wiling to confront and overcome, and the suffering they are willing to endure in the process. First-order desires can also be evaluated on a host of dimensions including the role they play in maximally affirming life, the opportunities to exhibit creativity they offer, the resistance they may encounter, and the ways they help craft the self.

Understood as a desire to desire, the will to power cannot be permanently satisfied; its essential nature is relentless activity. In essence, the will to power reflects an internal world of Becoming embodied by human beings. The process—the striving to confront and overcome resistance in service of fulfilling first-rder desires—constitutes and strengthens the will to power. As a microcosm of the world of Becoming, the will to power can never find a final resting point or realize permanent fulfillment; ongoing activity defines its nature.

As such, suffering is critical to the good human life. First, suffering is part of the process of overcoming resistance in order to fulfill first-order desires. Second, suffering marks the insatiability of the will to power: every satisfaction of a first-order desire thwarts the will to power's drive to have unsatisfied first-order desires that require overcoming resistance to fulfill. Third, suffering partially defines Nietzsche's understanding of human happiness.

In that vein, Nietzsche constantly reminds higher human types to cultivate worthy enemies (TI, "Morality as Anti-Nature," 3; Z I, "On War and Warriors;" Z III, "On Old and New Tablets," 21; GM I, 10). This instruction concerns the nature of the resistance to be overcome in pursuing the fulfillment of first-order desires: only powerful people and daunting obstacles can provide the most challenging resistance that offers the greatest opportunities for testing and developing the will to power.

Whereas hedonists take happiness to be the greatest balance of pleasure over pain and classical Greek philosophy describes happiness as internal peace and contentment arising from a harmonious soul, Nietzsche understands happiness as "all that heightens the feeling of power" (AC 2). What heightens the feeling of power? The feeling of power intensifies through the activity and results of confronting and overcoming significant, difficult resistance in fulfilling first-order desires. The more stubborn and recalcitrant the resistance that is faced, the greater feeling of power we experience when it is overcome—and the greater suffering we endure along the way. Thus, suffering is neither peripheral to nor an impediment to happiness: greatness requires significant suffering and is partly constituted by it. The greatness of deeds and achievements bespeaks of the greatness of the soul of the agent. Unlike hedonists and classical Greek philosophers, Nietzsche does not aspire to tranquility, serenity, or a permanent pleasurable rest—"the religion of comfortableness" (GS 338). Instead, he asks for greater, more challenging activity in service of an ever-more-robust will to power, which is the privileged, but not only human drive. Accordingly, part of Nietzsche's tragic view of life is that higher human types will nurture ever more challenging first-order desires that will present more challenging resistances that will probably eventually lead to greater defeats and possibly to death (Z IV, "The Drunken Song,"11).

In any case, for Nietzsche the world as a whole is inaccessible to us because we are within it. When he speaks of will to power as that which underlies all living things, it may seem that he is resorting to a metaphysical linchpin that makes the world as a whole accessible. But, in fact, will to power underscores the world's inaccessibility: the world eludes our fixed cognitive categories because it is in flux and becoming, and we impose contingent order and meaning upon it through interpretation. Will to power names the essence of all living things, but that essence is not a fixed set of characteristics; instead, it is the enigmatic process of struggle, assertion, resistance, submitting, and overcoming. The subtext of will to power is an attack on rigid distinctions, binary thinking, and dualistic oppositions. Thus, for Nietzsche the will to power is a primitive notion that resists specific definition.

Furthermore, will to power underscores Nietzsche's appreciation of deconstruction, reimagination, and re-creation. He is clear that "all great things bring about their own destruction through an act of self-overcoming; thus the law of life will have it, the law of the necessity of 'self-overcoming' in the nature of life" (GM III, 27).

Self-overcoming must be distinguished from self-destruction which arises from psychological neurosis, grave insecurities, internal self-contempt, and repressed hostilities. On the contrary, for Nietzsche, self-overcoming is part of self-aggrandizement, not self-destruction as such. Life is lived at the expense of other lives (because power and identity are relational notions) and at our own expense. Nature and life are dialectical forces, and the value of the self lies primarily in its ability to transcend itself in tacit understanding of the contingency of the world of Becoming. Because the world is in a continuous state of flux, truculent adherence to a particular, fixed self-understanding will interfere with the project of life.

Thus, the will to power is a metaphor for life; the eternal recurrence is a psychological test of the value and vivacity of one's will to power; and the overman is either the personification of the ideal will to power or merely a thought-experiment Nietzsche discards or another metaphor for self-overcoming and creative energy.

5. The Last Man and The Overman

Again, to prepare to even approximate a higher human type, we must pass through "three metamorphoses" of discipline, defiance, and creation. The spirit, like a camel, flees into the desert to bear enormous burdens (the process of social construction); the spirit, like a lion, must transform itself into a master, a conqueror who releases its own freedom by destroying traditional prohibitions (the process of deconstruction of and liberation from the past); but the lion cannot create new values, so the spirit must transform itself into a child, whose playful innocence, ability to forget, and capability for creative games signals the spirit's willing its own will (the processes of re-imagination and re-creation) (Z I, "On the Three Metamorphoses"). This cycle continues until we die or lose the human capabilities required to participate. This describes the full process of Nietzschean becoming—recurrent deconstruction, reimagination, and re-creation—the virtues of the active nihilist and grand striver.

As described earlier, passive nihilism represents an anti-Nietzschean reaction, a no-saying response to the understanding of inherent cosmic purposelessness. One type of passive nihilist is Nietzsche's "last man." Last men exert themselves minimally and avoid suffering religiously. They are shallow, narrow egalitarians, who pursue a superficial "happiness" that extinguishes their possibilities for intense love, creation, longing, striving, and excellence (Z I, "Zarathustra's Prologue," 5).

The highest ambitions of last men are comfort and security. They are the extreme case of the herd mentality: habit, custom, indolence, egalitarianism, self-preservation, and muted will to power prevail. Last men embody none of the inner tensions and conflicts that spur transformative action: they take no risks, lack convictions, avoid experimentation, and seek only bland survival. Nietzsche is not necessarily describing the middle-class mentality of his day, but rather the banality of the possible classless society of the future.

In contrast to last men, stands the *übermensch* or overman. The overman is Nietzsche's male-gendered symbol of human beings overcoming themselves to superior forms. Nietzsche does not give us a definite description, but the overman represents a superhuman exemplar that has not yet existed: "Never yet has there been an overman. Naked I saw both the greatest and the smallest man: they are still all-too-similar to each other. Verily, even the greatest I found all-too-human" (Z II, "On Priests"). "I teach you the overman. Man is something that shall be overcome. What have you done to overcome him?" (Z I, "Zarathustra's Prologue," 3). "Man is a rope, tied between beast and overman—a rope over an abyss . . . 'I am a herald of the lightning and a heavy drop from the cloud; but this lightning is called overman'" (Z I, "Zarathustra's Prologue," 4). "Dead are all gods: now we want the overman to live" (Z I, "on the Gift-Giving Virtue," 3). "Not 'mankind' but overman is the goal!" (WP 1001). "The Roman Caesar with Christ's soul" (WP 983).

Nietzsche's desiderata for higher human types include a host of general attributes:

(1) *Luxuriating in Contingency and Ambiguity*: the ability to marginalize but not eliminate negative and destructive impulses within oneself, and to transfigure them into joyous affirmation of all aspects of life; to understand and celebrate the radical contingency, finitude, and fragility of ourselves, our institutions and the cosmos itself; to regard life itself as fully and merely natural, as embodying no transcendent meaning or value.

(2) *Cultivating a Pure Spirit and Appreciation of Process*: to harbor little or no resentment toward others or toward the human condition; to confront the world in immediacy and with a sense of vital connection; to refuse to avert our gaze from a tragic world-view and, instead, to find value not in eventual happiness, as conceived by academic philosophers, but in the activities and processes themselves.

(3) *Pursuing Excellence*: to refuse to supplicate oneself before great people of the past but, instead, to accept their implicit challenge to go beyond them; to give style to our character by transforming our conflicting internal passions into a disciplined yet dynamic unity; to facilitate high culture by sustaining a favorable environment for the rise of great individuals; to strive for excellence through self-overcoming that honors the recurrent flux of the

cosmos by refusing to accept a "finished" self as constitutive of personal identity; and to recognize the Sisyphus-like dimension to human existence: release from the tasks described is found only in death. Given the human condition, high energy is more important than a final, fixed goal. The mantra of "challenge, struggle, overcoming, and growth," animating and transfiguring perpetual internal conflict, replaces prayers for redemption to supernatural powers. Part of our life struggle is to confront and overcome the last man within each of us, to hold our internal "dwarf" at bay.

The overman would be joyous, in control of his instinctual will to power, able to forge an admirable unity and style out of his inherent multiplicity, severe with himself, in control of his desires, a sublimator and refiner of cruelty, an unrepentant bearer of great suffering, a pursuer of "truth" who is aware of the essential unity of truth and illusion, a creator and imposer of values and meaning, who experiences his existence as self-justifying. The overman will remain faithful to this earth and not defer gratification in hopes of transcendent salvation in another world, he will possess great health and be able to experience the multiple passions he embodies, he eschews the easy path of last men, he understands the value he creates is simply what he embodies, he celebrates a justified self-love, he is free from resentment and revenge, he wastes no time in self-pity, he is grateful for the entirety of his life, he understands and maintains a clear distance between himself and the herd, and he exemplifies the rank order of life. The overman "shall be the meaning of the earth" in that the overman endows life with value and redeems the species' inherently meaningless tragic existence. In sum, the overman is a higher mode of being that approximates the human aspiration for transcendent greatness.

The overman represents the full process of Nietzschean becoming—recurrent deconstruction, reimagination, re-creation—the virtues of the active nihilist. To prepare to even approximate the joyful overman, we must pass through "three metamorphoses" of discipline, defiance, and creation. The notion of overman—as symbolic, dynamic, indeterminate—provides an ideal toward which to strive. It is as an (unattainable) ideal that the overman confers meaning and creates values.[8] The overman symbolizes a refashioning of our sensibilities and aspiration in service of an enhanced life. It points a direction rather than specifying a clear goal. Nietzsche warns readers not to view the overman as an evolutionary necessity or as an idealistic type of higher man (EH, "Why I Write Such Good Books," 1).

Nietzsche, by his own general philosophical framework, cannot prove or rationally establish the superiority of his vision. He can provide only aesthetic images of human types and ask us to which we are drawn. Remember, when Zarathustra describes the overman and the last man to the crowd, the masses yell back, "Give us the last man; turn us into these last men! Then we shall make you a gift of the overman!" (Z I, "Zarathustra's Prologue," 5). As always, the masses prefer the easier, less threatening, more comfortable alternative. They are unmoved by Zarathustra's artistry. This underscores Nietzsche's disapproval of the herd mentality and the minority (elitist) appeal of the overman.

Nietzsche's overman invites several questions: Is the overman, despite Nietzsche's denials, a remnant of hero worship? Is it another vestige of the Judeo-Christian morality he repudiates? Is the overman exemplified, or at least approximated, by the spiritualized will to power of philosophers and artists? Or is the warrior and conqueror of others a better, or at least a possible, approximation? Or is the overman nothing more than a signification of the process of deconstruction, reimagination, and re-creation that constitutes self-overcoming in a world of flux?

Some philosophers take Nietzsche's invocation of the overman to be the projection of his deepest fantasies, as the dream of the sickly, physically weak, little boy who yearned for conquests that eluded him in life. If so, the notion of the overman may be Nietzsche's most pathetic creation because its origins lie in his weakness, alienation, and estrangement from life. Such an objection applies the idea of genealogical critique, a Nietzschean staple, to Nietzsche's own work. As such, the objection claims to reveal the suspicious origins and craven spirit that allegedly generated the notion of the overman. In that vein, Frederick Copleston says, "[The Overman] is all that ailing, lonely, tormented, neglected Herr Professor Dr. Friedrich Nietzsche would like to be." Bertrand Russell adds, "There is a great deal in [Nietzsche] that must be dismissed as merely megalomaniac . . . in his day-dreams he is a warrior, not a professor." Alasdair MacIntyre concurs, "The [Overman belongs] in the pages of a philosophical bestiary rather than in serious discussion . . . [The Overman is] at once [an] absurd and dangerous fantasy."[9]

In response, Nietzscheans would point out that it is not even clear to what the overman refers. Is "overman" just another name for philosophers of the future or nobles or free spirits or Dionysian masters? Or does the term designate a being that stands above higher humanity? Or does "overman" confer quasi-divine status upon higher humanity?[10] Second, it is not clear whether the overman is a supra-human who has not yet appeared (See, e.g., Z II, "On Priests," and Z I, "Zarathustra's Prologue"), or whether the overman has sometimes appeared accidentally in the past, as a glaring exception to the common run of men (See, e.g., AC 3-4). Third, regardless of one's answers to the first two questions, there remains the issue whether the overman is intended to serve as an ideal, or as a metaphor, or merely as a thought-experiment that Nietzsche discards.[11]

But Nietzsche's critics shape an important point: to become preoccupied by the overman is unwise. Even by Nietzschean standards, analysis of the overman is problematic. Thus, a principle of charitable interpretation suggests that we should not permit too much of our evaluation of Nietzsche's thought to turn on our judgments about the overman.

Although Nietzsche, characteristically, was loose in his use of "overman," we should not equate the overman with nobles or with higher humanity, nor should we take the overman to confer quasi-divinity upon higher humanity. Instead, the overman, to the extent it can be viewed nonmetaphorically, is a supra-human ideal, someone who could fully affirm eternal recurrence and bellow to the sky, "*Amor fati!*" Whether even the greatest human exemplars, who are most in touch with the tragic dimension of life, are capable of such exuberance is questionable. In its fullest depiction, as a supra-human ideal of perfect affirmation of eternal recurrence and full commitment to self-overcoming, the overman has probably never appeared on earth.

Indeed, there is evidence that Nietzsche took overman merely as a thought-experiment whose importance withered (Z II, "On Redemption," and Z II, "The Stillest Hour"), but we can nevertheless understand the overman as a metaphor for the process of deconstruction, reimagination, and re-creation. Taken as this metaphor, overman is perfectly compatible with eternal recurrence, and in fact is just another way of underscoring the themes of self-overcoming, life-affirmation, and creative energy.

We should, however, be cautious when mixing the ideal and the metaphorical dimensions of overman. The ideal dimension permits a personified image toward which to strive but never reach, while the metaphorical dimension highlights Nietzsche's broad themes. Both dimensions are compatible with Nietzsche's commitments to dialectical transformation, the world of Becoming, and the need to become who you are.

Still, Nietzsche does sometimes talk as if the overman is a type of redeemer: "The attainment of this goal would require a *different* kind of spirit from that likely to appear in this present age: spirits strengthened by war and victory, for whom conquest, adventure, danger, and even pain have become needs . . . it would require even a kind of sublime wickedness, an ultimate, supremely self-confident mischievousness in knowledge that goes with great health . . . the *redeeming* man of great love and contempt . . . he may bring home the *redemption* of this *reality*" (GM II, 24). If the overman is a redeemer does not that reveal Nietzsche's *ressentiment* of this world, his desire for revenge, his effacement of *amor fati*, and his secular transformation of God?

Nietzscheans will rejoin that it is not clear whether that passage refers to the overman, to higher humanity, to a literary character such as Zarathustra, to prophets emerging during the death of God, or to something else. Perhaps we are better served by thinking of the "redemption" as movement toward accepting Nietzsche's broad themes, including their elements of self-undermining and self-parody. "Redemption" alludes to his understanding of greatness: self-integration and self-mastery, overabundance of energy, and a range and multiplicity that creates internal dialectical tension.[12] Approaching the ideal of the overman requires recurrent self-creation, which does not necessarily require conquest over others. For Nietzsche, though, refraining from conquest over others is not necessarily a manifestation of excellence. It becomes so only if one has the power to dominant others but has made a decision from strength to refrain from doing so. Higher human types, those who approach the overman, create themselves without regard for social conventions and values. Higher types are both great, because they have not been leveled by the herd mentality, yet fragile, because self-integration, overabundance of energy, and multiplicity form a combustible combination.

Accordingly, the "redemption" passage (GM II, 24) is dramatic and hyperbolic, but it does not necessarily manifest *ressentiment*, revenge, or renege on the value of *amor fati*. Just as affirming eternal recurrence is compatible with the constant self-creation and self-overcoming to which Nietzsche aspired, and just as negative psychology need not underlie personal transformation, the same can be said here.

As the son and grandson of ministers, it is unlikely that Nietzsche fully discarded his Christian background. We might take the overman literally and seriously and view it as a secular surrogate for God. But that reading is obtuse. Even if we reject the thought-experiment interpretation of overman and accept a strong version of the overman-as-ideal interpretation, the overman falls far short of a god. Indeed, the overman's mortality, recurrent personal change in a world of Becoming, and radical fragility embody anti-divine themes. Nietzsche does not seek redemption from the human condition; instead, he suggests that higher human types can renounce passive nihilism and embrace active nihilism.

Also, we should never lose sight of the personal nature of Nietzsche's thought: the eternal recurrence is his formula for greatness, the will to power is his interpretation of the cosmos, and the overman is his personification of, or metaphor for, or thought-experiment of greatness. Nietzsche fully lived the internal life and his writings were explicitly autobiographical. Thus he chronicles his own struggles with the human condition and reveals his own devices for "giving style to one's character."

6. Nietzsche on Jesus

Nietzsche is only obliquely concerned with revealing the true, historical Jesus and with dissecting Jesus' specific moral teachings. Instead, his main focus is describing and evaluating Jesus' inner life and demonstrating the psychological type of human being that Jesus exemplifies. Nietzsche admires the most general attributes of Jesus: his purity of spirit; willingness to confront and overcome strong resistance; distance from *ressentiment*; capability of living his philosophy; robust interior life; efforts to transvalue existing values; and Jesus' contrasts from the "good and the just" in his society. The "good and the just," those who venerate the status quo and who treat all potential social reformers as "destroyers," are prevalent in all societies. Pharisees, who valued their social status, reputation for superior blessedness, and perceived personal merit represent the good and the just in Jesus' time. Sensing the radical nature of Jesus' advocacy and religious interpretations, the Pharisees resisted his innovative overtures. His opposition to them turned Jesus away from this life (Z I, "On Free Death").

Nietzsche admires Jesus as a "free spirit," a person who goes beyond the dominant ideas of his society and whose meaning cannot be reduced to dogmas, creeds, or simple principles (AC 32). That he expresses his thoughts in parables is no accident. Jesus was interested in vividly portraying the trajectory of his general themes of unconditional love, forgiveness, mercy, and nonresistance. He was uninterested in legislating or parsing moral doctrines.

But, as always, Nietzsche, the master psychologist, peered into Jesus' soul in order to discern Jesus' underlying motivations and drives. The predominant image of Jesus in scripture is that of a gentle, passive prophet of nonresistance, unconditional love, and nonjudgmental relationships. Jesus embodies a pure heart that unwaveringly embraces even "enemies" and those bent on doing him harm. Along with that image is another, less frequently portrayed Jesus who castigates the religious leaders of his day, the Pharisees and Sadducees, and who alludes at retribution for those who do not follow his interpretations or way of life. Nietzsche dismisses a third rendering of Jesus—as the redeemer sent by God to die as atonement for all human sins—as the scurrilous invention of St. Paul. Nietzsche's understanding and evaluation of Jesus' life and teaching, then, is more of a psychological analysis of a certain rare human type than it is a scientific inquiry purporting to reveal the actual historical Jesus.

Nietzsche takes Jesus to embody the notion that the experience of eternity, the Kingdom of God, is genuine and accessible to anyone (AC 29). On Nietzsche's reading, eternal redemption and the Kingdom of God are not external, transcendent condition or events, but are instead found in a person's salutary inner life. Thus, Peter Berkowitz writes

> Jesus, the historical link between Judaism and Christianity, exemplifies in Nietzsche's eyes a form of life in which redemption is achieved without appeal to a transcendent moral order. And Nietzsche's portrait of Jesus as a man who achieves eternity within time takes on heightened significance.[13]

Still, Jesus betrays an "instinctive hatred of reality" and "the instinctive exclusion of any antipathy, any hostility, any boundaries or divisions in man's feelings" (AC 30). This combination of "an extreme capacity for suffering and a hypersensitivity to contract with or resistance from the external world"[14] engender a robust perspective on morality and a distance from the stifling conventional wisdom of Jesus' time. Jesus is free of the *ressentiment* that plagued his early followers and those, particularly St. Paul, who invented Christianity with its dogmas, prescribed faith, rituals, laws, orthodoxies, and religious formulae (AC 40). As Nietzsche understands him, Jesus discarded the existing notions of sin, guilt, and atonement. Jesus refashioned the received religious wisdom of his day in service of a higher vision: "Jesus said to his Jews: 'The law was for servants—love God as I love him, as his son! What are morals to us sons of God!'" (BGE 164) Nietzsche underscores approvingly Jesus' repudiation of the legalistic and formalistic interpretations of the Pharisees.

Nietzsche insists that those, such as Jesus, with extraordinary vulnerability and sensitivity are susceptible to "suffocating from pity." Even more than most human beings, those who are hypersensitive require "hardness and cheerfulness" (BGE 269). Nietzsche describes Jesus as a person afflicted with "the fear of pain, even of the infinitely small in pain . . . [who] feels contact too deeply" (AC 30). We are hard-pressed to depict the Jesus of scripture as hard or cheerful. Regardless of whether we take the historical Jesus to be merely a Cynic philosopher or an apocalyptic prophet or the Son of God, his soul admits little cheer and manifests no hardness: "My soul is very sorrowful, even to death" (Matt. 26: 38; Mark 14: 34); "I have compassion on the crowd" (Mark 8: 2); "When he saw the crowd, he had compassion for them (Matt. 9: 36); "And when he drew near and saw the city he wept over it" (Luke 19: 41); "'Where have you laid him [Lazarus]?' They said to him, 'Lord, come and see.' Jesus wept." (John 11: 34-35). Scripture does not record Jesus either laughing or failing to demonstrate compassion for those in need: hilarity and hardness of heart were not in his personal repertoire. For example, Jesus disapproves of those whose lives are filled with laughter: "Woe to you that laugh now, for you shall mourn and weep" (Luke 6: 25).

Nietzsche placed high value on laughter, dancing, stylistic movement, and playfulness as avenues to wisdom, knowledge, and as an expression of *amor fati* (GS 1, 107, 324, 327, 383; BGE 223; Z IV, "On the Higher Man," 16-20). He also prizes hardness, power, and strength as the antidote to feckless human reactions such as pity (Z II, "On the Pitying"; BGE 171, 201, 222, 260, 293; GS 118, 271, 338). When a person pities he "*loses force*" and the dynamic of pity saps the energy from life as "suffering itself becomes contagious" (AC 7). Laughter and spiritual hardness elevate energy and animate *amor fati*; whereas tears, pity, and excessive gravity have the opposite effect.

As a result, Nietzsche portrays Jesus as a "mixture of the sublime, the sick, and the childish" (AC 31). The combination suggests an extreme innocence and hypersensitivity coupled with an inability to access self-protecting mechanisms (such as laughter) that might ward off instinctive reactions of pity, leavened by a pure spirit that rises above bitterness and hostility. Because of his "extreme capacity for suffering," Jesus "feels every contact too deeply" and thereby hates reality and embodies "an instinctive exclusion of all aversion, all enmity, all feeling for limitation and distancing" (AC 30). Thus, because Jesus is morbidly vulnerable he adopts a lifestyle instinctively that inclines toward self-preservation: nonresistance, forgiveness, mercy, and unconditional love. Someone with Jesus' psychological vectors cannot endure enemies, opposition, or hostility (AC 32). Thus, Jesus way of life is the sole possibility available to him given who he is (AC 30). Jesus does not arrive at his moral prescriptions from epistemological insights, theoretical discoveries, or divine inspiration. For Nietzsche, Jesus' moral message is an expression of who he must be given his own psychology. Just as Nietzsche insisted that all great philosophy was autobiographical (BGE 6), so too, he was firmly convinced that Jesus' teachings were a subconscious confession of his temperament.

Although arising from extreme inexperience, hypersensitivity, and a morbid psychological condition, the result is Jesus' "blessed" and "sublime" heart (AC 31). Unfortunately, being a "mixture of the sublime, the sick, and the childish," Jesus was especially susceptible to the machinations of the good and the just: "Had he only remained in the desert and far from the good and the just! Perhaps he would have learned to live and learned to love the earth—and laughter as well!" (Z I, "On Free Death"). At bottom, Jesus' psychological pathologies lead him to adopt the way of life that he extolled as underwritten by the divine will. As always, Nietzsche connects a person's beliefs, choices, and actions to the person's psychological type.

Jesus' stance of nonresistance, unconditional love, and forgiveness flows, then, from his basic psychology: his extreme vulnerability to suffering and uncommon sensitivity to confrontation. As reality is inherently tragic, Jesus' stance is a way of withdrawing from reality, thereby minimizing the pain he would otherwise endure. Thus, for Nietzsche, Jesus evinces a type of decadence which is a symptom of a decline of power (AC 29). Through inner serenity underwritten by nonresistance, unconditional love, and forgiveness, Jesus attains the values of the Kingdom of God in this world and realizes the eternal (AC 33). Jesus nobly rises above decadence, but not heroically: Jesus does not artfully transform struggle, antagonism, and conflict into practical advantage. Rather, Jesus turns inward and adopts the only stance for living appropriate to his psychology (AC 30). Still, Jesus' nonresistance invites the "good and the just" in society to undermine his intentions, to subvert his moral message, and, ultimately, to destroy him. Although noble and free of *ressentiment*, Jesus' naivete and vulnerability presented him from harnessing his spiritual power in ways effective in this world.

Nietzsche concludes that Jesus harbored the "illusion" that he was the son of God and therefore enjoyed "complete freedom from sin." He advises us that this illusion "should not be judged too harshly" (HAH I, 144). More strikingly, Nietzsche describes Jesus as inexperienced, immature, naïve, even "childish" (HAH II, 2, 83; GS 138; AC 31, 32). As a corollary to his fundamental naiveté, Jesus loved the earth and laughter insufficiently (Z I, "On Free Death").

But Nietzsche holds out the possibility that had he lived longer he would have "recanted his teaching" (Z I, "On Free Death"). That is, Jesus' inherent nobility, tempered by his earthly suffering, would have drawn him away from some of his teachings had he lived long enough. The contrast here is between Nietzsche's admiration of Jesus' character and spirit understood holistically and Nietzsche's dissection of particular shortcomings flowing from Jesus' immaturity and his confrontations with the "good and the just" of his time. Jesus has the "warmest heart" (HAH 235) and his "inner lights" illuminate his entire nature (AC 32).

According to Nietzsche, Jesus comes to understand the inadequacy of human love and fantasizes divine love as a glowing substitute.

> It is possible that, disguised by the holy fable of Jesus' life, there is hidden one of the most agonizing martyrdoms of *one who knows the nature of love*: the martyrdom of the most innocent and most desirous heart that never had been content with any human love, that *demanded* love, wanted to be loved and nothing else, with mad determination and terrible outbursts against those who withheld love from him . . . and who, finally, having come to know everything about human love, had to invent a God who was nothing but love, nothing but the *capacity* for love, one who takes pity on human love because it is so feeble and so unknowing! He who does feel like this—*seeks* death (BGE 269).

Requiring discipline, knowledge, and effort, salutary human love must be learned (GS 334). Jesus yearned for such love, but found his desires unrequited. He was driven to martyrdom by the inadequacy of human love. Vulnerable and hyper-sensitive, Jesus required "hardness and cheerfulness more than other men," but fell prey to "the danger of suffocating from pity" (BGE 269). Jesus comes to understand the shortcomings, perils, and risks of human love as a result of suffering. As always, suffering and pain are paramount instructors about life. More important, they transform the human spirit (D 114). Unfortunately, the Romans, with the complicity of the "good and the just," crucify Jesus and he is never allowed to put into practice the lessons he has learned (and, possibly, distance himself from some of his prior teaching). Thus, Jesus died a "free death" in that he chose and even sought to die, according to Nietzsche. Still, he died "too early" and not "at the right time" because he was unable to put into practice the knowledge gained from his suffering and martyrdom (Z I, "On Free Death"). As always, Nietzsche reminds us that the extent to which "human beings can suffer" largely determines their place in "the order of rank" (BGE 270). We can only wonder what transformations in spirit and action would have occurred in a surviving Jesus.

For Nietzsche, that Jesus "wanted to die" (HAH II, 94); "was seized by a longing for death" (Z I, "On Free Death"); "sought death" (BGE 269); and provoked death (AC 35) is not surprising. Although Jesus' death is untimely—as it prevents Jesus from putting into practice what his suffering and martyrdom taught him about love and life—it allowed Jesus a final, dramatic way of underscoring his way of life. He does not resist the process by which he was sentenced to death, nor the officials who presided over it; he does not assert his civil rights nor cross-examine his accusers; he professes love for those bent on executing him; he casts no blame; and he expresses no hostility, much less *ressentiment* (AC 35). At his direst hour, Jesus' psychological condition impels him to reveal his blessedness through nonresistance and unconditional love. As such, he attains a certain victory of the spirit in martyrdom as he serves as an exemplar for those of similar psychology. Nietzsche insists that Jesus died not to redeem all human beings from the ravages of sin, but to demonstrate "how one ought to live" (AC 35).

Curiously, Nietzsche attributes to Jesus words while on the cross that are inconsistent with scripture. Nietzsche reports that Jesus responded to the thief being crucified next to him with "If you feelest this . . . *thou art in Paradise, thou art a child of God*" (AC 35). For Nietzsche, this signals that Jesus' notion of the Kingdom of God centered on experiencing the eternal while living, not attaining eternal life in a transcendent realm (AC 33). The Kingdom of God, on this reading, is not a state or a place, but a subjective experience fueled by the condition of one's soul now: "the *feeling* of perfection" (AC 34). Jesus and the thief can both attain the Kingdom of God while being crucified! The richness of inner reality can overcome and transform the degradation of external atrocities. These in fact are Jesus' "glad tidings": The Kingdom of God is *within* us! (AC 29)

The traditional Christian reading is much different. Scripture reports that the thief asks Jesus to remember him when Jesus attains kingly power, presumably at the onset of the Kingdom of God. Jesus replies, "Truly, I say to you, today you will be with me in Paradise" (Luke 23: 43). The implication is that Jesus is promising the thief a place in heaven after they both expire in a few hours. The Christian interpretation includes the promise of personal immortality in a blissful transcendent realm.

In fairness, Nietzsche is expanding upon his interpretation of Jesus' words to the Pharisees who ask when the Kingdom of God will arrive. Jesus responds, "The Kingdom of God is not coming with signs to be observed; nor will they say, 'Behold here it is!' or 'There!' for behold, the Kingdom of God is in your midst" (Luke 17: 20-21). Nietzsche takes this to connote that the Kingdom of God is not a place or state, but a description of an internal condition available to human beings who cultivate blessedness. Christians often interpret these words to mean that the Kingdom of God is already on a trajectory or that human beings can prefigure the Kingdom of God by internalizing and acting in accord with its values now.

7. Nietzsche on St. Paul and Christianity

Nietzsche insists that St. Paul transformed the life of Jesus and advanced the notion of resurrection to create "the Redeemer" (AC 43). The Church has become just another powerful force of conformity, dogmatism, and complicity with state power. It has extinguished Jesus' advice to distance ourselves from family in the quest for attaining perfection. Led by St. Paul, the Church has exploited Jesus in service of the values of the herd. Jesus is thus the bridge between Judaism and Christianity. Berkowitz concludes that

> Jesus' real significance for mankind . . . has everything to do with his own single-minded, utterly egoistic, inward-looking exercise in self-deification. Rather than teach a faith, Jesus showed how to experience eternity within the confines of finite human life; he became almost more than human by overcoming the spirit of revenge . . . Without faith in a personal God or speculations about a transcendent order, Jesus attains a kind of perfection. His legacy to mankind is his life as a model of the good life.[15]

For Nietzsche, Jesus counseled his disciples to strive for perfection now, on this earth in this life. Christianity, as fashioned by St. Paul, St. Augustine, and later by Luther and Calvin, casts its gaze on a transcendent world in the distant future. Obedience to the rituals and creeds of rigid religious institutions replaced Jesus' veneration of inner intentions and motives. Dogmatism and legalism ousted spirituality and the quest for self-perfection. The horrors of retribution, revenge, and *ressentiment* triumphed over forgiveness, mercy, and unconditional love. Allegiances of faith and retirement from robust living routed appeals to reason and adventurous deeds that fashioned souls. That Nietzsche disparages St. Paul as "a genius in hatred" (AC 42), and a "hate-obsessed false-coiner" (AC 42), a "frightful imposter" (AC 45), and a "moral cretin" (WP 171) is no accident.

The crux of Jesus' prescribed social practice was forgiveness of enemies; unconditional love of everyone; refusal to retaliate against or even actively resist evil; abrogation of the use of force and aggression; and refraining from moral condemnation (AC 33, 35, 39; WP 158-163, 211-212). Nietzsche concludes that in contrast to how Christianity developed, the underlying message of Jesus was that sin, guilt, and punishment should be "abolished" (AC 33, 41).

Even in the numerous places where Nietzsche disagrees with Jesus' specific moral prescriptions, he judges Jesus as noble even if naïve and excessively sensitive. In contrast, Nietzsche is unsparing in his psychological analysis of St. Paul whom he regards as mendacious, conniving, seething with *ressentiment*, and an annihilator of the passions. For Nietzsche, St. Paul, not Jesus, is the linchpin of slave or herd morality. St. Paul is the culprit who denigrates the spirit of *amor fati* by extolling the need for a transcendental justification of human existence and by denying that this world and life are the supreme values.

8. Nietzsche's Understanding of Jesus

Nietzsche's portrayal of the psychology of Jesus focuses on his unconditional love, nonresistance to evil, extension of mercy, and commitment to forgiveness. Nietzsche alludes to another image of Jesus in scripture: a person who scolds the religious leaders of his day, the Pharisees and Sadducees, and who threatens retribution for those who do not follow his interpretations or way of life. Yet Nietzsche virtually ignores that part of Jesus' mindset during his evaluations.

Thus, Jesus promises retribution for those who stray from the divine will. They will "be thrown into the outer darkness; there men will weep and gnash their teeth" (Matt. 8: 12); "The Son of man will send his angels, and they will gather out of his kingdom all causes of sin and all evildoers, and throw them into the furnace of fire, where there will be weeping and gnashing of teeth" (Matt. 13: 41-42); "And cast the worthless servant into the outer darkness, where there will be weeping and gnashing of teeth" (Matt. 25: 30). Jesus also castigates cities, such as Chorazin and Bethsaida, which fail to repent their transgressions: "You shall be brought down to Hades . . . it shall be more tolerable on the Day of Judgment for the land of Sodom than for you" (Matt. 11: 20-24; Luke 10: 13-15).

Moreover, Jesus is occasionally angry and rebukes or menaces other people or things. Thus, he "looked around at them [Pharisees] with anger, grieved at their hardness of heart" (Mark 3: 5); "he upbraided them [the eleven remaining apostles] for their unbelief [in his resurrection] and hardness of heart" (Mark 16: 14); "And he strictly ordered them [unclean spirits] not to make him known" (Mark 3: 12); "But he rebuked them [demons], and would not allow them to speak, because they knew that he was Christ" (Luke 4: 41); "But he turned and rebuked them [James and John]" (Luke 9: 55); When hungry, Jesus cursed a fig tree that was unproductive out of season: "May no one ever eat from you again" (Mark 11: 13-14), and "the fig tree withered at once" (Matt. 21: 18-19).

Jesus is fiery when he proclaims: "Do not think that I have come to bring peace on earth; I have not come to bring peace, but a sword" (Matt. 10:34). In that vein, he insists that families will be divided: "For I have come to set a man against his father, and a daughter against her mother, and a daughter-in-law against her mother-in-law; and a man's foes will be those of his own household" (Matt. 10: 35-36; Luke 12: 49-53). Jesus warns that a person who loves his or her parents or children "more than me is not worthy of me" (Matt. 10: 37).

Of course, the most dramatic expression of Jesus' anger is the scene at the Temple in Jerusalem where he attracted the attention of the Sadducees: "And Jesus entered the temple of God and drove out all who sold and bought in the temple, and he overturned the tables of the money-changers and the seats of those who sold pigeons. He said to them, " 'It is written, 'My House shall be called a house of prayer; but you make it a den of robbers'" (Matt. 21: 12-13; Mark 11: 15-17). On one account Jesus' weapon of choice was a "whip of cords" (John 2: 15).

Either Nietzsche refuses to include these parts of Jesus' psychology in his dissection—perhaps because he is convinced that they were later attributions conjured by the early Christians—or Nietzsche considers them aberrational or marginal events. But these depictions of Jesus in scripture coalesce uneasily with Nietzsche's rendering of Jesus as one to whom hostility, anger, aggression, and opposition were intolerable. While the naiveté, inexperience, hypersensitivity to suffering that Nietzsche highlights are undoubtedly part of Jesus' psychology, that they constitute its entirety is highly doubtful. In contrast to Nietzsche's psychological rendering of Jesus and in accord with Nietzsche's general understanding of human beings, Jesus embodied multiplicity, conflict, and inner complexity. He was not simply a child-like "idiot" (AC 29).

Clearly, Nietzsche opposes much of what Jesus holds dear. The value of *amor fati*, which glistens in engaged, highly creative, context-smashing actions in the world contrasts with Jesus' version of the good life: material minimalism; self-effacing service to those in need; distance from recognition, honor, and reputation; associating with and ministering to those stigmatized as socially undesirable; and the utter refusal to accept social hierarchies grounded in factual inequalities among human beings. Moreover, Jesus purports to reveal a new and better interpretation of God's law. While he breaks from the received opinions of his tradition and heralds a new way of life, he does so in service of God. Jesus' moral message is a far cry from Nietzsche's announcement that God is dead and the best of us must become our own gods.

Finally, Nietzsche's understanding of how Jesus rendered "the Kingdom of God"—as seeking eternity on earth internally and within time—is controversial and tracks most closely the conclusions of those who view the historical Jesus as a Cynic philosopher as opposed to those who perceive Jesus as an apocalyptic prophet or as the son of God. For Nietzsche, Jesus took the Kingdom of God to be the present condition of the human heart and soul such that we internalize the moral trajectory that Jesus prescribed. (In fact, Nietzsche, however, would probably not describe Jesus as a "philosopher" and he did take Jesus to be under the illusion that he was the son of God and thereby without sin.)

To perceive Nietzsche as signing on to many of Jesus' specific prescriptions for the good life is difficult. Nietzsche admires Jesus even though he cannot embrace most of Jesus' ideas and explicitly repudiates Jesus' followers and the religious institutions they conjured. For example, Nietzsche would impugn the notion of agapic love as hopelessly abstract as it aspires to apply to everyone and thus applies to no one in particular. Thus it ignores the rank order of human beings and invokes an insipid egalitarianism. He would regard attempts to render the notion more concrete—for example, by focusing on the principle of equal consideration of different needs—as insufficient. For Nietzsche, human love is much too fragile, confused, imbued with power struggles, and deceptive to be understood unconditionally. Misery and misunderstanding pervade even the best human loves.

Specifically, Nietzsche is unimpressed by the enjoinment to "love one's neighbor as one's self" and by the corollary to extend oneself and one's resources to all those in need. He takes these imperatives to be excessively abstract because they are indifferent to the specific psychologies of concrete individuals and fail to recognize the rank order of human beings. What kind of person would embrace these Christian bromides? Nietzsche suggests someone whose self-image is enhanced by exuding a tinny general benevolence to everyone, regardless of their constitutive attributes and personal merit. Perhaps such people bestow unconditional love in order to elevate their own self-esteem.

What Nietzsche admires in Jesus are his efforts in self-mastery, willingness to confront and overcome daunting obstacles, elevation of the inner life as definitive of greatness, and purity of spirit. Jesus leads an apolitical life liberated from *ressentiment*. Jesus willingly confronted suffering, acted according to his convictions, and embodied heightened aesthetic awareness. He was a moral radical whose life is exemplary for the few able to try to emulate it. No reasonable person could accuse Jesus of being a last man. At bottom, Nietzsche contrasts the blissful inwardness of Jesus to the *ressentiment* and conniving of St. Paul and the early leaders of Christianity. Jesus was free from the passions of ordinary people; he was a self-creator who confronted and overcame the weightiest burdens as he styled his character. As do most great human exemplars, Jesus lived his life on the edge of destruction and annihilation. Jesus died a "free death," although "too early" and not "at the right time" (Z I, "On Free Death"). In Nietzsche's view, the ossified, pretentious institutions of Christianity are unworthy of Jesus and untrue to the life he led (AC 39). Nietzsche goes so far as to describe Jesus as "the noblest man" (HATH I, 475) and the overman as "Caesar with Christ's soul" (WP 983).

> This 'bringer of glad tidings' [Jesus] died as he had lived, as he had *taught—not* to 'redeem men' but to show how one must live . . . He does not resist, he does not defend his right, he takes no step to ward off the worst; on the contrary, *he provokes it.* And he begs, he suffers, he loves *with* those, in those who do him evil. *Not* to resist, *not* to be angry, not to hold responsible—but to resist even the evil one—to *love* him (AC 35).

9. Jesus and Engagement in this World

Unraveling the relationship of Jesus to our world is a daunting task. What seems undeniable is that Jesus had an apocalyptic inspiration: the end of the world was imminent. As such, earthly events and activities faded in insignificance to the impending Kingdom of God. In fact, those who interpret Jesus as "only" a prophet of the apocalypse are convinced that his normative message had little or nothing to do with reforming social institutions or with prescribing a new morality. For such thinkers, Jesus was convinced that there was no long-run for which to be concerned. Instead, Jesus' moral message was a description of relations under the forthcoming Kingdom of God, which will come about only through divine agency. Apocalyptic prophets herald the good news that a transcendental power will soon ensure the total victory of the forces of good over the currently dominant forces of evil and inaugurate a paradise where the world and heaven coalesce perfectly forever. The Kingdom of God, in which the Son of Man will reign, ends the history of our world and inaugurates a new order.[16]

Still, even under this interpretation of Jesus, we should prefigure relations under the Kingdom of God today. Jesus' normative message cannot persuasively be understood as only applicable to the supposed coming order. Jesus insisted that we should act *now* in the ways he understood to define relationships under the Kingdom of God. We can, in a sense, attain the Kingdom of God within ourselves by modeling our behavior in accord with Jesus' example. In this fashion, Nietzsche is correct that Jesus understood the Kingdom of God as seeking eternity on earth internally and within time. But Nietzsche is incorrect in thinking that that is all Jesus meant by the Kingdom of God. Nietzsche adjusted Jesus' words to the thief crucified next to him in order to underscore his own interpretation of Jesus. In fact, Jesus was firmly convinced that the Kingdom of God was an actual, impending order of which Jesus' own actions and examples were signs. Part of that order was a judgment in which people will be accepted or rejected by God.

If this general interpretation of Jesus is correct, the question again arises: What is Jesus advising about engagement in this world today? One might conclude that Jesus would counsel indifference or withdrawal. The things of this world are not only inherently transitory, but they will soon evaporate under the coming Kingdom of God. Worldly goods and success are thus utterly insignificant. On this view, Jesus' extolling of material minimalism, forgiveness, mercy, and nonresistance arises, contra Nietzsche, not from Jesus' hypersensitive psychology but from his conviction that the inauguration of the Kingdom of God was near. Why bother with worldly trifles when an earth-shattering event was on its way? That Jesus' ethic seems impossible to implement in this world is unsurprising; it is in fact an ethic definitive of the Kingdom of God, an order much unlike the institutional structures characterizing this world. On this interpretation, Nietzsche was correct in concluding that Jesus distanced himself from of the prescriptions of *amor fati*: Jesus did not embody a maximally fulfilling attitude toward this world, but instead structured his life around the supposed imperatives of the Kingdom of God. That Jesus could attain eternity on earth internally and within time was a function of how he crafted his soul, but not a consequence of his embrace of *amor fati*.

In my judgment, to conclude that Jesus advised indifference to or withdrawal from this world is an error. Yes, the supposed glories of the Kingdom of God dwarf the significance of the baubles of this world. But this world remains a staging ground for salutary soul-crafting. By anticipating and acting upon the values definitive of the Kingdom of God now we prefigure the Kingdom of God internally. To think otherwise is to be committed to the odd view that Jesus is only describing relationships in a future world order and advising his audience to continue their worldly ways while this world remains extant, that Jesus is in effect saying, "Here is how things will be in the Kingdom of God, but you have no need to adopt this moral message today in the world as you know it." On the contrary, my position is that Jesus is advising his audience to act now *as if* the Kingdom of God is already in place. Instead of being indifferent to the world or counseling his audience to withdraw from it, Jesus is advising a self-transformative engagement with the world. Even if this world is soon to be extinguished by the new order of the Kingdom of God it remains valuable for an enterprise dear to Nietzsche's own heart: crafting the human spirit. That the apocalypse did not occur as soon as Jesus apparently suspected it would only brightens that conclusion. To follow the path of Jesus, how are we to live in this world: by following the dominant ideas about practical success or by prefiguring the values of the Kingdom of God? If a person argues that Jesus could ignore the consequences of acting upon his moral message because he was convinced that the world as he knew it was soon to end, we should ask what Jesus would have advised his audience had he been convinced that the Kingdom of God would not occur for, say, 100 or 200 years? Would Jesus have defined "neighbor" differently? Would he have advised currying favor with notables in high society and distancing oneself from social undesirables? Would he have suggested developing better armaments and keener military strategies? Perhaps learning new ways of exacting vengeance upon enemies?

My point is that those who state confidently that Jesus was indifferent to this world or advised withdrawal from it, and those who conclude assuredly that Jesus' moral message did not include prescriptions for acting in this world are overstating their cases. Instead, Jesus was describing how to become "perfect" (Matt. 19: 21) by anticipating the values definitive of the Kingdom of God and by crafting one's soul accordingly. That he also apparently believed that the inauguration of the Kingdom of God was imminent only affects the urgency and not the content of his normative message. The challenge for those who insist that Jesus' moral teachings were applicable only to the short period between the continued existence of this world and the supposed impending inauguration of the Kingdom of God is to articulate what Jesus would have taught had he thought that the Kingdom of God would arrive only in the distant future.

To underscore this point, the early history of Greek philosophy, that predated the birth of Jesus, is replete with philosophers who advised material minimalism, forgiveness, and moral virtue without an appeal to an apocalypse. Socrates, the Cynics, the Stoics, and the Epicureans all taught that the cultivation of the proper internal condition is more important than the typical barometers of worldly success. Some of these thinkers believed in an afterlife, but some did not. All sensed that people could not be harmed in the most fundamental ways without their own unwitting collaboration. That is, people could not embody a corrupt soul unless they permitted, knowingly or not, the contamination. As harboring a corrupt soul is the only genuine or at least the most damaging harm, our task on earth is to attend carefully to our internal condition. The wild variance between the prescriptions of this philosophical tradition and the dominant ideas of what constitutes success in society cannot plausibly be attributed to the belief that this world was soon to end. Thus, convictions about the dire future of this world are neither necessary nor sufficient for subscribing to Jesus' moral message.

Obviously, the existence of each human being ceases all too soon and his or her world terminates at that point. But the early philosophers and Jesus were convinced that living the good human life centered on nurturing a pure internal condition. In my judgment, like his Greek predecessors, Jesus' normative message does not depend on his apparent belief that the world was soon to be swept away by the inauguration of the Kingdom of God. On the contrary, Jesus was convinced that we should prefigure the arrival of the Kingdom of God by warmly embracing the values of that kingdom now. Why? We should embody and act upon those values because they constituted the highest goodness that defined the striving toward perfection.

In that vein, one can argue that, contra Nietzsche's interpretation, Jesus counseled vigorous engagement with this world, whether it was to end soon or in the distant future. Jesus, unlike some of the Hellenistic thinkers, did not advocate personal isolationism or distance from society. Instead, he extolled caring for those in need, connecting with those ostracized from society, and healing those plagued by infirmities. Jesus affirms this world by bestowing unconditional love even when beset by injustice, persecution, and defilement. In his own way, Jesus, like Nietzsche, affirms this world by viewing others through the lens of charity and compassion. Human beings must repent as a way of re-focusing their attention from the petty material and egoistic concerns of the self to a vision of God and neighbors. Preoccupation with self-preservation and self-amplification shrinks this world to the things, events, and people able to facilitate our vanities. Bestowing unconditional love and adopting an expansive understanding of our relations and responsibilities to neighbors engage the world more fully through heightened mutual vulnerability. In Jesus' understanding of robust engagement in this world, radical openness to others replaces the narcotic of safe-guarding the citadel of the self.

Whereas Nietzsche counsels a hardness of heart as the path toward honoring the rank order of human beings and striving toward individual greatness,

Jesus preaches that interpersonal barriers should be smashed and hierarchies repudiated in service of invigorating collective human engagement. For Jesus, the life turned inward and focused only on the affirmation of the self is partial, distorted, and ultimately unfulfilling. Untainted by *ressentiment*, fear, or the spirit of gravity, the inner state which Jesus embodied embraced this world as an arena of soul-making in a thoroughly collective context. Such artistry cannot be conducted in the dark, isolated, netherlands of the solitary individual. Service to others combined with an unwavering refusal to view others only at arm's-length extends the metaphysical boundaries of the self. My strictly egotistic concerns relinquish privilege of place to wider projects and a more profound affirmation of this world. While Jesus was passive and accepting on his own behalf, he was resolute in alleviating the distress of others. Whereas Nietzsche idealizes the glorious individual, the grand transcender who presumably justifies the human species, Jesus celebrates the transformative community devoted to radical, mutual vulnerability and spiritual sustenance. Whereas Nietzsche engages the world from the standpoint of the concerns of individuals striving for self-mastery, Jesus participates in the world from the vantage point of the salutary community that venerates collective activity.

10. Daunting Normative Ideals

The challenges posed by the respective ideals of Jesus and Nietzsche are disquieting. Jesus embraces a radical impartialism that requires, among other things, extending unconditional love not only to those with whom we are intimate but also to strangers and even to "enemies." Given the human difficulties, conceptual and practical, of bestowing unconditional love on *anyone*, the imperative to accord unconditional love on *everyone* is stunning. Perhaps such widespread, undifferentiated concern is possible in the Kingdom of God, but in our world such an effort would ignore seemingly relevant differences among people. Do we not owe more to those who have benefited us in the past, often at considerable sacrifice, time, and effort? Are not our own resources limited, making it impossible to lavish our concern indiscriminately? Must we abrogate the interests of those we love (specially) in deference to the supposedly weightier collective interests of the needy multitude? Can we maintain a robust sense of individuality when trying to fulfill the requirements of such a communally-demanding ethic?

Nietzsche's image is equally daunting. He demands a relentless dissatisfaction that requires continual deconstruction, reimagination, and re-creation. Nietzsche's grand striver is ever onward, brandishing a sense of aristocratic privilege, in pursuit of the deeds that warrant merited self-pride. But does Nietzsche appreciate sufficiently the human need for savoring the past, for security and peace, and for serenity and satisfaction? Does the grand striver relinquish much human good in his preoccupation with factual differences among people and the supposed rank order of the species? Does Nietzsche circumscribe too narrowly the grand striver's circle of concern—those of his own kind and rank? Is the glorious individualism of Nietzsche's ideal purchased at too high a cost: a potentially alienating departure from salutary community? Does the grand striver, while extolling freedom and creativity, in fact create his own chains and manufacture his own prison?

To address these questions further, we must examine more closely the respective versions of perfectionism advanced by Jesus and Nietzsche.

Four

THE PERFECTIONISM OF JESUS

Although their general images of the ideal track their respective understandings of the nature of the world and of human beings, both Jesus and Nietzsche advocate striving for perfectionism. To understand Jesus' quest we must return to his teaching that we should extend unconditional love to neighbors and to supposed enemies.

1. Perfectionism and Unconditional Love

Jesus taught that "You, therefore, must be perfect, as your heavenly Father is perfect" (Matt. 5: 48) and "If you would be perfect, go, sell what you possess and give to the poor, and you will have treasure in heaven; and come, follow me" (Matt. 19: 21). Striving for perfection includes adopting a default position of forgiveness and mercy, and extending unconditional love—caring for and loving strangers and even enemies.

In the parable of the Good Samaritan, Jesus illustrates his interpretation of the love commandment (Luke 10: 25-37).[1] After a lawyer asks him what a person must do to "inherit life," Jesus' response is to obey Jewish law: love God completely and love your neighbor as yourself. As always, Jesus begins in revealed scripture and Jewish law. Of course, this approach is especially pertinent when responding to a question posed by a lawyer. But incisive *interpretation* of scripture and law remains paramount. The lawyer intuits acutely that the expression "my neighbor" is not self-executing. How many other people must his circle of concern include? Only those people within geographic proximity? All and only those members of his religious and ethnic tribe, the Jews? All and only *righteous* Jews? Or must his circle of concern expand beyond tribal boundaries? So the lawyer asks for clarification, "And who is my neighbor?"

The answer to this question is of monumental importance. If the lawyer is required to expand his concern beyond the righteous would he not thereby be a condoner or even an enabler of sin? If he is required to love those outside of his religion would he not thereby be providing consolation for the godless?

Even after having established the proper answer to the question of the appropriate scope of a person's concern—even after we can identify our "neighbors"—other questions would emerge. What does it mean to "love" one's neighbor as oneself? Does that mean that the lawyer must risk as much to preserve the endangered life of a "neighbor" as he would sacrifice to maintain his own life? Does it imply that a neighbor has as great a claim on the lawyer's material resources as does the lawyer? Does it mean that a neighbor has as great a claim on the lawyer's time, effort, and consideration as does the lawyer? Does "loving" one neighbor require not only performing the appropriate deeds but also having the proper *disposition* toward others?

Clearly, the answers to such questions cannot be extracted neatly from the plain meaning of the text of Jewish religious law. Indeed, what it means to love God with one's entire "heart, soul, strength, and mind" also requires interpretation. But the focus of this parable is the meaning of "Love your neighbor as yourself." To render an interpretation of the phrase, Jesus might have advanced a host of moral principles, policies, and theories designed to illustrate the scope of "neighbor" and the extent to which loving a neighbor requires our sacrifice, risk, forbearance, and intervention. However, as do all great teachers of morality who reside outside the classrooms of higher education, Jesus appreciates that a story can more vividly and effectively convey moral conclusions and stimulate further reflection. Thus, Jesus tells the story of the Good Samaritan.

After kinsmen such as a priest and a Levite fail to render assistance to a wounded Jewish traveler, a Samaritan renders aid. The priest and Levite may have been concerned with obeying the purity laws that forbade contact with a corpse; they might have feared for their own safety (as the bandits who robbed and beat the wounded man may still have been in the vicinity); or they may have questioned whether the victim was Jewish (as the man had been stripped of his clothes and lay unconscious when they approached). In all these cases, the priest and the Levite could appeal plausibly to Jewish law to justify their refusal to act: the victim might not have been Jewish and thus not a "neighbor" to whom they owed a duty of assistance; the prohibition against defilement may well have been applicable; and they might have jeopardized their own lives had they stopped to aid the victim.

As is typical, the contrast is between a strictly formalistic rendering of Jewish law (as favored by Pharisees) and Jesus' more expansive rendering. For Jesus, the three possible justifications for inaction are all insufficient. The surprising hero of the parable is a Samaritan. The choice is surprising because the enmity between Samaritans and Jews was longstanding and profound. Jesus' choice of a Samaritan underscores his moral message that we must love and care for even those who are antecedently perceived as enemies.

The Samaritan assumes risks. As a follower of the Torah, the Samaritan bears some risk of defilement should he touch or come within six feet of a corpse. He also risks the possibility that the predators that had beaten and robbed the victim might be lying in wait for additional prey. Moreover, the Samaritan risks possible retaliation from the victim's family: "For in situations of violence, where revenge was commonly taken, an enemy (even one who helps) could easily become the object of a family's revenge."[2] Most strikingly, the Samaritan assumes these risks on behalf of a stranger, who is not, strictly speaking, a "neighbor," but is, instead, from a tribal perspective an enemy.

What does the Samaritan do for the victim? The Samaritan's immediate, intuitive response highlights that Jesus prizes the proper moral dispositions, not merely the appropriate deeds. The Samaritan is not merely doing the morally right act because logic—the rational elaboration of established moral principles and policies—declares that it is the morally right act. The Samaritan does not, thank goodness, anticipate Kantianism. Instead, the Samaritan feels compassion and responds accordingly. Remember, that religious law says "you shall love your neighbor as yourself," it does not merely demand that "you should fulfill your moral duties to your neighbor." People can fulfill their moral duties from a variety of motives that exclude love. To name only a few: people can fulfill moral duty because of their commitments to comply with the conclusions of moral logic; from hope of reciprocated benefit from others; and from belief that fulfilling moral duty will be rewarded in an afterlife. Jesus implies that all such motivations are inadequate. We must love our neighbors as we love ourselves. Our actions must flow from the appropriate internal dispositions. This is why the parable does not merely chronicle what the Samaritan did for the victim he comes upon. The parable must note that the Samaritan exuded the proper inner disposition toward this stranger-enemy: he feels "compassion."

The Samaritan pours "oil and wine" on the victim's wounds and binds them up. Commentators have noted the religious imagery: binding wounds is akin to God's actions in saving people; oil and wine are "sacrificial elements in the temple worship."[3] Of course, the Samaritan cannot leave the victim where he has found him. He places the victim on his own donkey and transports him to an inn. We do not know whether the Samaritan rode with the victim on the same animal or whether he led the animal, carrying only the wounded man, to the inn. If the latter, the Samaritan would have voluntarily placed himself in the role of servant in order to facilitate the wounded man's well-being. Moreover, once at the inn, the Samaritan remains overnight and cares for the victim. He has not only rendered immediate assistance, gone out of his way to secure safety for the victim, and delayed his own travel and business commitments, he has also revealed his identity to the innkeeper and perhaps other lodgers.

The Samaritan might have merely dumped the victim at the inn in the dark of night and fled. He might have even left some money to pay for the victim's lodging and medical care. (Although doing so might have been imprudent: innkeepers were not known for their honesty and generosity.) But the Samaritan remains with the victim and reveals his identity to others. Why? Because loving one's neighbor requires no less. Perhaps the safer path would have been enough for the Samaritan to fulfill his abstract moral duties to strangers, but the riskier course is required for those embodying the inner dispositions presupposed by the love commandment.

But the Samaritan is not finished. He gives two denarii to the innkeeper, promises to return, and to pay whatever more extensive amount the lodging and medical care of the wounded man tallies. The Samaritan's commitment is a natural extension of his compassion. At this time and place, people incurring debts that they could not honor were imprisoned. Had the Samaritan not pledged to pay beyond the two denarii, the wounded man would have either not been cared for or after being attended to would have been responsible for a debt he could not pay. Thus, the Samaritan must pledge to stand as surety for the wounded man and must return to the inn sometime after his business commitments are concluded. In sum, the Samaritan has extended himself in several dimensions: he has donated his time; he has endured much inconvenience; he has invested his efforts; he has expended his material resources; and he has exposed himself to risks. He did all this on behalf of a stranger, who if conscious, would have regarded him as an enemy. Through this parable, Jesus eviscerates the prevalent understanding that one's "neighbor" is defined by nation, tribe, or geographical proximity. Moreover, Jesus illuminates not merely the range of *acts* required to fulfill the love commandment, but also the *inner dispositions* that must animate those acts.

Notice that in the parable of the Good Samaritan, Jesus does not answer the lawyer's second question, "And who is my neighbor?" precisely. Like all parables, this story of morality requires the audience to reflect further. Clearly, the wounded stranger was not antecedently a neighbor of the Samaritan in any of the usual senses of that term. Instead, the Samaritan acted *as if* the wounded man was a neighbor; or he *became* his neighbor through his compassionate deeds; or he *acted as* a neighbor once he understood the wounded man's plight. The parable makes clear that moral duties and love to others is not circumscribed by the parameters typically recognized in Jesus' time: religion, nationality, tribe, or righteousness. The need of others and the opportunity of the moral agent to mollify their predicaments are crucial. Thus, no predetermined boundary exists that would carefully delineate who is and is not my neighbor.

2. Extending Unconditional Love

But how can I "love" strangers? Remember, to perform the proper deeds is not enough to fulfill the commandment; we must love our neighbors. Does it really make sense to think that the Samaritan in the parable could love the wounded stranger merely because the man had been victimized and was in dire need? Perhaps the Samaritan empathized with the victim and acted compassionately to ease his suffering, but could he actually love a person whom he had never met? After all, we have no evidence that the wounded man even recovered consciousness after the Samaritan's ministering.

Perhaps the best understanding is that we should embody a general beneficence toward humanity and an open-heart toward individuals. Although we cannot literally love everyone, especially those whom we have never encountered, from the outset, we can demonstrate warmth and good will toward all, and be prepared to love those whose paths cross ours. In any event, we should surely not exclude others antecedently from our beneficence based on artificial barriers such as race, ethnicity, religion, or our evaluations of their moral worth. That the conventional wisdom of our society brands some as "enemies" does not justify their exclusion from our moral concern. At times, we may be called upon to make such people our "neighbors."

The enjoinment to "love thy neighbor as thyself" can be understood as requiring justified self-love and self-respect as a condition precedent to loving neighbors. But, typically, human beings do not need instruction in self-love. We tend to prefer our interests and appreciate our well-being quite naturally. Accordingly, Jesus is probably not urging us to higher degrees of self-regard, but encouraging us to extend our typical concern for self to others in need. Moreover, excessive self-regard amplifies into selfish acquisitiveness, and utter selflessness deflates into subservience. Both self-love and love of neighbors are required for salutary dispositions, choices, and actions. In a sense, a proper understanding of self-love requires exercising the capability of loving neighbors. Instead of perceiving the love of neighbors as an add-on or as subsequent to the proper regard for self, Jesus suggests that the love of self and love of neighbors are mutually sustaining: neither is fully possible without the other. I, no less or more than others, embody intrinsic value and I genuinely love myself only when I love my neighbors. As such, my moral calculations should include the interests of self but not privilege them above the interests of others. My interests count no less or more than those of every other person affected by my contemplated action.

Jesus also recognizes a distinction between wrongful actions and wrongful omissions. The robbers beat and robbed their victim unjustifiably: they acted wrongly. The priest and the Levite inflicted no further harm, but they did not care enough to attend to the wounded man's suffering: they failed to act rightly. Moreover, the priest and the Levite probably appealed to established religious rules to rationalize their inaction. As always, for Jesus, formalistic interpretations and mechanical application of the results are inadequate to fulfill divine imperatives and to earn "eternal life."

But how much risk and sacrifice are we required to undertake on behalf of our neighbors? Typically, Jesus does not provide a precise answer. Even the level of the Samaritan's own risk and sacrifice are unclear. How likely was it that the bandits who robbed and beat their victim were still in the area waiting for new prey? Was this a common strategy of enterprising thieves in that area during that time? Assuming that the Samaritan was a business traveler, to what extent, if any, were his commercial interests adversely affected by his compassionate deeds? Given his material holdings, how great a monetary sacrifice did he make in paying the innkeeper for the wounded man's lodging and medical care? Even though the wounded man had been robbed would the Samaritan be reimbursed gratefully by the man's family once those members learned the sequence of events? Or would the family be inclined irrationally to seek revenge against the innocent Samaritan? These are only a few of the questions we need to answer prior to determining precisely how great a sacrifice and risk the compassionate Samaritan voluntarily assumed.

Of course, parables deliberately omit the detailed information on their subjects that would allow the audience to craft fastidious conclusions. Such stories yield a moral trajectory; they do not end with absolute, self-executing imperatives. What it means to "love one's neighbor as oneself" remains contestable. Suppose the Samaritan was required to risk his life more explicitly in order to rescue the wounded man? Would he still be required to undertake the task?

Suppose as the Samaritan approached the wounded man, the thieves, armed and dangerous, popped out of an arid sanctuary and issued an ultimatum, "Traveler, go on your way and you will not be harmed. But try to help the man we just beat and robbed and you, too, will meet his fate!" Would the commandment to love one's neighbor as oneself require the Samaritan to risk his own life in this concrete way in order to aid the victim?

Or suppose that all else in the parable is the same, but in order to pay for the wounded man's lodging and medical care the Samaritan would have to expend most of his material holdings. Moreover, the innkeeper recognizes the wounded man as a person without a family whose members might reimburse the Samaritan. Also, the Samaritan's own family will suffer significantly because of their patriarch's compassionate efforts on behalf of the wounded man. Under such circumstances, does the commandment to love one's neighbor as oneself require the Samaritan to relinquish most of his finances in order to aid the victim?

I could continue to pose countless hypothetical cases to press the general point: the parable of the Good Samaritan does not demonstrate precisely the scope and strength of the claim that a "neighbor" has on my effort, time, money, attention, and love. A literal interpretation of the love commandment might well conclude that a neighbor—all those in need whom we might aid?—has *as great* a claim on my effort, time, money, attention, and love as I do. If the notion of "claim" is off-putting—it would sound oddly offensive if my neighbor actually confronted me and claimed to have as strong a title to my effort, time, money, and attention as I do—then we can understand the imperative as placing us under the same duties toward our neighbors as we assume toward ourselves. Even if our neighbors cannot actually claim their due as a matter of right, we are obliged to extend our effort, time, money, attention, and love to them as much as we should to ourselves.

Yet, we must recognize that Jesus was not fond of literal renderings and code-book approaches to morality. While the benefit of parables flows from their vividness and emotional imprint, the morals they convey characteristically lack rigorous formulations. The proper scope of the commandment to "love one's neighbor as oneself" remains a matter of ongoing reflection. A soul yearning for perfection should not be constrained by antecedently imposed limits: we should not define "neighbor" in ways that include some and preclude others from the outset. Perhaps the commandment is more an ideal toward which to strive than a moral imperative which must be attained: flawed, fallible human beings cannot achieve moral perfection, but in our struggle toward that goal glorious self-transformation occurs. Perhaps by cultivating the proper inner dispositions toward other people, by casting off the limitations imposed by the insularities of nations and tribes, by translating our compassion into salutary deeds, and by developing the appropriate moral habits we can nurture our characters and sculpt our souls in ways that will maximize our chances of arriving at the correct moral solutions to particular cases. Perhaps a well-ordered spirit and a disciplined character are better guides to moral virtue than carefully crafted philosophical principles and policies ... perhaps.

Most important, the parable addresses not only the need of our fellow human beings and our duties to provide succor, but the effects of our actions on the people we are becoming. Surely, we should abrogate biased, prejudiced attitudes toward other groups and toward strangers. Yes, we should not accept arbitrary, artificial boundaries that carve human beings into "us" and "them." Thus, we should approach others with an open-heart, make anyone our "neighbor," or at least act toward them as if they were our neighbor. That part of the love commandment, as illustrated by the parable, may well strike us as compelling.

But does it follow that there are no boundaries as to what we owe our "neighbors"? Even if we accept that no boundaries can define who our neighbors are from the outset, we might well inquire as to how much we owe those whom we make our neighbors. Again, do we owe each neighbor *as much* as we would allot to ourselves? Is such a position possible to translate into action? If so, is such a social practice desirable?

Contemporary social science research casts chilling water on Jesus' enthusiasm for the possibility of widespread human unconditional love. For example, Jonathan Haidt concludes that

> It would be nice to believe that we humans were designed to love everyone unconditionally. Nice, but rather unlikely from an evolutionary perspective. Parochial love—love within groups—amplified by similarity, a sense of shared fate, and the suppression of free riders, may be the most we can accomplish ... if religion is a group-level adaptation, then it should produce parochial altruism. It should make people exceeding generous and helpful toward members of their own moral communities, particularly when their reputations will be enhanced. And indeed, religion does exactly this.[4]

3. Unconditional Love and Abstraction

However, to dismiss agapic love as hopelessly abstract and ethereal—as I was tempted to do earlier in this work—is too facile. Jesus' instruction in the parable of the Good Samaritan is that our neighbor is anyone we meet who is in need (or anyone who is in need, whether we meet them or not); loving our neighbor requires us to fulfill those needs if possible; and loving our neighbor requires more than the appropriate actions—it requires that we act from the proper dispositions of compassion. To regard our neighbors appropriately, then, requires an unconditional affection toward them that spurs us to fulfill their needs. Such love is not grounded in their merit, past service to us, or our hope for reciprocal benefit. Instead, Jesus insists we must love our neighbor agapically and concretely.

The question arises as to whether such love is possible. Perhaps a few people, totally devoted to service to others might approximate this ideal, but is the ideal of agapic love unreasonable for the overwhelming majority of people? Yes, a few exemplars such as Mother Teresa might stand as contemporary illustrations of the lessons of the Parable of the Good Samaritan, but can this ethic be universalized? The rest of us have families to raise, careers to foster, and responsibilities to discharge.

The radically egalitarian ethic of Jesus, however, paid little attention to careers, explicitly distanced people from their families, and took our highest responsibility to be nurturing our souls and those of our neighbors. When we bestow agapic love upon our neighbors we reflect an image of God's unconditional love for us. By surrendering to God's love, we open our hearts to higher purposes. In loving our neighbors agapically we recognize their inherent dignity and make them subjects of our concern, regardless of their personal deserts and other entitlements. We are in the world together as equal participants in the stream of life. Moreover, although agapic love is often depicted as affection that is utterly distinct from attention to the beloved's properties a more precise rendering is recommended. God's agapic love is directed toward his human creations and, thus, the property of "being a human creation of God" is implicated in divine agapic love. Human agapic love of neighbors also attends to a general property in the beloved: the image of God, the spark of the divine that every human being presumably embodies. Our regard for our neighbor is grounded in one unalterable, *universal* property of human beings, not in *special* attributes or traits that distinguish individuals. As such, each neighbor's well-being is equally important. Jesus did not enjoin human beings to love everything agapically, but only to love God and to love our neighbors unconditionally. As such, human agapic love is not truly a bestowal of value upon others after deliberation; instead, it acknowledges the value in others that God has already bestowed.

In the words of Soren Kierkegaard:

Your neighbor is every man, for on the basis of distinctions he is not your neighbor, nor on the basis of likeness to you as being different from other men. He is your neighbor on the basis of equality with you before God: but this equality absolutely every man has, and he has it absolutely.[5]

Because agapic love of our neighbors is neither preferential nor personal, it cannot serve as the basis or the starting point of erotic love or friendship love, both of which are inherently preferential and personal. An issue arises as to whether agapic love of neighbors is genuinely the love of a person. Stripped of all constitutive attributes, relationships, past deeds, deserts, other entitlements, and the like, what remains of the concrete individual? When we love our neighbor unconditionally, do we truly love her as a unique person? Surely, if we love agapically we do not love our neighbor because of who she is, but, still, we must focus on the concrete individual to determine the nature and extent of her needs and which of her needs we ought to fulfill. Each of our neighbors will be different in these regards, at least to some extent. That is, to structure the acts appropriate to express our unconditional love for our neighbors we must attend closely to their individuating characteristics and circumstances. Given that agapic love of neighbors requires both the proper affection and the appropriate deeds, the concrete individual does not disappear. Unconditional love cannot require identical treatment of all neighbors for so doing would ignore the fact that our neighbors do not always share the same needs; agape must focus, instead, on equal consideration of different needs. Accordingly, unconditional love of neighbors does not imply fungibility—that one neighbor is indistinguishable from and replaceable by another. I may well love all my children equally and unconditionally, but it hardly follows that I view them as indistinguishable from or replaceable by each other.

Although most of us can identify, at best, only a few practitioners of widespread unconditional love in our world, the enjoinment to love our neighbor agapically is not merely an abstract, contentless slogan. To approximate the ideal requires great sacrifice—relinquishing the pursuit of most of the values and prizes that the world cherishes, including robust family relations, individual status, and career possibilities—but that should not surprise anyone who attends to Jesus' moral message: we are to prefigure now the more genuine values and prizes of the impending Kingdom of God.

4. A Summary of the Perfectionism of Jesus

That Jesus taught largely through parables is a function of three convictions. First, Jesus was convinced that his audience should do some work in order to grasp the moral of his stories. Eschewing the legalism and formalism of the Pharisees, Jesus demanded that his audience interpret the parables within their social context but always with keen awareness of the love commandment. Second, Jesus was most interested in nurturing the inner condition of his audience, in assisting other people in cultivating the proper dispositions of character and in artfully crafting their souls. As such, Jesus guided people toward how they should *be* generally instead of prescribing dogmatically what they should *do* specifically. He was confident that people who embodied the appropriate intentions and motivations would perform the right deeds: the proper external actions will flow from the pure mode of being. Third, Jesus understood that complexities, nuances, and extraordinary circumstances will upset the most carefully sculptured moral rules. Parables will thus remain more vivid and memorable than a discourse on moral principles that will fade quite quickly. Accordingly, Jesus' normative message is less a rigorous system of thought and more a glorious moral trajectory.

The perfectionism of Jesus, which is simply another term for the proper nurturing of the human soul, is grounded in cultivating appropriate dispositions and performing prescribed deeds. The appropriate dispositions are defined in terms of extending unconditional love from the self to all others, and embracing mercy and forgiveness as virtually default responses to the shortcomings and transgressions of others. Jesus is seemingly convinced that attaining the proper dispositions is both necessary and sufficient for performing prescribed deeds. That is another reason why Jesus does not craft or argue for rigorous moral principles that might decide concrete moral cases mechanically and formalistically. Instead, Jesus understands that being a certain kind of human being is the best guide for determining what one should do in specific circumstances. Jesus also understands that no system of moral rules by itself can adequately take into account all possible aspects of all possible cases nor can it anticipate all fresh cases, those of first impression. This is why being a certain kind of human being is necessary for determining the right moral answer to particular problems. However, to say that being such a person is also sufficient for performing prescribed deeds may be too strong. Surely, Jesus recognizes weakness of will and human shortcomings: even where the righteous person recognizes moral duty he or she will at times fail because of weakness of will or because of some other human deficiency. To remain human is to ensure that perfection can at best be only approximated.

Extending unconditional love to all others requires distancing ourselves from the partiality and privileges of intimate family relations: singling out family members for special concern jeopardizes the radical impartiality of allocating effort, time, and sacrifice that is the cornerstone of Jesus' ethic. As no antecedent boundaries circumscribe how much effort, risk, and sacrifice we ought to expend or incur on behalf of others, particularly the needy, and whom we should include in our circle of concern, the special requirements of family can pose practical and spiritual problems. In that vein, pursuing material accumulation or person aggrandizement are also obstacles to perfecting the soul. Prefiguring the values of the Kingdom of God in a thoroughly secular world is no small task.

For Jesus, factual differences among human beings are insignificant and morally irrelevant. He is singularly unimpressed by the "greatest exemplars" in a society and accords them no special esteem. If anything, they represent souls diverted from the true path of redemption as they journey toward narcissism and inflated pride. Jesus emphasizes the social dimension of human fulfillment and the communal axis of the individual-community continuum. Displaying a resume glistening with attained goals, high cultural creativity, Nietzschean self-mastery, and the like to Jesus would not bring anticipated applause. Jesus is not concerned with what a person produced on those dimensions but on who the person is in terms of inner dispositions and what social actions the person performed. Clearly, Jesus values self-abnegation over self-pride grounded in the values of Nietzsche's grand striver. For Jesus, to those whom much is bestowed—in terms of innate talents, initial starting position, and early socialization—much communal service is required. The egalitarian ethic of Jesus is so extreme that the boundaries, so prized by modern ethicists, between moral duty and moral supererogation evaporate.

Therein lies the prime difficulty for Jesus' rendering of morality. His is an ethic seemingly suitable only for those with a special religious calling. A few dedicated paragons, willing to cast aside the allures of the secular world, such as Mother Teresa and Mother Cabrini, are the only suitable candidates for practicing Jesus' radical egalitarianism. Even if convinced by much of Jesus' message, the rest of us—burdened with responsibilities, careers, and families we cannot and do not choose to discard—will fall woefully short of the ideal. But perhaps that is the underlying message of any perfectionist ethic: understand that you will fall short of the ideal, but by crafting your soul and shaping your lives in the general direction of the ideal you will become a better human being than you would have been otherwise.

5. The Ethic of Jesus and Contemporary Philosophy

The contemporary philosophical works of Peter Singer and James Rachels provide practical examples of this point. The most influential contemporary applied ethicist, Australian Peter Singer, argues that we are morally obligated to do much more for others, even strangers, than conventional practices admit. He begins from an observation from nineteenth-century philosophy Henry Sidgwick that "The good of any one individual is of no more importance, from the point of view (if I may say so) of the Universe than the good of any other."[6] That is, from the vantage point of the cosmos—the external perspective of an indifferent observer or of Nature itself or a deity that values all human creatures equally—the importance of an interest or need does not depend on who embodies it.

Singer's argument, first enunciated in an article called, "Famine, Affluence, and Morality,"[7] can be summarized as follows:

(1) Suffering and death resulting from inadequate food, shelter, and medical care are bad events.
(2) If it is in our power to prevent something bad from happening, without thereby sacrificing anything of comparable moral importance, we ought, morally to do it.
(3) Millions of human beings are in fact suffering and dying from inadequate food, shelter, and medical care.
(4) Millions of human beings in affluent countries have it within their power to prevent much of this suffering and dying without thereby sacrificing anything of comparable moral importance.

Therefore, millions of human beings in affluent countries ought, morally, to prevent those sufferings and deaths.

Singer takes his first premise to be uncontroversial: that suffering and death arising from lacking basic necessities are bad events is unlikely to be contested seriously. He explains his second premise: "By 'without sacrificing anything of comparable moral importance' I mean without causing anything else comparably bad to happen, or doing something that is wrong in itself, or failing to promote some moral good, comparable in significance to the bad thing that we can prevent."[8] Although he is writing in the context of contributing to famine relief, he illustrates his principle by a Good Samaritan-type example: if a person is strolling past a shallow pond and sees a child drowning, who he might rescue easily at only the sacrifice of getting his clothes muddy, he ought, morally, to save the child. In that case, the rescuer would not be sacrificing *anything* morally significant, much less be sacrificing something of *comparable* moral importance.

The force of Singer's "ought" judgment is one of moral obligation: "'I have an obligation to' means no more, and no less, than 'I ought to.'"[9] Thus, in Singer's view, rescuing the child drowning in the pond and contributing to famine relief, under the circumstances described, are moral imperatives; they are not supererogatory actions—deeds that are good, go beyond the call of moral requirements, and thus are not wrong not to do.

His argument does not depend on the proximity of human need. Whereas the Good Samaritan of the Biblical parable came upon a beaten victim and would otherwise have never known of his need, Singer insists that "it makes no moral difference whether the person I can help is a neighbor's child ten yards from me or a Bengali whose name I shall never know, ten thousand miles away."[10] Human beings today have access to information and communications media unimaginable in Biblical times. Singer implicitly reminds us that these technological advances have moral ramifications for the questions

"Who is my neighbor?" and "What do I owe my neighbor?" While physical proximity to people in dire need typically means that it is more likely that we will aid them, for Singer it does not follow that we ought to help them instead of others who live farther away. Physical proximity to people in dire need may well result in our being in a clearer position to determine what must be done and to provide immediate aid—reasons that may well impel us toward helping them first. But physical proximity as such cuts no moral ice for Singer.

Moreover, Singer's argument makes no distinction between cases where I am the only person who can supply the required succor and cases where millions are in the same position to help. If I am one of a million bystanders who watch a child drown whom any of us could have easily rescued I am no more or less morally culpable than if I was the only bystander who refused to help. In such cases, moral culpability does not divide among those who are morally deficient and thereby lessen their blame; instead, moral culpability multiplies and those who are morally deficient, all other things being equal, all bear full moral responsibility for their inaction.

But *how much* are we morally required to sacrifice, in terms of physical risk and monetary disbursements, to alleviate the suffering and deaths of our fellow human beings who are in need? Singer's first answer to this question is severe:

> I and everyone else in similar circumstances ought to give as much as possible, that is, at least up to the point at which by giving more one would begin to cause serious suffering for oneself and one's dependents—perhaps even beyond this point to the point of marginal utility, at which by giving more one would cause oneself and one's dependents as much suffering as one would prevent [to those in need faraway].[11]

Singer recognizes the well-known principle of economics that the same amount of additional money will increase a person's well-being less, the wealthier he or she is: five extra dollars is more significant to a destitute person than to a rich person. Still, Singer struggles with the implications of marginal utility as the standard of moral obligation. He offers a lower moral standard as a possibility: "we should prevent bad occurrences unless, to do so, we had to sacrifice something morally significant . . . even on this surely undeniable principle a great change in our way of life is required."[12] So his considered view at this point was that the standard of marginal utility remained the most philosophically persuasive principle of distribution, but the more moderate standard—give or risk unless in doing so you must sacrifice something morally significant—would still have revolutionary effects.

In a later rendition, Singer softened even the moderate standard. Fearful that both of his previously offered recommendations might be viewed as too strenuous by almost everyone and that people might conclude that if they cannot fulfill their moral requirements they will not even bother to try, Singer suspects that "public advocacy of [the standard of marginal utility] is undesirable."[13] We will be better off—if our goal is the reduction of absolute poverty—to advocate publicly a reduced standard that more people will embrace even though the best philosophical argument supports a much higher standard. In that vein, while conceding that any such figure will be arbitrary, Singer concludes that 10% of one's income is an appropriate amount for those who are relatively affluent.

> [T]hose earning average or above-average incomes in affluent societies, unless they have an unusually large number of dependents or other special needs, ought to give a tenth of their income to reducing absolute poverty.[14]

Singer recognized the radically counterintuitive implications of his position. He was self-consciously a moral reformer—the core of his project was not to validate but to transform our current moral understandings. Where our moral standards and expectations are increased, he believes that our decisions will improve: rigorous moral arguments can augur salutary changes in moral practices.

What is clear is that Singer's answer to the question "Who is my neighbor?" is "everyone."[15] Clearly, Singer, as does Jesus, renounces tribalism, discrimination based on common religion, race, ethnicity, gender, and the like from the outset. He refuses to carve the universe into friends, acquaintances, and strangers—at least for the purposes of determining whose needs should count in our moral calculus.

His theoretical answer as to how much is owed my neighbors is as much as I have to the point of marginal utility. His practical answer to that question is I owe my needy neighbors aid as long as rendering assistance does not compel me to sacrifice something morally significant; at the very least, if I am relatively affluent I ought to contribute 10% of my holdings to help reduce absolute poverty.

As such, Singer's position is a contemporary interpretation of the parable of the Good Samaritan with a few modest adjustments. If taken literally, the parable of the Good Samaritan could be construed as calling for radical impartiality. To love my neighbor as myself might imply that I should allocate my resources—money, time, and effort—to others in the same way that I think I should allocate them to myself. Thus, in a forced choice situation, where I could distribute, say, a piece of food to another person or consume it myself, if all other factors are equal, then I should figuratively flip a coin to determine the recipient. That is, as between giving the food to the other person or consuming it myself, I should select the recipient randomly because under the conditions specified my "neighbor" has as much claim to the food as I do. Granted, Jesus was always suspicious of strict, code book understandings of religious and moral law, and Jesus' description of the Good Samaritan's actions does not automatically support the literal interpretation I suggest, but that understanding remains a live possibility.

In any case, Singer's theoretical prescription of giving one's material possessions to stymie world poverty and famine to the point of marginal utility—the level at which by giving more one would cause oneself and one's dependents as much suffering as one would alleviate for the needy—approximates radical impartiality. Moreover, Singer states explicitly that "we cannot, if we accept the principle of equal consideration of interests, say that doing [a particular] act is better . . . because we are *more concerned* about Y than we are about X. What the principle is really saying is that an interest is an interest, whoever's interest it may be."[16]

Unlike the biblical love commandment and the parable of the Good Samaritan that interprets it, Singer is not counseling universal love. His ethic is grounded in rationality and the principle of equal consideration of interests regardless of the affection one might have for the people who embody them. The biblical imperative is one of deed *and* affection, whereas Singer s ethic is only of deed. That is, Singer does not require that we feel as close emotionally to needy strangers as we do to family and friends. What he concludes—at least when he invokes the standard of marginal utility—is that any difference in affection should not translate into different treatment in terms of allocating our material resources where equal needs are at issue.

Taken at its most uncompromising, the radical impartiality thesis demands that we assume the perspective of an ideal, detached observer when arriving at moral judgments: I must attach no special weight to my own interests when determining moral action. Also, the fact that another person is my spouse, my child, or my intimate friend is morally irrelevant: it provides no moral reason to favor such a person over a complete stranger. An eighteenth- century English philosopher, William Godwin, sums the view up well when he considers whom he should save in a fire, an archbishop or a chambermaid, when he can save only one: "[if the chambermaid is my wife or mother] that would not alter the truth of the proposition [about whom to save] for of what great consequence is it that they are mine? What magic is there in the pronoun 'my' to overturn the decisions of everlasting truth?"[17] We may from a moral viewpoint discriminate between people—Godwin would save the archbishop not the chambermaid—but this may be done only on the basis of *non-relational* characteristics, those that would attract the assent of an ideal, detached observer.

We must understand that the debate about radical impartiality focuses on the level of concrete moral action. All major theories of morality agree that moral rules and principles should apply to everyone alike; that I cannot make myself an exception to the moral law. The debate over radical impartiality centers on the relevant criteria of moral choice under conditions of scarcity such that we cannot all have what we need and what we want.

Crucial to radical impartiality is the vantage point from which it flows. From the standpoint of a God or Nature or an Ideal Observer each of us is equal and none of us has a legitimate claim to privilege based on identity alone. The Parable of the Good Samaritan, along with Godwin and Singer take this God's Eye or cosmic view. But human beings making moral choices in our flawed, fallible world also have personal perspectives that seem relevant. As Sidgwick pointed out

> It would be contrary to Common Sense to deny that the distinction between any one individual and any other is real and fundamental, and that consequently 'I' am concerned with the quality of my existence as an individual in a sense, fundamentally important, in which I am not concerned with the quality of the existence of other individuals: and this being so, I do not see how it can be proved that this distinction is not to be taken as fundamental in determining the ultimate end of rational action for an individual.[18]

Brushing aside Sidgwick's imperial reference to "Common Sense" (in upper case, no less), his point is telling. Unlike the answer flowing from an Ideal Observer operating from a cosmic perspective, from a personal perspective identity is significant. If the chambermaid is my mother or wife I would surely rescue her to the detriment of an archbishop should I not be able to save both. In doing so, I would not be succumbing to the talismanic power of a pronoun ("my"), but would, instead, be acknowledging that based on our relationship I owe my mother or wife more than I owe a stranger. Should I select randomly and rescue the archbishop, thereby allowing my mother or wife to die, I would be subject to moral disapprobation.

Singer softens what he takes to be the best philosophical standard—give to others to the point of marginal utility—in deference, I believe, to the existence of the personal perspective. Thus, his practical answer to the question of how much should we give needy strangers is to the point where we do not sacrifice something morally significant; and, at the very least, if I am relatively affluent I ought to contribute 10% of my holdings to help reduce absolute poverty.

Of course, practical considerations of limited time, effort, and resources will limit our duties to fulfilling the needs of others, even when those needs are recognized and the others are not distant strangers but known community members. Moreover, special obligations to others we have voluntarily contracted by dint of our occupations or personal relationships will further limit our capability of fulfilling the needs of others.

Still, radical impartiality has stunningly counterintuitive consequences for family life. While Singer ultimately does take into account people with "an unusually large number of dependents or other special needs," which leads to common objections to his general view: What about my family, even if not "unusually large"? Don't I owe them much more than I owe strangers? Should I reduce my spouse and children to the point of marginal utility for the sake of strangers? Don't I owe family members more than I do others even if those other people are needier? Would not contributing even 10% of my holdings—Singer's most modest proposal—reduce the well-being of those closest to me?

Such questions are addressed by another contemporary secular philosopher, James Rachels. He argues that privileging family members in our moral calculus, even if deeply embedded in conventional moral wisdom, is fatally flawed because it wrongly privileges irrelevant considerations, such as luck, with moral significance:

> Suppose a parent believes that, when faced with a choice between feeding his own children and feeding starving orphans, he should give preference to his own. This is natural enough. But the orphans need the food just as much, and they are no less deserving. It is only their bad luck that they were not born to affluent parents; and why should luck count, from a moral point of view?[19]

Rachels endorses the view that "universal love is a higher ideal than family loyalty, and that obligations within families can be properly understood only as particular instances of obligations to all mankind."[20] Finally, the conception of morality captures "something deeply important that we should be reluctant to give up. It is useful, for example, in explaining why egoism, racism, and sexism are morally odious, and if we abandon this conception we lose our most natural and persuasive means of combating those doctrines."[21]

Rachels advances a number of insights here. First, he disparages good fortune as morally irrelevant. In a world with radically unequal distribution of resources, a world which praises lavishly the partiality shown by parents to their children and by intimate friends to one another, a child's well-being is wrongly connected to facts beyond the child's control: initial starting position, material circumstances of birth, and the genetic lottery. Second, when he addresses family duties as derived from more general duties to all humans and impartiality as essential to blocking racism and sexism, Rachels is stressing that the entire history of progressive moral thinking is a story of widening our circle of concern. Tribalism is dangerously parochial from a social and moral standpoint. Carving out carefully and narrowly circumscribed loops designating "them" and "us" reflects and fosters misunderstanding and terrorizes deeper moral sentiments. We might expect this from gangs of socially deprived adolescent boys, but not from moral philosophers.

He points out that his ethic leaves room for partiality of affection ("universal love," then, should not be understood literally):

> Love involves, among other things, intimacy and the sharing of experiences. A parent shows his love by listening to the child's jokes, by

talking, by being a considerate companion, by praising, and even by scolding when that is needed. Of course these kinds of behaviors also show partiality, since the parent does not do these things for all children.[22]

In that vein, Rachels offers a concession. He implicitly undercuts Godwin's position and concedes that those who advocate no difference between a person's moral requirements toward one's own children and toward other children would appear "morally deranged."[23] Nodding to the strictures of practicality and concluding that the appearance of moral derangement counts against the most radical versions of impartiality, Rachels softens his verdict and renders it in three tiers. First, if a parent is confronted with a choice between providing the basic necessities for one's own children or providing for the like needs of other children, the parent may prefer the interests of his or her own children. So where equal needs are in play, we may permissibly prefer—"perhaps you even ought"[24] to prefer (perhaps!)—to provide for the needs of our children. Second, where the choice is between providing a benefit for our own children or a *slightly* greater benefit for other children, we may prefer fulfilling the interests of our own children. But, third, "if the choice is between some relatively trivial thing for one's own and necessities for other children, preference should be given to helping the others."[25] The overall effect of Rachels' position is that parents may provide the necessities of life for their own children first, but they are not morally justified in providing their own children luxuries while other children lack the necessities of life. Given the number of children who currently lack the necessities of life in our world, the results of accepting Rachels' moral doctrine would be revolutionary.

What constitutes a "luxury" is, of course, contestable. More stringent interpretations would classify almost anything beyond essential food, clothing, and shelter as "luxuries." Thus, even parental funding of his or her child's college education—much less the purchase of cell phones, expensive toys, fancy clothes, and exotic vacations—would count as a luxury. Looser interpretations might accept higher education as a necessity of sorts, but distinguish between the costs acceptable at a state university and the "luxurious" expense of a private institution.

The call to deemphasize partiality to family members resonates in the words of Jesus. The Kingdom of God must be sought above all else. Family, relatives, and friends are of trivial concern by comparison. Jesus goes so far as to say that people must "hate" their family as a prerequisite for being a genuine disciple (Luke 14: 26; Matt. 10: 37). Although we need not take "hate" literally, the term and context surely advise followers to distance themselves from their families. Jesus' own family relations were strained as evidence exists that they rejected his message and that he distanced himself from them (Mark 3: 31-34). Jesus was keenly aware that family divisions would dog his message (Luke 12: 51-53; Matt. 10: 34-46; Mark 13:12). Those who view the historical Jesus as an apocalyptic prophet conclude that Jesus

> [W]asn't teaching about the good society and about how to maintain it. The end was coming soon and the present social order was being called radically into question. What mattered was not, ultimately, the strong family ties and social institutions of this world. What mattered was the new thing that was coming, the future Kingdom. It was impossible to promote this teaching while trying to retain the present social structure.[26]

Those who take the historical Jesus to be a Cynic philosopher would see him as spreading the Cynic creed of radical individuality which rejects the view that family affiliation and affections are required for personal fulfillment. Such interpreters would view Jesus as offering a revolutionary social program somewhat independently of the advent of the Kingdom of God.[27]

The appeal to impartialism challenges those who embrace conventional wisdom to sharpen their position. Those aspiring to retain a robust preference for family and friends over the general needs of strangers might revisit the link between differences in affection and differences in material allocation. Either impartialists permit (a) no differences in our affectionate concern for family and our "love" for strangers or (b) they do permit such affectionate differences but conclude that they should not translate into differences in the way we allocate our material resources (or, at the very least, those differences in allocation should be severely limited). I'll call the first impartialist view *universal or general benevolence* and the second impartialist view *affectionate difference*.

Who has ever held the universal benevolence position? The answer is not clear, but Jesus is surely a candidate. A strict understanding of the biblical love commandment and the parable of the Good Samaritan that interprets it makes Jesus a strong possibility. After all, the love commandment is not merely about deeds and the allocation of resources, but also relates to the distribution of our affection. The Good Samaritan was not simply acting on some principle of reason that established his moral duty; he was acting from his "compassionate" heart and was responding viscerally to a stranger's (an "enemy's") need.

Although Godwin has an extreme impartialist view, he need not be interpreted as requiring a universal benevolence or an undifferentiated affection; Singer avoids speaking about affections and proudly positions his view as demanded solely by reason; and Rachels understands explicitly the need for parents to lavish more affection on their own children than upon children generally. Thus, they are not candidates for the universal benevolence view.

How might an advocate of conventional wisdom undermine the universal benevolence approach? First, a defender of family partiality might argue that the universal benevolence approach has an impoverished understanding of the value of personal relationships. In a world where people are equally fond of everyone, strangers and family alike, the good news is that the maladies of racism, sexism, religious intolerance, and the excesses of tribalism would vanish. We could well speculate that the overall amount of global happiness would increase. Still, the bad news is that the special joys of intimacy, family affection, and deep love would also evaporate. Radical impartiality of feeling is incompatible with the kind of profound personal relationships that distinguish a robustly meaningful human life. Moreover, we might argue that the sorts of dispositions and virtues—such as honesty, loyalty, caring, patience, empathy, and the like—that comprise the moral enterprise can be learned only from personal relations characterized by partiality of concern.

Although this is a reasonable argument, the universal benevolence approach has a plausible response: Is it so obvious that the overwhelming majority of human beings would choose our present world over a world embracing universal benevolence? The answer may well depend on whom we ask. Certainly those of us who have a reasonably satisfying network of personal relations would agree with the advocates of conventional wisdom; but those of us who suffer from intense, unsatisfied basic needs and who have experienced mainly stormy, frustrating personal relations may dissent. Taken as a world survey, which group predominates?

Second, a defender of family partiality might argue that personal relations have an inherent value and a phenomenology that transcends the requirements of impartial benevolence. Personal relations are not merely different in degree from impersonal relations, they are different in kind: the metaphors of mutual bonds, connectedness, attachments, although faintly capturing the truth, are too effete. Two Sicilian slogans from my youth are helpful in expressing the metaphysical differences between familial and impersonal relationships: *sangu du me sangu* ("blood of my blood"—to indicate the metaphysical links among grandparents, parents, and children) and *nun aviri famigghia e comu essiri un nuddo miscatu cu nenti* ("to be without family is to be a nobody mixed with nothing"). Our families, relatives, and closest friends do not merely interact with us at a distance; instead, they partially constitute who we are: they help define our values, they help sculpt our self-understandings, and they widen our subjectivity beyond the self. If we substitute a tepid universal benevolence for the partiality of intimate relationships, we alter personal identity in dangerous ways. Moreover, the very notion of "love" presupposes partiality. I cannot love everyone even if I am disposed to do so. Love, as opposed to a general benevolence toward all humankind, requires, among other things, participating in common enterprises, sharing information about oneself that is not available to the general public, and spending more time with the beloved than with acquaintances and strangers. Thus, I cannot "love" everyone if for no other reason than I am strictly limited in terms of time, geographic location, and general resources. Brushing aside factors such as my incompatibility with certain personality types, my inability to find numerous other people yearning for intimacy with me, and the like, the phenomenology of love is inherently partial. Accordingly, the imperative of general benevolence inaugurates the doom of interpersonal love.

Again, this is a powerful argument from the standpoint of current social theory and practice, but the prophets of general benevolence have a plausible response. Defenders of Jesus could argue that the alleged present benefits of family partialism arise only because our present world is fragmented and tribal. In a world characterized by invidious comparisons, ongoing zero-sum contests, and stark distinctions between friends and foes, the consolations of family and intimate relationships seem irresistible; such connections offer refuge from and succor within a generally hostile environment. But the prophets of general benevolence call upon us to eclipse our present world and transform the planet. In a world where principles of general benevolence were widely embraced, the phenomenology of our needs and satisfactions would change. We would no longer require the comforts of oases from general hostility and estrangement because the overall environment would be one of caring and concern. Although teasing out the specific details of a world we have never known would be overly speculative, the point is that critics of the principle of general benevolence cannot assume present social conditions and the phenomenology of intimate relations as unalterable givens without begging the most important questions at issue (that is, assuming as true that which must be proven as true).

Third, a defender of family partiality might argue that to require people to determine all of their important decisions by impartial consideration of global needs is to destroy the notion of personhood itself. The assumption here is that personhood presupposes partiality in the sense that one's identity and personal integrity must consist in part of projects, aspirations, and life's plans that have unique status in a person's priority of values simply because they are hers.[28]

An interesting question arises. Could a prophet of general benevolence respond that with the proper moral education and socialization the general welfare, at least insofar as it involves satisfying the basic needs of everyone, could in fact become our project, life's plan, and highest aspiration? Is there necessarily an incompatibility between thinking and acting impartiality, and one's integrity? Could it not be the case that the reason partialists now suspect that there is such an incompatibility is that as an empirical and contingent matter most people are radical partialists? But is this an inevitable feature of human nature? Or is it a sad commentary on the primitive, parochial level of our moral education and socialization?

John Cottingham, a contemporary English philosopher, would be unconvinced by the questions I have raised on behalf of general benevolence:

> A world in which I accorded everyone at large the same sort of consideration which I accord to myself, my children and my friends would not be

'one big happy family'; it would be a world in which affection no longer existed because the sense of 'specialness' had been eliminated. It would be a world where much of what gives human life preciousness and significance had disappeared.[29]

One of Cottingham's points is that an ethic of general benevolence transforms each of us into a type of dispassionate, bloodless, conscientious bureaucrat who never displays favoritism when allocating public resources. To partialists, this even-handedness constitutes a feckless moral ideal because two of the paramount points of the moral enterprise are personal transformation and social nonfungibility.[30]

We return to the questions which haunt advocates of general benevolence: Despite their protestations to the contrary, can they truly accommodate a moral universe where individuality and intimacy remain? Is a universe of impartiality truly a better world on balance than the partialist world that presently dominates our moral thinking?

Defenders of Jesus could retort that many of the charges hurled by partialism are question-begging. They may charge that partialists, instead of establishing that currently accepted notions are necessary features of human beings, merely presuppose the values of the dominant social order and then simply show how the ideal of general benevolence fails to instantiate those values. If so, then all the partialist has done is show that when judged by partialist standards, the principle of general benevolence will fail. But after all, part of the general benevolence program is to unsettle and transform precisely those partialist values and standards. The advocates of general benevolence may argue that instead of exposing embarrassing implications of general benevolence, all the partialist has done is restate part of the program of general benevolence and register shock. But this response was to be expected from the outset: the entrenched social order is unlikely to welcome a threatening challenger.

Fourth, partialists will insist that the principle of general benevolence is utopian in a pejorative sense. Invoking the "common sense" of Sidgwick, partialists will point out that human beings neither parcel out their affection nor their material goods indiscriminately. We devote much more care, time, and resources to our own plans and projects, and to our own self-development and fulfillment, than we can even begin to conceive of devoting to the needs of humanity generally.

As an empirical matter, partialists are correct. But surely the advocates of general benevolence do not deny this description of current and past practice. The real debate is whether our dominant social practices can and should be transformed. Partialists take the prevalence of common practices as strong (dispositive?) evidence that the ethic of general benevolence is beyond our grasp. Because partialists are also firmly convinced that any concentrated effort to strive for the ethic of general benevolence is accompanied by devastating costs—loss of genuine personal relationships, compromise of the individual's integrity and self-identity—they argue that the quest for this impossible dream is ignoble: we cannot achieve general benevolence and we should not struggle for it.

The advocates of general benevolence ask us to look around this world and see what the dominant practices have wrought. They perceive partialists as overly pessimistic and point out that wide acceptance of general benevolence would not be onerous on any one individual, group, or nation, and would facilitate great overall benefits in the world. Instead of viewing prevalent past and current practices as data for circumscribing what is possible, advocates of general benevolence view them as embodying numerous moral errors that should be repudiated: to limit artificially our social possibilities by accepting the past as dispositive of the future destroys moral progress.

On the level of reason, the debate between the conventional wisdom of partialism and the revolutionary aspirations of general benevolence is inconclusive. Most readers probably find themselves favoring a version of the partialist position, for most of you, by virtue of being in a position to read literature of this type, are not engaged in a brutal struggle for survival. Your probable distance from necessity permits innovative reflection on the terms of social life. But you also have or possess a reasonable chance for a network of relatively satisfying personal relations, and have deeply assimilated dominant social and moral norms. You are the readers to whom partialists can confidently appeal when favorably comparing "our" world with the hypothetical conditions of general benevolence. You appear to have much to lose and relatively little to gain, both materially and emotionally, from a conversion to general benevolence. Furthermore, even if you sympathize with the aspirations of general benevolence, and I speculate that most of you do, you will probably suspect that the burden of persuasion rests with the advocates of general benevolence. That is, no conclusive argument is available on questions such as these: Is human nature inherently and inevitably partialist? Can personhood exist in a world of general benevolence? Can intimacy persist where we do not favor some people in terms of the emotional and spiritual? Therefore, the advocates of general benevolence must convince us to change our minds because our default mindset registers partialism. Also, most readers will be undoubtedly very skeptical about the prospects that the institutions of family and intimate associations can be restructured in a way that preserves their unique values to personal integrity and growth, yet embody an ethic of general benevolence.

Advocates of general benevolence focus on the principle of equality, as interpreted from a cosmic vantage point, as definitive of morality. Indeed, Jesus describes relations in the Kingdom of God and invites human beings to prefigure those associations today. In fact, the principle of equality is only one of many principles required for full moral assessment; and the cosmic vantage point is only one interpretive perspective. Accordingly, partialists may well claim that advocates of general benevolence generate disturbing implications only because they wrongly reduce morality to one of its component principles and judge from one interpretive perspective. Although I am not convinced that general benevolence can be proved logically unsound or empirically impossible, neither can general benevolence persuasively alter our default moral theory and practice. Paradoxically, general benevolence might be most successful in an atmosphere of relatively abundant resources where universal benevolence would be less taxing for us all: precisely the atmosphere where general benevolence would be least necessary. Where general benevolence is most needed, in circumstances of deprivation and scarcity, it may be least persuasive because great numbers of people are preoccupied with a brutal struggle to obtain life's necessities.

This paradox suggests another facet of the problem: a serious coordination problem attending general benevolence. Even those who deny the partialist conclusion that our world is preferable to a world of general benevolence must grapple with the fact that an individual's choice is not simply between our world and one of general benevolence; instead, the choice is between our world and acting *as if* we are in a world of general benevolence. Acting as if a world of general benevolence existed does not, in the absence of millions acting likewise, establish the presumed paradise. The pressing question is whether I prefer acting in accord with the partialist norms of our present world or acting in accord with the norms of general benevolence while the vast majority of human beings are acting in accord with the partialist norms of our present world. Accordingly, even someone who is moved by the ideal of general benevolence and who is seduced by its transformative possibilities has a further question to address: Does it make moral and practical sense for me to act on that ideal while millions of other human beings remain partialists?

The philosophical impartialism of Singer and Rachels does not require general benevolence of sentiments. Rachels' ethic explicitly allows parents to love their children more than the children of others. He understands that parental love will demonstrate partiality when sharing experiences and nurturing intimacy: parents cannot foster such sharing and nurturing with all children. Furthermore, an insipid general benevolence would inadequately provide for children's emotional needs: children need to be regarded as special in a way that general benevolence makes difficult, if not impossible.

Although accepting affectionate differences, Rachels adopts a three-tiered impartialism as described above. The critical feature of Rachels' ethic is that the interests of one's children should not always be paramount when the interests of other children are at issue. When the choice is between benefiting one's children and benefiting other children equally then fulfilling the interests of one's children may (even should) assume priority; when the choice is between benefiting one's children and benefitting other children only slightly more, Rachels' ethic, again, permits privileging the interests of one's children; but if the choice is between bestowing a luxury on one's children or providing necessities for other children, priority should be given to aiding the other children.

The rhetoric trick here is to label the fulfillment of certain interests as "luxuries," a phrase that carries morally pejorative baggage and obscures the real choices most parents face. Because the basic needs of children range beyond the merely material (as Rachels concedes), any reasonable interpretation of where to draw the line between basic needs and luxuries may leave most parents—even those antecedently drawn to impartialism—with precious few material and emotional resources to even consider allocating to the basic needs of strangers. Moreover, the application of Rachels' three-tier ethic is murky: a large chasm exists between what rises only "slightly" above a basic need and what might reasonably be viewed as a "luxury."

Suppose I provide my children a meal that is slightly more costly than the most abstemious entrée available. Would that be permissible under the second tier? Probably, because food is a basic need for both my children and other children. Would funding a typical birthday party for my child qualify? On one hand, it seems part of making my child feel special, but, on the other hand, whether it amounts to a basic need is contestable. Would not contributing that money to famine relief be a better choice under Rachels' ethic? While buying my child a Mercedes Benz automobile strikes us as an obvious luxury, how should we feel about the choice of buying my child a used Chevrolet versus taking that money and contributing to the basic needs of strangers? In our time and place is ownership of a motor vehicle a luxury? Should parents consider funding their child's college education at a state university a luxury? Or does luxury come into play only when they support their child's decision to go to a pricier, more prestigious private institution? Rachels admits that "Clearly, the line between the trivial and the important can be drawn at different places."[31] But I would submit that where we draw that line is critical for understanding our moral obligations under his ethic. The task is especially important for the vast majority of parents who are in a position to confer few "luxuries" of any sort upon their children.

The strength of Rachels' ethic is that he accepts affectionate differences. On his view, we can regard certain people as special: We can enjoy their company more than that of others; mourn their deaths more than the deaths of strangers; revel in their happiness and successes in a way in which we do not rejoice in those of others; spend more time with those whom we see as special and care for them in circumstances and in ways in which we would not look after others. In short, Rachels' ethic distances itself from a radical equality of allocation of emotional and spiritual resources. As a result, Rachels' version of impartialism can accommodate the type of personal relations many of us cherish.

Still, an issue arises as to the relationship of intimacy, in the sense of one's emotional and spiritual allocations, and the distribution of one's material and service goods. That is, while it may be true that Rachels' ethic allows us to see certain people as special, mourn their loss more than those of others, and rejoice in their happiness, can we also distribute material goods and provide aid in sufficient measure to our intimates than to others? Surely, unlike Godwin, Rachels would permit us to rescue the chambermaid who is our mother and not the archbishop; after all, the choice is between equal basic goods. But what if my choice is this: if I save my mother she will survive as she was prior to the incident, but the archbishop will perish; if I save the archbishop he will survive as he was prior to the incident, and my mother will struggle to safety, survive, but remain in a predominately vegetative state until she perishes 20 years later? The cases no longer involve exactly equal needs. Is saving my mother a "luxury" as she will not die in either case? Should I save the archbishop, who is a stranger, but who will otherwise die?

The key here is to unravel the connection between acting, on emotional and spiritual levels, like someone is your intimate friend and thus special, and often remaining impartial when allocating paramount material and service goods. Is it plausible to act as if someone is your friend, to tell that person that you are friends, yet at the moment of need toggle to a default moral position of impartiality where equal basic needs are not involved? If adherents to Rachels' ethic must embody a moral schizophrenia toward their family and friends then the general criticism that impartialists cannot truly integrate a coherent understanding of personal relations may persist. That is why drawing the lines among (a) equal basic needs, (b) slight additional benefit to intimates, and (c) luxuries is so crucial.

Singer seems unconcerned about emotional attachments. At its most uncompromising his argument derives its conclusion from impartially considering interests and needs wherever they may exist and to whomever they may belong. For Singer, the moral point of view requires the principle of equal consideration of interests: we must give equal weight in our moral deliberations to the like interests of all those affected by our actions. An interest is an interest, whoever's interest it may be. The principle of equal consideration does not depend on a belief in factual equality, the belief that all people of all interest-bearers are actually equal in relevant physical and mental respects. Instead, the principle depends on the conviction that the most important interests, such as the interests in avoiding unnecessary pain, in developing one's talents, in fulfilling basic needs, in enjoying personal relationships, and in being free to pursue projects, are not affected by factual inequalities. Thus, the moral point of view requires that my own interests cannot, simply because they are my interests, count more than the interest of anyone else. In this fashion, moral reasons are universal—they rise above our own likes and dislikes and ascend to the standpoint of the impartial spectator or ideal observer—which elevates them from the merely relative or subjective.

From the application of the principle of equal consideration, he derives his philosophically preferred position: the standard of marginal utility—relinquish your material holdings to fulfill the basic needs of others up to the point where further donations would render you and yours to the same level of destitution that you seek to ease. His two later renderings—give to the point where you are not thereby sacrificing something morally significant and the 10% solution—are made only in deference to the difficulty of persuading people in a thoroughly partialist world to accept a stronger obligation to help those in need than they presently recognize.

Singer's standard of marginal utility does not reflect our biological inclinations, which decidedly favor partialism. Can we retain deeply felt love-bonds, but mete out our resources and service goods impartially? Does a type of moral schizophrenia result that undermines personal integrity? Does Singer mistakenly privilege only the cosmic perspective, that of the ideal observer—and thereby betray Sidgwick's "Common Sense" that the personal perspective should not be marginalized?

Of course, Singer retreats from the standard of marginal utility for practical reasons, some of which may be reflected in the rhetorical questions I have just posed. But I would argue that those questions do not merely reflect *practical* difficulties in implementing the standard of marginal utility, but cut to the very core of its *philosophical* acceptability. In that vein, regarding my time, effort, and material holdings as public resources reneges on my self-conception as an individual. Much of life can be viewed as a negotiation between our need for robust individuality and our competing need for intimate community. Each yearning offers great reward, but, if amplified, morphs into great disappointment. Thus, my yearning for robust individuality nurtures a feeling of specialness and uniqueness, underwritten by autonomy and freedom; but if I inflate my sense of individuality I may unwittingly invite estrangement, alienation, and hostile isolation. Meanwhile, my yearning for intimate community attaches me to projects, interests, and purposes that widen my subjectivity and connect me to larger concerns, thereby fulfilling my need to share my life and cooperate closely with others; but if I inflate my sense of community I may unwittingly suffocate my individuality, retreat too broadly from autonomy and freedom, and reduce myself to a pathetic drone in the social hive. Singer's standard of marginal utility may well be viewed as distorting the dimension of community to dangerous caricature. If so, a critic might well conclude that a healthy dose of individualism and the personal perspective is required to balance communal obligations and to produce a salutary morality. When the cosmic perspective reigns supreme, we are acting as impersonal spectators or detached deities, not as human beings.

Moreover, the standard of marginal utility jeopardizes the principle of personal desert. Typically, we accept that people deserve the holdings that they have justifiably earned through their labors. Some of these holdings, the ranting of libertarians to the contrary notwithstanding, are properly relinquished, usually through taxation, to enterprises facilitating the common good. But, if in the name of morality, the demands on our sacrifices are pushed to the standard of marginal utility then the principle of desert is under siege. To say that I initially deserve my holdings, but I must, morally, use them to fulfill communal needs up to the point of marginal utility renders my initial claim vacuous. Why not simply appoint a Marquis of Morality who removes the requisite amount from my holdings straightaway? In which case, the notion of initially deserving my holdings evaporates in the name of full disclosure. Of course that would be coercive and involve an identifiable third party, whereas Singer's principle is designed to convince right-thinking people to disgorge their holdings voluntarily. But that seems a minor detail for those antecedently committed to the alleged moral point of view. The acceptance of the standard of marginal utility produces the same effect as would the hypothetical Marquis of Morality. Once a well-intentioned agent voluntarily accepts Singer's standard of marginal utility, he or she is committed to the same results as a person who voluntarily remains in a land ruled by the Marquis of Morality. In both cases, the principle of desert struggles for its existence on life-support. The call "from each according to ability, to each according to need," may resonant in a communist paradise of material abundance, but it rings a sour note under the typical conditions of economic scarcity. Paradoxically, the standard of marginal utility and the Marxist slogan of economic distribution are most convincing under the conditions where they are least needed.

Finally, Singer's methodology is subject to several objections. First, he may be guilty of wrongful reductionism when he derives his concrete moral conclusions from only a few moral principles and observations. Just as libertarians can conclude smugly that all economic redistribution and taxation is theft because they operate only from the moral discourse of negative rights and duties, Singer can conclude that massive redistribution is morally required because he employs only the discourse of equality of interests. Both positions ignore a host of other morally relevant considerations that might alter their conclusions. Second, Singer's analogy between saving a victim in a pond and contributing to famine relief is problematic in that the number of destitute people who are starving is enormous, while the number of people we encounter drowning in ponds whom we could rescue is probably zero or at most a few. If we encountered or knew of countless drowning victims whom we could save—if their number was comparable to the amount of people presently starving—our intuitions about what we owe to such victims might well change. At some point, very early I would think, we would conclude that we had given or risked enough and that it was time for others to assume their fair share of the burden.

But why spend time trying to whipsaw the standard of marginal utility when Singer retreats from that demand and offers two more reasonable alternatives: giving to the point where we are not thereby sacrificing something morally significant and the 10% solution? First, Singer continues to cling to the standard of marginal utility as his philosophically preferred position. His later modifications are only pragmatic concessions. Second, and more important, the standard of marginal utility and the approach of general benevolence may well best reflect Jesus' understanding of the love commandment as interpreted by the parable of the Good Samaritan.

Jesus privileges the cosmic perspective. Of course, his ideal observer is God. Jesus is unwilling to pay homage to Sidgwick's "Common Sense" and acceptance of the personal perspective as a critical factor in drawing moral conclusions. Moreover, living in a culture and at a time when luxuries were fewer and less splendid than today, Jesus is concerned almost exclusively with matters of the soul. Whether we understand the "Kingdom of God" to mean eternal bliss in the hereafter or the imminent reign of the divine on earth or a state of mind attainable in the present, Jesus advocates that we prefigure the Kingdom of God in our intentions and actions. Whether we conclude that the historical Jesus was precisely as he is depicted in the canonical scriptures or that he was an apocalyptic prophet or a Middle Eastern Cynic philosopher does not alter that message. Whether Jesus was only talking about short-term moral behavior because he was convinced that the reign of the divine on earth was imminent or whether his was a long-term Cynic prescription does not change his radical interpretation of the love commandment. Furthermore, Jesus does not subscribe to what we now take to be bedrock family values. Parents, siblings, spouses, children, and friends have minimal importance when compared to the Kingdom of God. He advised his followers to renounce, among other things, their families (Luke 14: 26). Jesus recognized the counterintuitive aspects of his teaching and insisted that his message will divide, not unite, families (Luke 12: 51-53).

Thus, Jesus would reject the justifications of partiality to families that I have lodged. Also, in many Biblical parables (for example, the Parable of the Laborers in The Vineyard) Jesus distances himself from a conventional understanding of the principle of personal desert. Often in such parables, people will be given more than they deserve and others who resent that allocation will be scolded for their hardness of heart. (But in such parables people never receive less than that to which they are entitled. Does that complicate matters?) Finally, and most strikingly, Jesus takes God to be the genuine owner of everything. Thus, when we give to the poor we are not actually relinquishing what we initially deserved through our labors; instead, we are merely redistributing God's holdings in accord with God's law. In effect, by respecting religious and moral law, we are giving back to God what is God's. From such a perspective, Jesus would rule irrelevant virtually everything I have sketched in my brief for conventional moral and political wisdom.

6. Jesus' Enduring Message

Whether we view Jesus' ethic as short-term preparation for the Kingdom of God or a long-term solution to human social interactions, his moral perspectives vary radically from the conventional moral wisdom of his time and of ours. Although they do not rely upon religious appeals, Singer and Rachels offer us ways that are grounded in secular philosophy that permit us to move in the direction but fall short of Jesus' perfectionist teachings. Their efforts can be reasonably understood as crafting a salutary compromise between Jesus' stringent message and the practical realities of our world.

Even if we cannot embody and evince radical egalitarianism, impartiality, and unconditional love, we can certainly be more forgiving, more merciful, and more accepting of others. We can refuse to dismiss the claims of the needy, soften our natural inclinations toward harsh retribution, and appreciate the higher potentials of other human beings (especially strangers and "enemies"). We can move away from the project of creating a citadel of the self, immune from the vicissitudes of the outside world and complacent in its own worth, and cultivate a heightened mutual vulnerability with others and a greater estimation of social action. Even if the loud echoes of perfectionism are heard only by the hero, martyr, or saint, the rest of us can learn much from the dim whispers that resound to us. Perhaps this is the enduring truth in the message of Jesus' perfectionism.

Five

THE PERFECTIONISM OF NIETZSCHE

Under perfectionism, nurturing and refining the properties constitutive of human nature define the good life. Human beings should strive to maximize their higher potentials. Perfectionism need not and should not presuppose that attaining perfection in this regard is possible. Thus, Nietzsche is not a perfectionist in the sense that he believes that human nature is perfectible or that the majority of human beings will maximize their higher potentials or that there is one final goal to which all human beings should aspire or even that human beings can attain a final goal or constitute a finished product; but he is a perfectionist in the more modest sense I have outlined.

Nietzsche's perfectionism is individualistic and aristocratic. As such, he does not intend that his normative message be embraced by everyone. In fact, he speaks only to the few who have the potential to understand fully the tragic nature of life yet affirm life in all its dimensions. The crucial ingredients that define higher human beings, for Nietzsche, are the capability of enduring great suffering and turning it to practical advantage; the impulse to exert high energy and enthusiasm into projects requiring uncommon creativity; and full participation in the ongoing process of personal deconstruction, reimagination, re-creation. For the greatest among us, our paramount artistic project is crafting a grand self.

1. Nietzsche's Vision

Whether or not self-mastery and self-perfection are the sole focus of the will to power, they clearly are the prime concerns of Nietzsche's work. Neither state idolatry nor discredited supernatural images can provide human beings enduring consolations for their unresolvable existential crises. Instead, a new image of human beings is necessary.

Nietzsche's desiderata for higher types includes the ability to marginalize but not eliminate negative and destructive impulses within oneself, and to transfigure them into joyous affirmation of all aspects of life; to understand and celebrate the radical contingency, finitude, and fragility of ourselves, our institutions and the cosmos itself; to regard life itself as fully and merely natural, as embodying no transcendent meaning or value; to harbor little or no resentment toward others or toward the human condition; to confront the world in immediacy and with a sense of vital connection; to refuse to avert one's gaze from a tragic worldview and, instead, to find value not in eventual happiness (based on the accumulation of pleasure and distance from pain) but in the inherent activities and processes themselves.

To strive for perfectionism is to refuse to supplicate oneself before great people of the past but, instead, to accept their implicit challenge to go beyond them; to give style to one's character by transforming one's conflicting internal passions into a disciplined and dynamic unity; to facilitate high culture by sustaining a favorable environment for the rise of great individuals; to strive for excellence through self-overcoming that honors the recurrent flux of the cosmos by refusing to accept a "finished" self as dispositive of personal identity; and to recognize the Sisyphus-like dimension to human existence—release from the tasks described is found only in death. Given the human condition, high energy is more important than a final, fixed goal. The mantra of "challenge, struggle, overcoming, and growth," animating and transfiguring perpetual internal conflict, replaces prayers for redemption to supernatural powers.

The individualism Nietzsche suggests is neither the atomistic individualism of libertarianism nor the humanistic individualism of liberalism. Nietzsche, unlike atomistic individualism, does not see the individual as the fundamental unit of politics or the self as the embodiment of inviolable freedom; instead, he talks about the essential unity of the world of flux, the interrelationships that constitute existence, and the individual as a dynamic multiplicity. There is no stable self or single identity: the "individual's" uniqueness lies in the ordering of his or her internal impulses. Nietzsche, unlike humanistic individualism, does not see human life as inherently sacred or as embodying intrinsic dignity and value; nor does he subscribe to a regime of moral equality or equal consideration.

Nietzsche promotes the individualism of the highest human types while understanding that values are initially established by peoples. The "individuals" of libertarianism and liberalism are themselves a creation of a people, not a metaphysical fact (Z "Prologue," 9; Z I, "On the New Idol"). Lacking intrinsic value, human beings create the value they embody by living experimentally and by nurturing an environment that propagates great people and high culture. It is still "as aesthetic phenomenon that existence and the world are justified" in the sense that the highest artistic creations are great human beings themselves.

To understand, even vaguely, the new human image Nietzsche celebrates, it is important to sketch the roles of laughter, love, pity, and suffering. Laughter is an appropriate response to the inherent absurdity of human existence. It reminds us that we do not inhabit a special place in the universe, that our inclination to take ourselves too seriously is misplaced, that our quest for certitude is futile, that the cosmos is indifferent to our standards and aspirations, that despair is the refuge of passive nihilists, and that when allied with wisdom it offers us possibilities for the robust, active nihilism that constitutes high culture. A tragic worldview should be accompanied by appreciative comedy. To laugh at ourselves spices our affirmation of life.

To laugh at oneself as one would have to laugh in order to laugh *out of the whole truth*—to do that even the best so far lacked sufficient sense for the truth, and the most gifted has too little genius for that. Even laughter may yet have a future. I mean, when the proposition 'the species is everything, *one* is always none' has become part of humanity, and this ultimate liberation and irresponsibility has become accessible to all at all times. Perhaps laughter will then have formed an alliance with wisdom (GS 1; See also, GS 107, 324, 327, 383; BGE 223; Z IV "On the Higher Man," 16-20).

Love is an essential part of passing the test of greatness. Nietzsche tells us that "the spiritualization of sensuality is called *love*" (TI, "Morality as Anti-Nature," 3).To love is to affirm, to affirm is to value, to value is to find meaning. First, one must learn to love oneself: "One must learn to love oneself—thus I teach—with a wholesome and healthy love, so that one can bear to be with oneself" (Z III, "On the Spirit of Gravity," 2). Second, one must love the earth: "There are many good inventions on earth, some useful, some pleasing: for their sake, the earth is to be loved" (Z III, "On Old and New Tablets," 17). Third, one must love life itself: "I fear you [life] near, I love you far; your flight lures me, your seeking cures me: I suffer, but what would I not gladly suffer for you? . . . Who would not love you, you innocent, impatient, wind-swift, child-eyed sinner?" (Z III, "The Other Dancing Song," 1). Fourth, one must love eternity: "Never yet have I found the woman from whom I wanted children, unless it be this woman whom I love: for I love you, O eternity. *For I love you, O eternity!*" (Z III, "The Seven Seals," 1-7). Fifth, one must love others, particularly friends. While Nietzsche disparages the purity of such love—for where there is love there is always self-interest and the will to power, and there is sometimes inadequate self-creation—he appreciates that love can nurture the lovers' quest for perfection: "I teach you not the neighbor, but the friend . . . one must learn to be a sponge if one wants to be loved by hearts that overflow. I teach you the friend in whom the world stands completed . . . in your friend you shall love the overman as your cause" (Z I, "On Love of the Neighbor") and "all great love . . . wants to create the beloved" (Z II, "On the Pitying").

Nietzsche warns of the dangers of sexual love, reiterates his appreciation of friendship, and underscores his view of salutary love as a yearning and struggle for perfection. Sexual love is a lust for power as the lover yearns for unconditional possession of and aspires to become the supreme value of the beloved: "Here and there on earth we may encounter a kind of continuation of love in which this possessive craving of two people for each other gives way to a new desire and lust for possession—a shared thirst for an ideal above them. But who knows such love? Who has experienced it? Its right name is *friendship*" (GS 14; see also GS 334, 363). Salutary love requires hardness and exertion because it focuses on the recurring struggles of mutual self-perfection and self-overcoming.

The will to power is most robust and attains its highest possibilities for facilitating self-mastery and self-actualization in accord with Nietzschean values when it is unfettered by the paralyzing chains of the dominant ideas of societies grounded in egalitarian notions of reason, guilt, and sentiment. Again, the will to power is not fundamentally a will to life, understood as the yearning for self-preservation. Instead, the will to increase power and perfection sometimes requires risking one's life in service of higher values and achievements (BGE 13; GS 349; WP 650-651). Nietzsche is contemptuous of hedonistic ethics that insist that human beings do and should desire pleasure (BGE 228; WP 30; TI, "Maxims and Arrows," 12). Active nihilism includes transvaluing values and going beyond good and evil in allegiance to the normative standard of life's own self-surpassing. To the extent that they are able, each person must affirm his or her own life as a requirement of independence (Z II "On Self-Overcoming:). Within us all is an element of herd mentality, a "dwarf," that must be resisted if we are to fully engage the prescribed Nietzschean process of deconstruction, reimagination, re-creation. To become who you are demands that you recognize and abide by your own inclinations and aversions. One's initial starting position and early socialization often hinder this aspiration (GS 269), while weakness of will—knowing the proper path to self-mastery but taking a different route because it is easier, more convenient, or less arduous—is a major human imperfection (WP 46). Weak human beings pursue less valuable intentions and diminish the value of their goals.

Nietzsche places great value on solitude: "If we are always surrounded by another, the best of courage and goodness in this world is rendered impossible" (D 464) and on "keeping to one's own way" (GS 338). Solitude offers "a distant perspective" that allows us "to think well of things" (D 485). Solitude offers "brightness," "openness," "lighter feet," and "cleanliness" (Z III, "The Return Home"). Within solitude the restraints manufactured by the herd instinct fall away and we are "most beautiful" (D 499). He advises us to "choose the good solitude, the free, playful, light solitude that gives . . . the right to remain good in some sense" (BGE 25). Attaining excellence in isolation is a recurrent Nietzschean theme: if we are too deeply implicated in each other's lives we become officious intermeddlers and hamper each other's striving for greatness: "Live in seclusion so that you *can* live for yourself" (GS 338; see also BGE 44, 61).

In that vein, Nietzsche derides the "morality of pity" which implies that losing one's own way in order to come to the assistance of a neighbor" is virtuous (GS 338). For Nietzsche "the religion of pity" provides an excuse to stray from the hard path of self-actualization that is "remote from the love and gratitude of others." Pity is the enemy of salutary love. Pity reneges on the affirmation of life and the value of *amor fati*: it desires that things were otherwise, refuses to transfigure suffering into spiritual advantage, devalues life, and indulges weakness. Beyond its general complicity in the herd mentality, pity masks its motives: its grounding in feelings of superiority, negative evaluation of its object, and disguised resentments (GM III, 14; BGE 225; D 133-134; GS 13; AC 7). The decadence of pity is the elevation of the sharing of suffering and the marginalization of striving for mutual self-perfection. For Nietzsche, the individual who pities another person trespasses on the subordinate's pride and underscores his shame. The subordinate, if astute, will not respond with gratitude but with resentment at having had his degradation highlighted by the pitying person's alleged charity. In the end, the act of pity causes more suffering than it purports to ease (Z II, "On the Pitying"; BGE 171, 201, 222, 260, 293; GS 118, 271, 338).

Even war, with all of its dangers and sacrifices, attracts numerous people who are subconsciously "dodging their goal" of self-mastery in the context of the three metamorphoses (GS 338). But the will to suppress and dominate others is equally suspicious. The impulse to degrade others either arises from unworthy *ressentiment*, which betrays a lack of self-worth and self-love, or from a self-love that fails to apprehend the implications of its self-knowledge and thus degenerates to an egoism that mistakenly takes its own self-worth as the only human good (GM II, 11).

Nietzsche understands that greatness necessarily involves suffering and the overcoming of grave obstacles (BGE 225, 228). He evaluates peoples, individuals, and cultures by their ability to transform suffering and tragedy to spiritual advantage. We cannot eliminate suffering, but we can use it creatively. Suffering and resistance can stimulate and nourish a robust will to power. By changing our attitude toward suffering from pity to affirmation, we open ourselves to greatness. For Nietzsche, joy and strength trump the "happiness" of the herd, which is too often grounded in the values of last men.

Clearly, Nietzsche's new image of human beings is not projected for or achievable by all. It is an explicitly aristocratic ideal that is pitched only to the few capable of approximating it. Greatness and genius are fragile and vulnerable: they bring about their own destruction but arise stronger than ever. In the end, however, the only way to evaluate Nietzsche's new image of human beings is to live it (UM, "Schopenhauer as Educator," 8).

Accordingly, Nietzsche is not looking for disciples who will examine his work for a specific formula for discovering meaning and value, or those who will contemplate and analyze his thoughts abstractly. Instead, he is seducing and persuading those few human beings who combine a Nietzschean attitude with the potential for transvaluing values through creative action: "one has to compel men to take [philosophy] seriously, that is to say to let it inspire them to action, and I consider every word behind which there does not stand such a challenge to action to have been written in vain" (UM, "Schopenhauer as Educator," 8).

The meaning of life, for Nietzsche, focuses on stylistic movement—graceful dancing, joyful creation, negotiating the processes of a world of flux with panache and vigor—rather than goal achievement. Indeed, there is no ultimate, reachable goal, only development through recurrent personal and institutional deconstruction, reimagination, and re-creation. Our exertion of our wills to power in the face of obstacles, with the knowledge of inherent cosmic meaningless, and with profound immersion in the immediacy of life, reflects and sustains our psychological health.

Overcoming personal and institutional shortcomings and obstacles will permit us to become who we are: radically conditional beings deeply implicated in a world of flux. By affirming life in all its dimensions we joyously embrace life for what it is and regard it (and ourselves) as part of a grand aesthetic epic: "We may assume that we are merely images and artistic projections for the true author, and that we have our highest dignity in our significance as works of art—for it is only as an *aesthetic phenomenon* that existence and the world are eternally *justified* (BT 5; See also, BT 24).

Having detailed all this, Nietzsche, nevertheless, returns to one of his broad themes: readers cannot merely adopt his views and proclaim themselves his disciples: "When I imagine a perfect reader, he always turns into a monster of courage and curiosity; moreover, supple, cunning, cautious; a born adventurer and discoverer." (EH, "Why I Write Such Good Books," 3). Jesus advises his disciples: "whoever denies me before men, I also will deny before my Father who is in heaven" (Matt. 10: 33) and "he who does not take his cross and follow me is not worthy of me. He who finds his life will lose it, and he who loses his life for my sake will find it" (Matt. 10: 38-39). In contrast, Nietzsche repudiates the Christian notion of discipleship: we cannot merely follow a redeemer and overman because no such paragon has emerged. Instead, we should strive to go beyond even our best teachers and human exemplars. Whereas Jesus announces, "I am the way, and the truth, and the life; no one comes to the Father, but by me" (John 14: 6), Nietzsche's Zarathustra insists, "'This—is now *my* way—where is yours?' Thus did I answer those who asked me 'the way.' For *The* way—it does not exist!" (Z III, "On The Spirit of Gravity," 2). Nietzsche's epistemological perspectivism, as always, is incompatible with universal prescriptions grounded in the will of a transcendent source.

Thus, to follow Nietzsche in his broad themes is to reject servile parroting of Nietzsche's specific conclusions: compliant imitation honors neither teacher nor student. Instead, students must demonstrate their loyalty by overcoming, through joyous exertion of their wills to power, the teacher himself. Like all great instructors, Nietzsche understands that his most glorious task is to guide students on the art of teaching themselves, thus making the teacher obsolete.

One repays a teacher badly if one always remains nothing but a pupil . . . You are my believers—but what matter all believers? You had not yet sought yourselves: and you found me. Thus do all believers; therefore all faith amounts to so little. Now I bid you lose me and find yourselves; and only when you have all denied me will I return to you (Z I, "On the Gift-Giving Virtue," 3; See also, EH "Preface," 4).

2. Aristocratic Privilege

Karl Marx argued that human species-being is best fulfilled through social production. Human beings are productive in that we transform nature through creative labor and we are social in that our highest productivity is accomplished co-operatively under unalienating conditions. In contrast, Nietzsche stresses the productive dimension of human fulfillment: we are most worthy when our wills are most powerful and aligned with the appropriate values. Although Nietzsche praises high creativity and self-mastery, he does not highlight the social dimension of human productivity. As always, his is an explicitly aristocratic ethic that celebrates the rank order of human beings. Nietzsche unsqueamishly extols an aristocratic class that would "use the great mass of people as their tools" (WP 660; BGE 257). The goal of his imagined aristocratic society is to advance of the interests and perfections of the most outstanding individuals; he is unconcerned about the sum or average perfection of the mass of people. For Nietzsche factual differences among people have normative implications: sharing social resources equally will stymie the possibilities of the potentially greatest among us; nurturing an egalitarian mindset will reduce culture to its lowest common denominator. A person's greatness flows from his "range and multiplicity, in his wholeness in manifoldness" (BGE 212).

How might Nietzsche quantify his perfectionism? He instructs us that "Many die too late and a few die too early . . . Die at the right time . . . He who has a goal and an heir will want death at the right time for his goal and heir" (Z I, "On Free Death"). The rest of the passage supports the view that for Nietzsche "goal for each life is the greatest average perfection per day or year lived and its overriding goal the greatest lifetime value in history."[1] On this rendering, a life that extends beyond the higher ranges of a person's productivity jeopardizes his or her overall average perfection. Quality living is always preferred to quantity of life on this view. This is consistent with Nietzsche's conviction that the last man, like the flea beetle, lives the longest, and higher human types are more likely to blaze the spectacular but briefer paths of shooting stars. A person of Nietzschean higher rank who continues to live although he can no longer advance his creative goals is lowering the overall quality of his life. Thus, judged by Nietzschean criteria, Nietzsche's final 11 years of biological life, when he was catatonic and cared for by his mother and sister, decreased the overall value of his biographical life.

The simplest and most common objection to an averaging approach[2] to quantifying perfectionism can be summarized thusly: Suppose a person has lived a thoroughly productive life for, say, 50 years when judged by Nietzschean criteria. Let's stipulate that her average perfection is 90 units per year over that period (where perfection as such is scored as 100 units). She can live, say, 20 more years but her average perfection over that period will be only 60 units per year. Under an averaging approach to quantifying perfection she would be "dying at the right time" and she should thereby prefer to die at age 50: her overall average score would be 90 per year, whereas if she died at age 70 her overall average score would be just over 81 per year. But surely this is wrong. Our hypothetical person's overall total of perfection would be much higher should she live the additional 20 somewhat less productive years. Specifically, if she dies at age 50, her overall total (not average per year) of perfection would be 4500 units. Should she die at age 70, her overall total of perfection would be 5700 units. How can adding 20 years of more value to a life make that life worse? In Nietzsche's own case—where his final 11 years of biological life added virtually nothing to the overall total of perfection and detracted significantly from his average perfection per year, his averaging approach to perfection resonates. But that his averaging approach to perfection is persuasive in the hypothetical case is far from clear.

The averaging approach must insist that by continuing to live and falling below one's own prior achievements and standards one's overall life is made worse. On this view, the value of a life depends on its trajectory and the same extraordinary creative efforts if followed by a lengthy decline diminish the life when compared to death at the zenith of production. This gives credence to the snarky comment attributed to a Hollywood agent at the tragic death of James Dean (or was it Elvis Presley?): "Good career move." The presumption was that Dean (or Presley) had died at his career peak and had he lived decades longer his professional luster would have been dulled.

My view is that the averaging approach to perfectionism is most persuasive where the decline phase of a life is steepest. Thus, when applied to Nietzsche's own life, to say that he would have been better off had he died in 1889, at the moment of his incapacitation, instead of 1900 is reasonable. The averaging approach would also be persuasive where the decline phase of a life is less steep than that afflicting Nietzsche but still significant.

In cases, such as my hypothetical, the averaging approach to perfectionism is far less compelling. To conclude that living 70 years at an average of just over 81 units of perfection a year and an overall total of 5700 units is preferable to living 50 years at an average of 90 units of perfection a year and an overall total of 4500 units is reasonable. This conclusion becomes even clearer when we understand one of the limits of Nietzschean perfectionism: it defines the pursuit of perfection only or primarily in terms of individual production and individual self-realization. But even where, as in my hypothetical, a person's final 20 years are less productive and less self-actualizing they can embody other crucial values, particularly those glistening with communal dimensions. For example, living an additional two decades and watching one's grandchildren grow and flourish may have little or nothing to do with the grandparent's creative productivity or even their self-actualization but it may bestow valuable gratifications. The same can be said about growing old with one's spouse and a host of other experiences that are available to us only in the later years of life. Nietzsche's emphasis on productivity as the measure of perfection and his seeming indifference to social aspects of human fulfillment spawns suspicious implications.

Nietzsche's version of perfectionism becomes ever less compelling when we add what I will call his "principle of nobility": each person's overriding goal, in most cases, should not be his or her *own* greatest average per year perfectionist score, but the greatest average per year perfectionist score of the *greatest individual or few greatest individuals* in society. That is, my goal, as a person who cannot plausibly argue that he is a higher human type from a Nietzschean perspective (at best, I am only a member of the "scholarly oxen" class) should be expending my time, effort, and resources to advance the interests and perfectionist quest of the greatest exemplars in my society: "Mankind must work continually to produce individual great human beings—this and nothing else is its task . . . How can your life, the individual life, retain the highest value? . . . only by your living for the good of the rarest and most valuable specimens" (UM, "Schopenhauer as Educator, 6; see also, BGE 126, 199, 265, GS 23) and "The essential characteristic of a good and healthy aristocracy . . . [is] that it accepts with a good conscience the sacrifice of untold human beings who, *for its sake,* must be reduced and lowered to incomplete human beings, to slaves, to instruments" (BGE 258). In sum, Nietzsche's perfectionism instructs the vast majority of us to devote ourselves only to nurturing the excellences of the greatest exemplars in our society and empowers the greatest exemplars to embrace our sacrifices and use our services with a good conscience.

The principle of nobility, the crux of Nietzschean aristocratism, is Nietzsche's ballast for his averaging approach to perfectionism, which prefers the greatest average perfection per year of a person with the overall goal being the greatest average lifetime value in history. An individual's value—what is to be averaged—is determined, in rare cases, by his or her approximation to the highest human exemplars or, more commonly, by his or her contribution to the production of the highest human exemplars. Nietzsche recognizes that insofar as all human beings embody the will to power, and power is the standard of excellence, all human beings have some value. [3] Even the most decadent, passive nihilists exhibit power and value in muted form and meager degree. But the principle of nobility grades the quantity and quality of value by aristocratic criteria.

The principle of nobility repels modern readers because it recognizes that the masses have value (beyond minimum species worth) only insofar as they serve a few "great" people who in turn care about the masses only to the extent that the masses can serve them. Even if you weaken the force of the principle of nobility by adding intermediate principles that recognize a hierarchy of graded degrees of excellence, the principle is still noxious. The intermediate principles would give more reason to care for the "non-great" to the degree, however slight, to which they approach greatness, but would still not satisfy basic egalitarian inclinations. The principle of nobility celebrates accomplishments and creative greatness by severing them from the lives that sustain them. Nietzsche, again, ignores concrete human beings and wrongly amplifies artistic, philosophical, musical, scientific, and military creation in the abstract. He would willingly sacrifice human lives for great works.

The principle of nobility thereby obscures the suffering of numerous human beings by glorifying the cultural artifacts generated by a few. Nietzsche's seemingly fatuous aristocratism and reptilian indifference to the lives of the masses are the low point of his work. All human beings, mediocre or potentially great, need a deep sense of purpose in their lives. Nietzsche would have us believe that such purpose should center on becoming great or serving those who can become great, where "greatness" translates to the creation of cultural artifacts and a vague type of self-mastery. Nietzsche may well be charged with focusing excessively on the self to the exclusion of real intimacy and community. We must find meaning, one would suppose, outside the self and beyond cultural creations. We need communal involvements in causes greater than nurturing cultural superstars. Would Nietzsche have us believe that Mother Teresa's life—at least the part spent ministering to the poor and diseased — was in vain? Is she only the queen of the herd? Does she merely waste time resuscitating the replaceable?

Nietzsche too easily identifies the masses with fungibility, as if all the nongreat are akin to sparrows whose lives are indistinguishable. But, contrary to Nietzsche, greatness is not found only in art, philosophy, music, and science. Greatness is often embodied by those whose lives are among the simplest and who lack public renown. Such greatness is not focused on Nietzschean creativity or the trendy donning and discarding of personal masks. Instead, it is centered on love, caring, making the world a better place by deeply influencing those around you in uniquely positive ways, speaking to our higher instincts rather than obsessing about power and domination. Our choices are not simply herd conformity or Nietzschean greatness.

Of course, Nietzsche might sneer and claim that I have described only another manifestation of power. And given the broadness of his use of the term, Nietzsche could make a case. But, even under his background assumptions, there are different forms of power embodying different values. Critics could still insist that the "power" described above is psychologically and, yes, morally preferable to the manifestations honored by the principle of nobility.

Greatness comes in more forms than Nietzsche suggests. As reflective people grow, they come to realize that there were heroes all around them. Men and women of strength, honor, and courage who are capable of stunning self-sacrifice because they perceived themselves as part of a wider subjectivity, as a link in a generational chain that often stretches from the old country to the new. They are the giants upon whose shoulders you and I stood. Heroes do not always get their names in the newspapers; they do not always create great art, music, philosophy, or science. While Nietzsche rants and raves about the herd, and self-servingly positions himself above it, many of us will retain our faith in the immediacy of flesh-and-blood and in redeeming intimacy.

The Nietzschean response is predictable: Not all human beings are equal. Only a few can invent their own lives. The vast majority simply follow established societal teachings and habits. The few are better human beings than the many. The best human exemplars are indifferent to the valuations of the masses. The many are last men: they aspire to material comfort and indolence; they do not even "strut and fret their hour upon the stage" but, instead, somnambulate through life leaving no mark other than promulgating more of their kind. Nietzsche measures people by non-moral criteria: by their excellences, personal achievements, intelligence, and creative powers. He centers human uniqueness on creativity. The greatest human beings relish the immediacy of life, neither dwelling on the past nor overly anticipating the future. For Nietzsche, vengeance and *ressentiment* cannot issue from robust self-love and love of life. Only insecurity, self-doubt, and the repressed hostility of inferior for superiors generate vengeance and resentment.

The Nietzschean response is inadequate. Excellences, personal achievements, intelligence, and creative powers can all be exemplified by common people. We are not all either herd animals or cultural geniuses. Nietzsche identifies, as do most philosophers, excellence too closely with intellectual activity. Apart from his romantic worship of military battle, he sees genius only in art, music, philosophy, and science. He also oscillates between valuing creativity as such and valuing creativity in terms of its social effects. The former interpretation values creativity independently of effects on others; for example, under this view *Thus Spoke Zarathustra* is a wonderful creation regardless of whether anyone reads it other than its author. The latter interpretation values the book because of its cultural impact, hopefully, its role in nurturing highly creative people.

While we should not easily disparage the life of the interior, it is woefully insufficient for engaging the world. Private fulfillment is less purposeful than public involvement that requires passionate identification with particular communities. Such activity, horror of horrors, means mingling with the herd. Human beings have a need for belonging and much fear, insecurity, selfishness, and anxiety arise from the frustration of that need. This need does not flow from a herd instinct, at least not in a pejorative sense, but is a prerequisite for a highly textured and meaningful life. The lack of a robust sense of belonging undermines the development of the self.

Another aspect of Nietzsche's evaluations of human beings, a corollary to the principle of nobility, may also be troubling. Suppose that a person, Rizzo, through uncommon effort, will, and determination actualizes most of her higher human capabilities. The final product is someone who is only average or perhaps a smidgen above average when judged by Nietzschean vectors of creativity, zest for adventure, high artistic production, and the like. Rizzo has (nearly) maximized her potentials given her innate talents, initial starting position, and early socialization. For the sake of comparison, let's stipulate that she has attained, say, 90% of her capabilities. She has become (nearly) all that she could possibly be. Her neighbor, Leonardo, exerts less effort, will, and determination; he fails to actualize many of his higher human capabilities. But Leonardo enjoyed distinct advantages over Rizzo in terms of innate talents, initial starting position, and early socialization. As a result, although he attains, say, only 67% of his capabilities, Leonardo, when judged by Nietzschean vectors is clearly well above average in terms of final product. Leonardo has become only about two-thirds of what he could possibly be, but this still places him ahead of Rizzo when judged in terms of creativity, zest for adventure, high artistic production, and the like.

The question for Nietzsche is this: Who is the higher human type—the "average" person who became such by nearly maximizing her potentials or the "well above average" person who was blessed with much greater innate talents but developed only two-thirds of his potentials? The case for Rizzo is clear: she accomplished nearly everything she could possibly attain given her nature and environment; she became virtually all she could be; what more can we ask of a human being? The case for Leonardo lies in final product: he is simply more accomplished than Rizzo; perhaps Rizzo deserves a round of applause—in the same way that a donkey who gave its all in a thoroughbred race only to lose by three-quarters of mile merits a cheer for attaining its personal best time—but Rizzo's best simply pales before Leonardo's superior development even if we can reasonably claim that Leonardo underachieved (that he failed to become what he might and should have become given his innate talents).

The choice is between measuring greatness by (a) achieving one's maximum potential (the Rizzo standard) or by (b) one's overall development as such (the Leonardo standard). Nietzsche, it would seem, would be far more likely to embrace the Leonardo standard. In the instant case, he would surely conclude that neither Rizzo nor Leonardo is a higher human type—both fall short of Nietzsche's highest aspirations. But when ordering the rank of human beings, Nietzsche seems to invoke the Leonardo standard. For Nietzsche, becoming all that one could possibly become is woefully insufficient for greatness in those cases where innate talents are ordinary. The higher human types are such by their exceptional attainments—as judged by Nietzschean vectors. Probably the greatest among us must have Leonardo's talents and gifts combined with Rizzo's drive and diligence, but surely to qualify as a higher human type invoking the Rizzo standard is insufficient in Nietzsche's view.

Repelled by the principle of nobility and, perhaps, by its corollary, egalitarians might be tempted to disparage Nietzsche's entire philosophical outlook from the vantage point of immanent critique. Thus, we might conclude that Nietzsche's self-serving celebration of hierarchy and division is merely his psychological defense against loneliness, isolation, and alienation. His obsession with genealogy leads him to beliefs bordering on predestination, genetic determination, and overly simple categorization of human beings. The master of multiplicity is too often seduced by pedestrian reductionism, which occurs when he attributes one cause or origin to complex, dissimilar phenomena. His self-obsession, psychological defense mechanisms, and embarrassing self-promotions reveal that the university professor, the mere academic, never overcame his origins. Nietzsche's irritating misogyny, while perhaps explainable by his upbringing, underscores his emotional separateness. That he wrote a stirring life while living a sad one highlights the desperation of his cry "*amor fati*!" His quest for protean transcendence masks his personal dissatisfaction and lingering need for redemption. The strident proclaimer of the death of God still needed idols, despite his vitriol to the contrary. His constant screams for attention, compulsive need to provoke, and adolescent daydreams of glory betrayed a life and a person that were easily ignored. Nietzsche's recurrent illnesses, eventual insanity, and shameful expropriation by his sister and the Nazis were a tragic-ironic metaphor of his view of life.

Such judgments bear currency, but should not be taken as the final verdict on Nietzsche and his work. Perhaps by jettisoning the principle of nobility we can salvage Nietzsche's general trajectory about the quest for human perfection. Much of what Nietzsche says resonates with modern readers. For example, Nietzsche insists that we understand fully the tragic dimensions of life and accept the challenges of active nihilism. He unmasks the conceits and disguises of dominant society, and forces us to confront the "truth." He casts suspicion where smug assurance had reigned, and reminds us that striving toward worthwhile goals is accompanied by meaningful and valuable hardship. Nietzsche counsels love, laughter, and joy where resentment, mendacity, and suffering had prevailed. He seeks disciples among the strong, hard, courageous, and creative, and then he implores them to go beyond his teaching. He insists that the cosmos is inherently meaningless, but emphasizes that the imposition of value and meaning on our world is part of the human quest.

Nietzsche shares insights on the most important human themes: the inescapability of inner conflict; the perspectival nature of truth; the links between psychological types of human beings and their embrace of different truth claims; and the need to perceive reality from multiple perspectives. He connects writing and life; stresses the inability of language to capture life's complexities and fluidity; denies absolutism; and underscores the need to impose order and meaning on the world of Becoming. Nietzsche celebrates the salutary rhythms of deconstruction, reimagination, and re-creation; the need to recognize and welcome the tragedy and contingency that constitute life; the importance of replacing the task of objectively disproving truth claims with the project of casting suspicion upon their origins and the psychology of those who embrace them; the value of the project of self-overcoming, which includes subjecting one's own theoretical and practical commitments to the strictest scrutiny; and the call to luxuriate in the immediacy of life. As such, Nietzsche rejoices in life despite suffering and obstacles that would destroy lesser men. He vivifies our imagination and demands that philosophy relate to life. Reading Nietzsche is a refreshing change from being students of those who teach philosophy merely as an academic discipline and not as a way to live. These considerations, too, must be factored into any overall assessment of Nietzsche and his writings.

3. A Summary of the Perfectionism of Nietzsche

Nietzsche's perfectionism is grounded in his highest value, *amor fati*, an unconditional love of life. The mark of the good human life is a merited self-pride which arises from the accurate conclusion that you have succeeded in fulfilling the Nietzschean vectors of value: you have endured great suffering and turned it to practical advantage; you have exerted high energy and enthusiasm into projects requiring uncommon creativity; and fully participated in the ongoing process of personal deconstruction, reimagination, re-creation. As such, you have given style to your character; forged unity out of the multiplicity of drives you embody; and learned to love yourself, this world, life, eternity, and others of your rank. You have avoided the pitfalls of pity—being drawn back into the mindset of the herd and away from the hard path of self-realization—and have reveled in the joys of solitude. You have understood that factual differences among human beings bear normative implications.

For Nietzsche, to those to whom much is bestowed—in terms of innate talents, initial starting position, and early socialization—much more is owed. The most gifted among us supposedly justify our species; it is their interests and self-realization that the rest of us should serve. To whom we owe moral duties and the amount we owe is not determined by the needs of others nor by the imperatives of unconditional love; instead, the respective places we occupy in the rank order of human greatness determines who owes moral duties to whom and the amount that is owed. Paradoxically, we owe more to those with the least needs but with the greatest capabilities of high creativity. Unless we are of the same rank, the least among us have the faintest claim to our aid.

Nietzsche is unimpressed with material accumulation, but enthralled with the products of high creativity. Much risk, suffering, sacrifice, and effort should be expended in service to high creativity. Our greatest artistic project is our ongoing sculpting of our selves. Critical to this project is participation in the production of grand culture. What is most common is least valuable. Nietzsche's radical aristocracy is grounded less in cooperative social endeavors and more in the productive capabilities of the glorious individual. Nietzsche derides the call for unconditional human love of others and service to those in need as the hallmarks of a person who instinctively despises this world and is hypersensitive to pain.

Much of Nietzsche's perfectionism is repugnant: the unabashed aristocratism; the principle of nobility; his averaging approach to measuring perfection and its corollary, what I have called the "Leonardo standard"; his failure to appreciate the marks of greatness of common people and his infatuation with the products of high culture and their creators; and the normative implications he derives from the existence of factual differences among human beings.

But a revised Nietzschean, one that discards the repellant aspects of his philosophy, can be crafted from his general philosophical themes. His image of the grand striver can be refashioned in a more inclusion manner, one which we allow more of us to approach what I have called the "Rizzo standard:" actualizing and maximizing our higher human capabilities, whatever they may be. In so doing, more of us may be able to attain the values of individualism but within the context of robust community. Some important contemporary philosophy, influenced but going beyond Nietzsche, points in that direction.

4. The Perfectionism of Nietzsche and Contemporary Philosophy

The romantic-heroic tradition of the nineteenth century, which influenced Nietzsche who in turn deepened its image, furnishes the ideal of the grand striver. The themes of overcoming obstacles, engaging in epic struggles, continuously pursuing new goals, relishing recurrent novelty, and transcending existing patterns define the grand striver. Along with Nietzsche, contemporary philosophers Roberto Unger and Robert Nozick have been greatly influenced by this ideal.

Unger claims that "problem of contextuality" is part of the human condition.[4] We experience ambivalent feelings of being necessarily embedded in a thick cultural and social context which seemingly defines the limits of the possible and impossible, yet we recognize that we are able to transcend cultural contexts and limits as we experience modes of thought and being that cannot be translated adequately by the logic and language of current norms. According to Unger, the paramount animating drive of human passion is to transcend the cultural contexts that are provided by the established forms of personal relations, intellectual inquiry, and social arrangements.

Unger is concerned with our existential dilemma, which manifests itself as simultaneous yearning and fear when in the presence of others. The passions are centered around the duality of our undeniable need for others and our felt danger at their approach. What Unger calls our "existential dilemma," I have earlier identified as the individual-community continuum: our oscillation during our lives between the quest to define a robust self and our yearning to fulfill our need for intimacy with others. Unger suggests that in order to advance self-understanding and mediate our existential dilemma, we must open ourselves to a full life of personal encounter, thereby giving full expression to our need while accepting the accompanying danger.

Unger accepts a thin theory of human nature: there is only one noncontingent fact of human nature, contingency itself. That is, the capability of human personality to transcend the limits of the culturally determined possible and impossible is the only noncontingent fact of human nature. For Unger we are most truly ourselves when engaging in activity in which we deny the false necessities generated by the structures of social life. For it is during such activity that we celebrate the possibilities of our infinite personalities. Implicitly acknowledging the contentlessness of the contingency claim, Unger seeks a normative conception of human personality which fuses description and prescription, but does not fall prey to skepticism or abject relativism.

According to Unger, four main images of personality are reflected in literature and philosophy: the heroic ethic, fusion with an impersonal absolute, Confucianism, and the Christian-Romantic ideal.

1. The *heroic ethic* attracts those who combine devotion to collective tasks with skepticism about the possibility of moral insight. Assuming a task at the margins of society and often in violation of some of its norms, the hero engages in limit-breaking activity. Heroes assign unconditional value to a conditional task; they exalt pride at the expense of faith; and disengage themselves from ordinary concerns. Heroes are willing to sacrifice themselves if required by the goals they serve. They embody overabundant energy and aggressive enthusiasm as they defy obstacles. The heroic ethic is the image of personality dearest to Nietzsche's heart.

2. *Fusion with an impersonal absolute* accepts a contrast between our illusory phenomenal world, where the principle of individuation holds sway, and the plane of absolute reality, where distinctions between individuals and things vanish. Seen most clearly in Hinduism and Buddhism, adherents take either the path of the recluse or accept their social role while remaining aloof from it. In either case, this world is seen as pervaded by suffering and inferior to absolute reality.

3. *Confucianism* accepts a particular list of social relations and ordering of the emotions. Viewing people as completely defined by fixed social roles and a particular political order, this vision mistakes a specific system of social order as the solution to conflicting conduct and assertion. Clinging desperately to tradition, this image exudes a strong conservative (*status quo* preserving) bias.

4. The *Christian-Romantic* notion puts personal attachments up for

grabs. This vision acknowledges that the qualities realized in faith, hope, and love override the claims of given social categories and concludes that advances in self-understanding occur as we open ourselves to personal encounter. Christian-Romanticism is beset by a deep ambivalence between a moralistic obsession with fixed rules and a fantasy of the super-individual who defies all obstacles while asserting his will.

Unger argues that if we take these four images and cleanse them of aspects which deny the infinite quality of personality, we will discover that the remaining theoretical ideas converge and give us similar answers to our most important normative questions. The resulting conception of human personality includes the primacy of personal encounter and love, and a commitment to social iconoclasm. Aggrandized mutual vulnerability is a prerequisite for advancing self-understanding, and, according to Unger, we are most empowered and most truly ourselves when we engage in context-transcending activity informed by faith, hope, and love. Unger insists that the concept of infinite personality allows us to avoid relativism, while the phenomenon of convergence offers us a reason to accept a normative conception of human personality that escapes contentlessness.

Unger uses what he takes to be the only noncontingent fact of human personality, its ultimate plasticity, and contends that political and social arrangements, instead of being depicted classically as a set of concrete social institutions defining a fixed and closed structure, should incorporate destabilization mechanisms that undermine existing social arrangements and unsettle hierarchical relations before they firmly solidify into entrenched power. Thus, instead of advancing a particular, substantive political situation, such as socialism, liberalism, or republicanism, toward which all societies should aim, Unger concentrates more on the process and necessity of social change. Unger's goal is to acknowledge the contingency of our institutional and social arrangements and open them to transformation. His project can be viewed as placing a radical framework on the classical method of arriving at normative conclusions from a conception of human nature.

The significance of Unger's work lies in how he links human personality with the image of the grand striver. For Unger, the process of recurrent deconstruction of existing social arrangements, reimagination of new social practices, and re-creation parallels Nietzsche's description of an individual's responsibilities for self-making. Whereas Nietzsche confines the image of the grand striver to the highest human exemplars, Unger sees the image as central to human personality and to moral and political action.

Robert Nozick imagines an experience machine that can give us any experience we desire.[5] Our brains could be stimulated so we would think and feel that we were winning the Nobel Prize, having dinner with our favorite celebrity, breaking Barry Bonds' home-run record, engaging in a torrid love affair with the person of our dreams, or anything else we want to experience. All the while we would be floating in a tank with electrodes attached to our brains. We could, if we wished, plug into the machine for life and program our entire life's experiences. Or we could program some time out of the tank every two years or so to select the experiences for the next period of our lives. While in the tank we will not know we are there. We will be firmly convinced that everything we experience is grounded in reality. Assuming all other logistics could be resolved (for example, a team to monitor the tank, ways to fulfill our nutrition needs, required medical care, arranging the blissful death that must eventually come), would we choose to enter the tank for an extended period?

In an age of developing virtual realities, Nozick's thought experiment is less bizarre than might first seem. He argues that we would reject the experience machine for at least three reasons. First, doing things is more important than having the sensations of doing them. More matters to us than merely how our lives feel from within. Second, we want to become a certain type of person, not simply float in a tank as a bland receptacle of sensations. Third, the experience machine limits us to an artificial environment which prevents actual contact with any deeper reality. The experience machine lives our lives for us instead of helping us live our own life. However sophisticated we imagine the machine, its major function is to remove us from reality and prevent us from making any difference in the world. Nozick introduces the thought experiment of the experience machine for a purpose that Nietzsche would applaud: undermining hedonistic views of the good life. If hedonistic accounts of the good life were compelling then we would rejoice at the possibilities offered by the experience machine—an existence consisting of the maximum cumulative pleasurable sensations; but in fact we would reject extended occupation in the experience machine for the reasons that Nozick offers; therefore, hedonistic accounts of the good life are deficient.

Our rejection of an experience machine that encloses us within a framework of just our own experiences, suggests that connecting with things and values beyond our individual experiences is crucial. Nozick takes meaning in life to involve transcending our limits. The narrow and more restrictive the limits of a life, the less meaningful it is. The more intensely people are involved and the more they transcend their limits, the more meaningful their lives are. For inherently limited human beings finding meaning requires connecting with something that is itself meaningful or valuable. To avoid infinite regress, the chain that grounds meaning must end with something that is either intrinsically meaningful or valuable or Unlimited. Thus to inquire about the meaning of a life is to ask how it is connected to other things.

For Nozick, then, meaning is relational, it concerns our connection with external value or other relational meaning, and it involves transcending our limits, going beyond our own value. Human beings have limited transcendence: as we go beyond our limits to connect with a wider context of value, that value is itself limited. Thus our lives yield limited, finite meaning. Only if an

Unlimited or Absolute exists to ground infinite meaning could our lives be otherwise.

The relationship between value and meaning is primary for Nozick. When discussing value, he begins from an aesthetic-scientific model. A painting has aesthetic value when it successfully integrates great diversity of material into a vivid, striking unity. In science, theories are evaluated by their ability to fashion unity out of diversity. He concludes that something has intrinsic value to the degree it is organically unified: the greater the diversity that gets unified, the greater the organic, intrinsic value. Thus the intrinsic value of something centers on how integrated it is within its own boundaries.

Both value and meaning, then, are important. Value provides the internal dimension of unity, meaning provides the external dimension of transcending limits and making new connections. Nozick is clearly influenced by the image of the grand striver or what Unger calls the heroic ethic: overcoming obstacles, breaking bonds, epic struggle, continuous striving for new goals, and recurrent novelty all belong to the realm of meaning. But he moderates these themes by the equally important image of the unifying creator: diverse materials are ordered, structured, styled, and integrated.

Most important, Nozick prizes the ongoing process of alternating creation and transcendence. Unlike a passive nihilist such as Schopenhauer, Nozick understands keenly that processes can have value and can provide contexts in which meaning flows. The rhythms of the process, ordering diverse material, introducing new material and disaggregating the old, ordering anew, and disrupting the new order by new material, form a continuing cycle combining meaning and value.

Nozick's similarities to Nietzsche and Unger are striking. Nozick takes meaning to involve transcending our limits and connecting to external meaning and value. Nietzsche talks about going beyond ourselves, self-overcoming, and negotiating the processes of a world of flux with panache and vigor, rather than seeking a final goal. Unger cherishes the capacity of human personality to transcend the limits of the culturally determined possible and impossible as the only noncontingent fact of human nature.

Yet all three understand the value of unity. Nozick takes organic unity as the definition of intrinsic value. Nietzsche insists on giving style to one's character and creating order out of multiple, conflicting impulses. Unger understands the necessity of creating larger, temporary social contexts. All three thinkers glorify, in different ways and through different words, the process of human life: there is no ultimate, reachable goal; what remains is only robust development through recurrent personal and institutional deconstruction, reimagination, and re-creation.

Unger calls for social structures that allow the fullest amount of social conflict consistent with his commitment to honor and facilitate the infinite human personality. But his notion of progress seems puzzling. He tells us that, despite our inability to transcend all conditionality, progress is possible as we loosen the limits of conditionality. But if progress means that some conditional forms are less conditional than others, or that some conditional forms are better than others, Unger may be presupposing a standard by which to evaluate conditional forms which itself is not conditional. Alternatively, if progress acknowledges that all forms are equally conditional, a democracy of conditionality, then it is not clear to what progress amounts. Is progress the explicit recognition that our modes of discourse are conditional, and the appreciation of the freedom we exercise when we continually recombine and reimagine contexts? Or is progress the process of recombination and reimagination itself? Finally, that the prescription to accelerate revision follows from the assumption that all forms of social life and all modes of discourse are conditional is unclear. We might well decide that given the fact of conditional forms and modes we should not accept any given structure as ultimate truth; we might well allow a reasoned process of change in our structures and modes; but why choose to accelerate revision? In the absence of evidence indicating that such a change would be an improvement, a higher form of conditionality, a closer approximation to a nonconditional standard, or a realization of freedom, why advocate change for change's sake?

Unger would probably reply that his model is based on a modern view of science. Science progressed from the Euclidean paradigm to another paradigm. The best science is viewed as capable of accelerating self-revision; recognizing and absorbing anomalies and incongruous perceptions; but without destroying itself or repressing the facts it has found. Science might be viewed by Unger as transforming the fact of conditionality into an intellectual advantage and theoretical method.

More fundamentally, progress can be defined in terms of Unger's one unconditional fact of human nature: its ultimate plasticity. Unger acknowledges that the act of context-smashing creates a new context; we are never unencumbered and unsituated. However, we progress as we ascend to looser contextual structures which encourage their own destabilization, thereby giving currency to human personality. We are not engaged in self-defeating rebellion for its own sake, but transform contexts for a purpose: to liberate human personality so that its one objective aspect can flourish. We never discover the Archimedean point which might arrest all future context-smashing; we never create a nontranscendable context which is indisputably superior to its competition; but neither are we trapped by a democracy of conditionality. There is a nonconditional standard by which to evaluate various conditional contexts: the one objective feature of human personality. Some conditional contexts are superior to others based on their flexibility and acceptance of destabilization. The contrast here is between rigid structures that resist attempts at destabilization and flexible structures that facilitate their own transformation. Moreover, Unger tries to document how plasticity has been paramount in military, economic, and social triumphs throughout history.

Accordingly, we should accelerate revision in order to precipitate an understanding of ourselves and as a requirement of worldly success.

Unger might reiterate that the fear of context-smashing is simply another manifestation of the paralyzing effects of the illusion of necessity communicated by mainstream ideology. Instead of accepting the alleged longing of the masses for security as a basic independent fact of human nature, Unger would perceive it as damning evidence that mainstream ideology has been successful in retarding the flourishing of our infinite personalities. Accordingly, we could take the critics' charge as further proof of the need to liberate the masses from the political *status quo*, and not as a demonstration of any presumed inadequacy in Unger's account.

Unger does not advocate relentless deconstruction for its own sake. That would be too much like Sisyphus's eternal task and would lack real purpose. Given that he believes in one objective nonconditional fact of human personality, Unger cannot go all the way and claim that everything is always up for grabs. To do so would court a passive nihilism which he denies. Instead, he provides a structure which is designed to allow the fullest amount of social conflict consistent with his commitment to honor and facilitate the infinite human personality. Once he denies that everything is contingent, Unger must build from what is objective. Unger is not seduced into extolling a condition of permanent indefinition, a ceaseless flux of conflict and transformation. Instead, he acknowledges the need for relatively tranquil periods of stability, time for rest and reflection. He places no faith in communitarian arguments that presuppose citizens share fundamental ends. Acceptance of these arguments too often paralyzes innovation and nurtures crippling austerity.

Still, Unger does not tell us how we are to act but only what it is to act and that we should act. I question whether Unger ultimately overrates the human need for context-smashing activity and underrates the human need for context-preserving activity. These two types of activity correspond to the human needs for adventure and security, and it should be clear that the relative attraction of these needs differs radically among people of varying education, age, gender, socioeconomic class, and aggressiveness. Offering no guarantees and exhilarated by the promise of empowerment, Unger heightens social risks: heroism and tragedy may be inextricably joined. Will "everyday people" be attracted to such a vision? Will the many people who are less politically inclined than Unger truly be empowered by the activity he and other intellectuals cherish? Does Unger demand too much of us when he insists that we risk mutual vulnerability and gamble with our deepest fears? Can human beings achieve much the same benefit with less risk by smashing contexts that are local and personal, and thus less intractable than Unger's grand institutions?

The romantic notion of deconstruction, reimagination, and re-creation stirs our fantasies and ennobles our spirits. But the advice to fashion a sequence of serial selves can foster lack of definition and a hunger for authenticity. The context-smashing self risks a robust sense of identity at the altar of expanded consciousness. Perhaps forging a unity out of multiplicity and self-mastery softens the possible excesses of the notion, but the dangers remain. If we are nothing more than a series of selves, we may not be anything.

Nozick's rendering of organic unity as the standard of value is also troubling. Intuitively, some organic unities need not be valuable at all. What diversities are unified, how they are unified, and for what purposes are independent factors that help determine whether and to what extent an organic unity is valuable. We can imagine, for example, a highly diversified group of people unified tightly under a program of dispensing evil. Thus human attitudes and the activity of evaluation itself affect judgments of value. The structure of something is not the sole, or even most important, criterion of its value.

Seeking a trait common to all valuable things, Nozick seizes on an aesthetic model. But why should we value art for the same features that we value a morally praiseworthy act or a cognitive value? Are morally praiseworthy acts more organically unified than evil acts? Can we judge the respective value of two acts on the basis of their comparative organic unity? Different things are valuable for different reasons and in different contexts. Any unified account of value will be suspect. Even as an aesthetic notion, organic unity does not reign supreme. The minimalist movement in art, for example, explicitly distances itself from forging unities out of multiplicities.

Nozick's understanding of meaning is also contestable. Whether our linking with an Unlimited or Absolute connects us with meaning is unclear. If the question of meaning arises only with limited beings, an Unlimited would be beyond the question. But to rise above the categories of meaning-meaninglessness is not necessarily to be meaningful. To ground human meaning the Unlimited must itself be meaningful. An Unlimited that transcends the categories of meaning and an Unlimited that must be meaningful are not identical.

Brushing this aside, if all human beings are connected to the Unlimited this might suggest that each human life is equally meaningful. This seems extravagantly counterintuitive. Or perhaps human beings must have the proper sort of connection to the Unlimited to acquire meaning. If so, what human action can produce the appropriate connection?

Nozick's sense of limitation is itself limited. He contrasts "limitation" with the "Unlimited" and sometimes ascends to the cosmic perspective of the Ideal Observer. If he had contrasted "limitation" to the "finitely possible" he would have remained firmly in the human perspective. The advantage of the latter strategy lies in pictorial symmetry: viewing human activity from a cosmic perspective ungenerously shrinks our achievements and calls the value of our existence into serious question; instead, I would argue that a humanly meaningful life requires only what is significant from a human perspective.

Nozick undoubtedly has some available responses. The link with the Unlimited is only one possibility he entertains. This possibility, unsurprisingly, raises issues surrounding theism. But Nozick never commits himself to the existence of the Unlimited. Finite human meaning is available as we link to other, finitely meaningful things and to value. His account of meaning does not depend on a theistic commitment.

Against Unger, I doubt whether human nature embodies only one non-contingent fact, contingency itself; whether we are most human only when we are transcending current social arrangements; and whether political structures necessarily govern best that destabilize themselves most.

In general, we should be suspicious when philosophers unveil what they take to be the elements of enduring human nature. Too often, it seems that these thinkers merely peer into their mirrors, discover activities they prefer, and then project those preferences as universal aspects of human beings as such. For example, Plato yearns for internal peace and harmony grounded in contemplation and rational activity. He then argues that these conditions and activities define the healthy human soul which marks the highest human fulfillment. Marx most enjoys creative activity over which he has complete control. He then argues that our species-being, his thin version of human nature, yearns for creative labor in the social context of an unalienating environment. Engaging in such labor translates into the highest human fulfillment. Gramsci most appreciates political activity designed to broaden democratic participation in setting the terms of social existence. He argues that human nature is most fulfilled when we are engaged in creating the ideological hegemony that will define our society. Unger is fondest of context-smashing action that animates institutional transformations that liberate us from the chains of stultifying false necessity. He then argues that the only unconditional aspect of human nature is contingency itself.

The list of philosophers lured into this trap extends far beyond the four examples I have cited. The tendency to universalize one's preferences and anoint them as definitive of enduring human nature is close to irresistible.

Against Nozick, I doubt that organic unity is the independent standard of all value; that meaning is best defined as overcoming obstacles, breaking bonds, and continuous striving, while value is defined as order, structure, and integration; and that the character of value is independent of human attitudes and evaluations.

Nozick argues that meaning is achieved by transcendence to a wider framework. But his principle has no logical stopping point until we aspire to an overarching Absolute that includes all actualities and all possibilities, a framework which cannot be dwarfed by imagining anything more. His strategy is analogous to those who demand permanence as a condition of meaning. Both strategies struggle with the power of the cosmic perspective to dwarf human accomplishments. The permanence principle insists that our accomplishments produce meaning only if they endure. But no human creation endures so human life must be meaningless. Nozick insists that ultimate meaning can only be secured by linking to an overarching framework. But if no such framework exists, then the cosmic perspective, to which we cannot link, can always dwarf our deeds.

However, we should not permit technical difficulties in Unger's and Nozick's accounts to obscure their contributions. Adding twists, turns, and vivid images to some of Nietzsche's account, they provide ways of achieving finite meaning and value in life. They may not give us the only way human beings can find meaningful lives, but this is a glad tiding. Given human diversity in temperament, personality, and embodied value, it would be sad if only one path was available for all.

A question lingers: Is the image of the grand striver, so prized by Nietzsche, Unger, and Nozick, different from Schopenhauer's gloomy eternal rut? Schopenhauer analyzed human experience in dualistic categories. We strive to attain what we lack or have insufficiently. Either we fail to attain our goal or we succeed. If we fail we suffer. If we succeed, momentary pleasure is soon followed by letdown and boredom. So we strive again to attain another goal, and the dreary pendulum continues.

Compare the image of the eternal rut to the image of the grand striver: a recurrent process of constructing, deconstructing, reimagining, and re-creating the self, personal relations, and social arrangements. Granted, Schopenhauer exaggerates the boredom, underplays periods of zestful triumph, and artificially limits the process to discrete desires and goals. But we can still question the point of the process of the grand striving. Is relentless striving merely a sign of discontentment? Is the grand striver merely a chameleon who changes color because of an inadequate sense of self? Is the forced activity of the grand striver merely a way to forget the pain of human life? Is there any difference between the grand striver and the greedy materialist who is never satisfied and who accumulates more and more wealth as an end in itself?

I am convinced numerous differences exist between Schopenhauer's eternal rut and the image of the grand striver. First, the process of the grand striver is committed to progress. The process is not viewed as a pendulum which swings back and forth, occupying the same space repeatedly. The grand striver, if successful, develops and creates. Whether viewed as Nietzsche's self-overcoming to a higher human form, Unger's creation of more flexible social institutions, or Nozick's connection with more meaning and value, the grand striver does not occupy the same space repeatedly. Second, the process of the grand striver, unlike Schopenhauer's endless pendulum, does not seek a final termination of the original goal and does not implicitly embrace permanence as a high value. Third, the grand striver finds deep meaning and value in the process itself as activity, creation, and continuing development flow. Finally, the attitude of the grand striver toward life is enthusiastically positive, while the disciple of Schopenhauer withdraws and tries to simulate union with the Absolute.

While I doubt that the image of the grand striver captures the entire deep truth about human personality and that it shows the only way to a meaningful life, it highlights important insights. Human beings are not static creatures. We flourish most vividly through ongoing creative development. Regardless of the view from afar, the process of this creative development furnishes the meaning of our lives. Even if the cosmos is inherently meaningless, pessimism need not result.

The image of grand striver, heroic and romantic, is appealing. Yet, taken to an extreme, it invites charges that it is adolescent and fatuous. For those of us close enough to the immigrant experience, those of us whose parents and grandparents endured hardships while living unremarkable lives in remarkable ways, the image of grand striver is too expansive. Our immediate ancestors, for example, led meaningful lives. They loved, worked, created, and instilled values. They were blue-collar workers, hardly part of the gifted artist class, but I refuse to believe they merely added more zeros to zeros, or that their proper function was to serve Nietzsche's artistic creators.

The image of the grand striver attracts us because it speaks to our sense of adventure, our individualism, our need to experience intensely. But we are much more than grand strivers. Unger and Nozick, even Nietzsche, recognize this. Our sense of community, our need for peace and respite, and our yearning for narrative structure are also part of human personality. We need to be distinct individuals, but if this impulse is exaggerated we become isolated and alienated. We need to be intimately connected to others, but if this yearning is unchallenged we become suffocated and overly dependent. The trick is to achieve the best measure of each impulse. Neither Romanticism nor Stoicism is sufficient. Each image speaks to only part of the human condition. We need to transcend grandly but we also need internal unity and integrated identities.

5. Jesus and Nietzsche: Toward a Synthesis

Imagine two choices: (a) our world as we know it, with much human suffering but significant human creativity or (b) a revised world where human suffering has been eliminated but no significant creativity occurs. I am not assuming that eliminating human suffering would result in extinguishing human creativity (although Nietzsche might well assume this) or any other causal relationship between suffering and creativity. I am posing two choices only to help focus our value priorities. Nietzsche would undoubtedly choose our world as we know it, whereas Jesus, based on his emphasis on alleviating suffering, would seemingly select the revised world. Which would you choose?

The hypothetical I have posed and the antinomies of the individual-community continuum invite us to consider synthesizing the views of Nietzsche and Jesus. Is it possible to strip the more extreme positions from each thinker and arrive at an ethic that can be lived in the world as we know it?

The respective background epistemological and metaphysical presuppositions of Nietzsche and Jesus are incompatible. Whereas Nietzsche extols perspectivism and the need to perceive reality from multiple vantage points, Jesus takes himself to be advancing conclusions that are eternal truths flowing from an Archimedean point that is the Divine Mind. Whereas Nietzsche rejoices in our world of Becoming, Jesus augurs the supposed imminent arrival of the world of Being that is the Kingdom of God. Whereas Nietzsche understands the cosmos to be inherently meaningless and our task to be the creation of fragile meaning within it, Jesus accepts the cosmos as instilled with meaning by Divine agency and our task to be the discovery of the proper path to attain that meaning. Whereas Nietzsche is firmly convinced that the cosmos is neither rational nor just, Jesus anticipates a Final Judgment that will reveal intrinsic rationality and justice. Whereas Nietzsche mocks the notion of permanent, fixed value, Jesus takes himself to be revealing precisely such worth and our capability to access and connect to it. Whereas Nietzsche derides the idea of a final culmination to our lives, Jesus advises us to prepare for exactly that event. The list could continue.

Because these sets of epistemological and metaphysical presuppositions are so radically opposed, any attempt at reconciliation would be fatuous. One might try to synthesize the opposing sets by appealing to human reason as the adjudicating agent. But any such effort would produce a question-begging distortion of the respective views of Jesus and Nietzsche. For example, one would think that either an anthropomorphic deity exists or it does not. To posit an utterly different type of deity as the product of reconciling Jesus and Nietzsche is to do irreparable violence to the views of both thinkers.

But the normative conclusions of Jesus and Nietzsche are quite another matter. As should now be clear, despite the title of this work, our choices were never either Jesus or Nietzsche in unadulterated versions of their teachings. Each thinker can be used creativity to mollify the excesses of the other. In my judgment, the contrast between Nietzsche's embrace of *amor fati* and Jesus' alleged distance from this world is misconceived. The more genuine difference is between engagement in the world that inclines toward individualism and that which is directed toward community. Viewing Nietzsche as articulating our greatest hopes and evoking our deepest fears about the values of individualism, and Jesus as expressing our highest aspirations and provoking our most profound aversions to community is reasonable.

The tension between individualism and community in Nietzsche is stark when a person of potential greatness is surrounded by a thoroughly mediocre community, one fervently committed to egalitarian values that ensure a lowest common denominator standard of value, meaning, and significance. In that vein, Nietzsche's individualism seems restricted only to higher human types. He consigns the rest of us to serving the interests and facilitating the perfection of the paradigms of our society. As such, most of us are relegated to advancing the narrow interests of a few, which hardly speaks to our individual empowerment. Thus, we must reject Nietzsche's aristocratism, his principle of nobility, and their corollaries straightaway if we are to understand his philosophy as radically individualistic.

Nietzsche offers the exhilaration of the values of uniqueness, autonomy, freedom from abject conformity to dominant ideas, and self-realization; he makes this offer at least to those who are potentially higher human types. But he unwittingly stokes our fears of alienation, estrangement, loneliness, and isolation. Jesus inspires us with his images of robust communal action, human solidarity, and universal love. But Jesus unintentionally incites our apprehensions of being suffocated by the oppressive collectivity, of being used only as a resource to fulfill the need of others, and of being mired in pathetic self-abnegation. Nietzsche and Jesus, then, vividly illustrate the hopes and fears of the individual-community continuum.

Understood in Hegelian terms, Jesus articulates the thesis of communitarianism, while Nietzsche represents the antithesis of individualism. We must provide the synthesis that would underscore and refine the strengths, and soften the concerns generated by each perspective. My synthesizing agent is the existential force of the individual-community continuum. I take this force to be part of the human condition and thus an aspect of human nature. Thus, my attempt to begin to reconcile the respective normative conclusions of Jesus and Nietzsche has a basis in our biological makeup. My animating assumption is that Jesus emphasized excessively our communal impulse, while Nietzsche overestimated our individualistic instinct. Trying to synthesize their respective views is thus possible and reasonable.

By discarding Nietzsche's aristocratism, principle of nobility, and their corollaries, we can refashion the image of the grand striver in concert with the Rizzo standard: we can all rejoice in the personal quest of self-realization defined by the process of deconstruction, reimagination, re-creation. Actualizing and maximizing our higher human potentials is not a process restricted to only the greatest exemplars among us. Instead, this process of self-realization can define a robustly meaningful and valuable human life. Our focus of concern need not be only on high cultural creativity or extraordinary artistic production. Often, relatively ordinary human action performed with brio and a sense of mission can cultivate our higher human potentials. But our yearning for solitude should be seasoned with a deeper appreciation of the intimacy only communal attachments can provide. Our measure of success should not be gauged by the superiority of our productivity in relation to others, but the extent to which our efforts, sacrifices, risks, and suffering facilitate the actualization and maximization of our particular set of higher human potentials and those of other people. We must understand that our mutual journey toward restyled "perfection" is not a zero-sum contest such that my success can arise only from your failure. In principle, at least, we can all attain the deserved self-pride emanating from fulfilling the Rizzo standard of actualizing and maximizing our higher human potentials. Although factual differences among human beings place limits on our respective possibilities, they should not bear aristocratic normative implications for how we should relate.

The image of the last man persists as an illustration of a person who refuses to assume the projects of the refashioned grand striver. The last man fails to take responsibility for the person he is becoming; offers facile excuses for his shortcomings; seeks only the blandest hedonistic comforts; and conforms abjectly to dominant social ideas in order to highlight his nonthreatening nature and to satisfy his compulsion for external validation. As such, the last man represents the path of least resistance: easy accommodations and effete aspirations replace the arduous task of self-realization.

Most important to this revised Nietzschean-inspired vision is recognizing that Aristotle was correct: human beings are social creatures and require engagement with an appropriate social environment to realize their higher human potentials. High energy and relentless enthusiasm are not only their own rewards but they also animate the truth that we generally reap what we sow: what we extract from a project is commensurate to what we contributed to it.

By admitting that attaining the most radical aspects of Jesus' teachings is possible for only the hero, martyr, or saint, we can ease our fears of self-abnegation and suffocation within the grand collectivity. Most of us will be unable to embrace and practice radical egalitarianism, utter impartiality, and unconditional love. But all of us can cultivate a more forgiving, more merciful, and more accepting approach to the perceived shortcomings and transgressions of other people. We can also examine the claims of the needy more seriously; restrain our natural inclinations toward stern retaliation; and encourage the development of the higher potentials of other human beings, especially strangers and "enemies." We can move away from the project of creating an invulnerable self, inoculated against the harshness of the external world and content in its own value, and, instead, cultivate a heightened mutual vulnerability with others and a deeper appreciation of salutary social action. Again, our most profound human project is not only realizing and maximizing our own higher human potentials but also helping other people realize and maximize their higher human potentials. In this manner, perfectionism exudes both individual and communal dimensions.

Knowing what to do in particular cases requires the virtues of the person of Aristotelian practical reason: moral sensitivity, perception, imagination, and judgment informed by experience. Jesus and Nietzsche were more concerned with crafting the proper inner dispositions and attitudes of their respective human exemplars; neither was obsessed with crafting general rules that could be applied to individual cases mechanically or formalistically. I will thus repress the urge to issue a host of general moral principles that would purport to resolve precisely how much we owe to others in particular cases or what we must do when confronted by specific moral dilemmas.

My sketch of the beginnings of a synthesis between Jesus' moral message and Nietzsche's normative conclusions does not depend on adopting the particular metaphysical and epistemological presuppositions of either thinker. Both those who are committed theists and those who are convinced that the cosmos is inherently meaningless could embrace the general trajectory of the synthesis. However, their respective lives would differ when each group of agents fills in my sketch with specific, substantive normative imperatives. To conclude that metaphysical and epistemological differences do not imply normative disagreements would be an error.

For example, followers of Jesus, who thereby believe that they are obeying the dictates of a Supreme Being, will fill out the framework of the synthesis differently from those who subscribe to Nietzsche's broad metaphysical and epistemological themes of contingency and conditionality. Believing, as did Jesus, that fixed, eternal normative principles are accessible to human beings coalesces uneasily with the neo-Nietzschean conviction that accelerated revision of the self and the social institutions within which it operates is wise. Believing, as did Jesus, that human beings must prepare for the arrival of the Kingdom of God rests uncomfortably with the Nietzschean creeds that this world and this life are all human beings can experience.

Specifically, followers of Jesus will be much more suspicious of distributing social resources on the basis of the principles of desert and entitlement than will Nietzscheans who aspire to social allocations grounded precisely on those principles. Followers of Jesus will be more sensitive to claims arising from need and will promote more enthusiastically responses flowing from mercy and compassion than will Nietzscheans. Both sets of believers will insist that the proper measure of human beings should not be what they possess or what they have accumulated materially, but who they are and what internal dispositions they have cultivated. They will also agree that those whom society disparages as "undesirables" or "aberrational" are not thereby automatically unworthy. Jesus and Nietzsche were consistently suspicious of the dominant understandings flowing from "the good and the just" in society and from mass opinion.

Nevertheless, in any case we confront a world not of our making and must transverse its vicissitudes with style, aplomb, and humility. Synthesizing the individualism of Nietzsche and the communitarianism of Jesus into a general framework is a step in that direction. Paraphrasing Nietzsche: this is my way, now what is yours?

NOTES

Introduction

1. John Dominic Crossan, *Jesus: A Revolutionary Biography* (San Francisco: Harper SanFrancisco, 1994); *The Historical Jesus: The Life of a Mediterranean Jewish Peasant* (San Francisco: HarperSanFrancisco, 1991); F. Gerald Downing, *Jesus and the Threat of Freedom* (London: SCM Press Ltd., 1987); B. Mack, *A Myth of Innocence* (Philadelphia: Fortress, 1988).
2. Bart D. Ehrman, *Jesus: Apocalyptic Prophet of the New Millennium* (New York: Oxford University Press, 1999); E.P. Sanders, *The Historical Figure of Jesus* (London: Allen Lane/Penguin Books, 1993): John. P. Meier, *A Marginal Jew* (New York: Doubleday, 1994).
3. This is the standard account of Christian religions. See, for example, Michael J. Wilkens and J.P. Moreland (eds.), *Jesus under Fire* (Grand Rapids, MI: Zondervan Publishing House, 1995).
4. S.G.F. Brandon, *Jesus and the Zealots* (New York: Scribner Books, 1967); G.W. Buchanan, *Jesus: The King and His Kingdom* (Macon, GA: Mercer University Press, 1984).
5. Richard A. Horsley, *Jesus and the Spiral of Violence* (Minneapolis, MN: Fortress Publishers, 1987).
6. Elisabeth Schussler Fiorenza, *In Memory of Her* (New York: Crossroad, 1983).
7. Morton Smith, *Jesus the Magician* (San Francisco: Harper & Row, 1978).
8. B. Thiering, *Jesus and the Riddle of the Dead Sea Scrolls* (San Francisco: Harper SanFrancisco, 1992).
9. Don Cupitt, *Jesus & Philosophy* (London: SCM Press, 1988), 25, 69, 70.
10. Crossan, *Jesus: A Revolutionary Biography*, 56, 121.
11. Ehrman, *Jesus: Apocalyptic Prophet of the New Millennium*, 142, 143.
12. Ibid., 181.
13. My sketch of Nietzsche's life borrows freely from Karl Jaspers, *Nietzsche: An Introduction to the Understanding of His Philosophical Activity* (1935), trans. Charles F. Wallraff and Frederick J. Schmitz (Tucson: University of Arizona Press, 1965), 27-115; and Walter Kaufmann, *Nietzsche: Philosopher, Psychologist, Antichrist*, 4th ed. (Princeton: Princeton University Press, 1974), 21-71.

One: Jesus: The Nature of Our World and Our Mission in It

1. Some Christian religious denominations, perhaps in order to preserve Mary's presumed virginity, insist that Jesus was an only child. Such denominations conclude that references to the "brothers" and "sisters" of Jesus in the gospels of Matthew and Mark do not refer to biological siblings but to his wider community of disciples and followers.
2. John Dominic Crossan, *Jesus: A Revolutionary Biography* (San Francisco: Harper SanFrancisco, 1994), 60.
3. Bart D. Ehrman, *Jesus: Apocalyptic Prophet of the New Millennium* (New York: Oxford University Press, 1999), 244.

4. See, for example, Raymond Angelo Belliotti, *Seeking Identity* (Lawrence, KS: University Press of Kansas, 1995, 1-38; "Honor Thy Father and Thy Mother and to Thine Own Self Be True," *Southern Journal of Philosophy* 24:2 (1986): 149-162; "Parents and Children: A Reply to Narveson," *Southern Journal of Philosophy* 26:2 (1988): 285-292; "Blood is Thicker than Water: Don't Forsake the Family Jewels," *Philosophical Papers* 18:3 (1989): 265-280.
5. Crossan, *Jesus: A Revolutionary Biography*, 69.
6. This section has been informed by Joel Feinberg, *Doing and Deserving* (Princeton: Princeton University Press, 1970); John Kleinig, "The Concept of Desert," *The Philosophical Quarterly* 8:1 (January, 1971); David Miller, *Social Justice* (Oxford: Oxford University Press, 1976); Julian Lamont, "The Concept of Desert in Distributive Justice," *The Philosophical Quarterly* 44: 174 (1994); Brian Barry, *Political Argument* (London: Routledge & Kegan Paul. 1965); George Sher, "Effort, Ability, and Personal Desert," *Philosophy and Public Affairs* 8:361 (1979); Fred Feldman, "Desert: Reconsideration of Some Received Wisdom," *Mind* 104:413 (1995); John Rawls, *A Theory of Justice* (Cambridge, Mass.: Harvard University Press, 1971); Robert Nozick, *Anarchy, State, and Utopia* (New York: Basic Books, 1974); Michael A. Slote, "Desert, Consent and Justice," *Philosophy and Public Affairs* 2:323 (1973); Alan Zaitchik, "On Deserving to Deserve," *Philosophy and Public Affairs* 6: 370 (1977).
7. Feldman, "Desert," 418.
8. Aristotle, *Nicomachean Ethics*, trans. by Martin Ostwald (Indianapolis, IN: Bobbs-Merrill, 1962), 1155a26-28.
9. See, for example, *United States Nursing Corp. v. Saint Joseph Medical Ctr.*, 39 F.3d 790, 792 (7th Cir. 1994).
10. Robert A. Hillman, "Debunking Some Myths About Unconscionability," 67 *Cornell Law Review* 1 (1981).
11. F. Gerald Downing, *Jesus and the Threat of Freedom* (London: SCM Press Ltd., 1987), 162.
12. Don Cupitt, *Jesus & Philosophy* (London: SCM Press, 1988), 98.
13. See, for example, E.J. Hobsbawn, *Primitive Rebels* (New York: Norton & Company, 1959), 57-58, 183.
14. The section on the concept of forgiveness has been informed by Lucy Allais, "Forgiveness and Mercy," 27 *South African Journal of Philosophy* (2008): 1-9; Nicholas Wolterstorff, "Jesus and Forgiveness," in *Jesus and Philosophy*, ed. Paul K. Moser (Cambridge: Cambridge University Press, 2009); "Does Forgiveness Undermine Justice," in *God and the Ethics of Belief*, eds. Andrew Dole and Andrew Chignell (Cambridge: Cambridge University Press, 2005); Jeffrie G. Murphy, "Remorse, Apology, and Mercy," 4 *Ohio State Journal of Criminal Law* (2007): 423-449; Jeffrie G. Murphy and Jean Hampton, *Forgiveness and Mercy* (Cambridge: Cambridge University Press, 1988).
15. Wolterstorff, "Jesus and Forgiveness," 208.
16. Ibid.
17. See, for example, Raymond Angelo Belliotti, *Seeking Identity : Individualism Versus Community in an Ethnic Context* (Lawrence, KS: University Press of Kansas), ix-x, 157-158, 191-193.

Two: Nietzsche: The Nature of Our World and Our Mission in It

1. Ken Gemes, "Nietzsche's Critique of Truth," *Philosophy and Phenomenological Research* 52 (1992): 47, 51.
2. Ibid., 54.
3. Ibid., 55.
4. Alexander Nehamas, *Nietzsche: Life as Literature* (Cambridge: Harvard University Press, 1985), 68.
5. Ibid., 65-68.
6. Bart Kosko, *Fuzzy Thinking: The New Science of Fuzzy Logic* (New York: Hyperion, 1993), 101.
7. Ibid., 6, 102-103.
8. Ibid., 102; Stanley Rosen, *The Limits of Analysis* (New York: Basic Books, 1980), 200.
9. Charles Altieri, "Ecce Homo," in *Why Nietzsche Now?* ed. Daniel T. O'Hara (Bloomington: Indiana University press, 1985), 395.
10. Steven D. Hales and Robert C. Welshon, "Truth, Paradox, and Nietzschean Perspectivism," *History of Philosophy Quarterly* 11 (1994): 101, 111-116.
11. Ibid., 113.
12. See, for example, Alexander Nehamas, "Who Are 'The Philosophers of the Future?'" in *Reading Nietzsche*, ed. Robert Solomon and Kathleen Higgins (New York: Oxford University Press, 1988), 62-63, 65.
13. See, for example, Karl Jaspers, *Nietzsche: An Introduction to the Understanding of His Philosophical Activity* (1935), trans. Charles F. Wallraff and Frederick J. Schmitz (Tucson: University of Arizona Press, 1965), 184-185.
14. See, for example, Leslie Paul Thiele, *Friedrich Nietzsche and the Politics of the Soul* (Princeton: Princeton University Press, 1990), 58.
15. Albert Camus, *The Myth of Sisyphus and Other Essays* (1942), trans. Justin O'Brien (New York, Vintage Books, 1960).
16. Jonathan Haidt, *The Righteous Mind* (Mew York: Pantheon Books, 2012), xiv.
17. Ibid., 43.
18. Ibid., 44.
19. Ibid., 278.
20. Ibid., 376.
21. Walter Kaufmann, *Nietzsche: Philosopher, Psychologist, Antichrist*, 4th ed. (Princeton: Princeton University Press, 1974), 225.
22. See, for example, Jerry H. Combee, "Nietzsche as Cosmologist," *Interpretation* 4 (1974): 38, 45-46; Arthus C. Danto, *Nietzsche as Philosopher* (New York: Columbia University Press, 1965), 206-208; Laurence Lampert, *Nietzsche's Teaching* (New Haven: Yale University Press, 1986), 258-259. See also WP 1062-1064, 1066-1067.
23. Raymond Angelo Belliotti, *Stalking Nietzsche* (Westport, CT: Greenwood Press, 1998), 78-79, 87-89.
24. See, for example, Jaspers, *Nietzsche*, 363-364.
25. See, for example, Lester H. Hunt, "The Eternal Recurrence and Nietzsche's Ethic of Virtue," *International Studies in Philosophy* 25 (1993): 3, 6.
26. See, for example, Kathleen Higgins, *Nietzsche's Zarathustra* (Philadelphia: Temple University Press, 1987), 175; Martin Heidegger, "Tragedy, Satyr-Play, and Tell-

ing Silence in Nietzsche's Thought of Eternal Recurrence," trans. David Krell, in *Why Nietzsche Now?* ed. O'Hara, 35.
27. See, for example, Richard White, "Zarathustra and the Progress of Sovereignty," *International Studies in Philosophy* 26 (1994): 107, 110-111.
28. See, for example, Robin Small, "Three Interpretations of Eternal Recurrence," *Dialogue* 22 (1983): 91, 108-109; Keith Ansell-Pearson, *An Introduction to Nietzsche as Political Thinker* (Cambridge: Cambridge University Press, 1994), 113.
29. See, for example, Ansell-Pearson, ibid., 111, 112.
30. Thiele, *Nietzsche and the Politics of the Soul*, 131, 134.
31. Ibid., 135.
32. See, for example, Pierre Schlag, "Missing Pieces: A Cognitive Approach to Law," *Texas Law Review* 67 (1989): 1195; Raymond Angelo Belliotti, *Justifying Law* (Philadelphia: Temple University Press, 1992), 211-220.
33. See, for example, Nehamas, *Nietzsche: Life as Literature*, 20-21; Lampert, *Nietzsche's Teaching*, 45: Kaufmann, *Nietzsche*, 85: Michael Tanner, *Nietzsche* (New York: Oxford University Press, 1994), 57.
34. Thiele, *Nietzsche and the Politics of the Soul*, 134.
35. Nehamas, *Nietzsche: Life as Literature*, 14, 15-16, 19, 27.
36. Ibid., 23.
37. Jaspers, *Nietzsche*, 409, 411, 412.
38. Patrick Gardiner, "Schopenhauer," in *The Encyclopedia of Philosophy*, ed. Paul Edwards, vol. 7 (New York: Macmillan, 1967), 328.
39. Kaufmann, *Nietzsche*, 281.
40. Ibid., 153.
41. Bruce Detwiler, *Nietzsche and the Politics of Aristocratic Radicalism* (Chicago: University of Chicago Press, 1990), 147-148.
42. Ibid., 148.
43. Ibid., 162-163.
44. Ibid., 165-166, 168.

Three: Fundamental Understandings of Human Beings: Unconditional Love and the Will to Power

1. The section on the interpretation of the parable has been informed by Klyne R. Snodgrass, *Stories with Intent* (Grand Rapids, MI: William B. Eerdmans Publishing Company, 2008); Craig L. Blomberg, *Interpreting the Parables* (Downers Grove, IL: InterVarsity Press, 1990); Richard N. Longenecker (ed.), *The Challenge of Jesus' Parables* (Grand Rapids, MI: William B. Eerdmans Publishing Company, 2000); Kenneth E. Bailey, *Poet & Peasant Through Peasant Eyes* (Grand Rapids, MI: William B. Eerdmans Publishing Company, 2000).
2. Bailey, *Poet & Peasant*, 203.
3. The section on agape has been informed by Neera Kapur Badhwar, "Friends as Ends in Themselves," in Clifford Williams, ed., *On Love and Friendship* (Boston: Jones and Bartlett Publishers, 1995); Anders Nygren, "Agape and Eros," in Clifford Williams, ed., *On Love and Friendship* (Boston: Jones and Bartlett Publishers, 1995); Barbara Hilkert Andolsen, "Agape in Feminist Ethics," in Clifford Williams, ed., *On Love and Friendship* (Boston: Jones and Bartlett Publishers, 1995); Robert C. Solomon, *The Passions* (New York: Anchor Press, 1976); *Love: Emo-*

tion Myth, and Metaphor (New York: Anchor Press, 1981); *About Love: Reinventing Romance for Our Times* (New York: Simon & Shuster, 1988); Robert Nozick, "Love's Bond" in *The Examined Life: Philosophical Meditations* (New York: Simon & Shuster, 1989), Irving Singer, *The Nature of Love, Volume 3: The Modern World* (Chicago: University of Chicago Press, 1989); Gene Outka, *Agape* (New Haven: Yale University press, 1972); Soren Kierkegaard, *Works of Love*, trans. Howard and Edna Hong (New York: Harper and Brothers, 1962).
4. Badhwar, "Friends as Ends," 210, 213.
5. Nygren, "Apage and Eros," 137, 131.
6. Ibid., 132-133.
7. See, for example, Bernard Reginster, *The Affirmation of Life* (Cambridge, MA; Harvard University Press, 2006), 103-147.
8. Karl Jaspers, *Nietzsche: An Introduction to the Understanding of His Philosophical Activity* (1935), trans. Charles F. Wallraff and Frederick J. Schmitz (Tucson: University of Arizona Press, 1965), 166-168.
9. Frederick Copleston, *A History of Philosophy*, vol. 7, pt. 2 (Garden City, NY: Doubleday, 1946-1965), 414. Bertrand Russell, *A History of Western Philosophy* (New York: Simon & Schuster, 1945), 767. Alasdair MacIntyre, *After Virtue*, 2d ed. (Notre Dame: University of Notre Dame Press, 984), 22, 113.
10. See, for example, Daniel W. Conway, "Overcoming the übermensch: Nietzsche's Revaluation of Values," *Journal of the British Society for Phenomenology* 20 (1989): 211-212.
11. See, for example, Laurence Lampert, *Nietzsche's Teaching* (New Haven: Yale University Press, 1986), 258 (teaching of the overman is provisional and superseded by the doctrine of eternal recurrence); Conway, "Overcoming the übermensch" 215-216 (the overman ideal is Zarathustra's not Nietzsche's and Zarathustra abandons that ideal); Leslie Paul Thiele, *Friedrich Nietzsche and the Politics of the Soul* (Princeton: Princeton University Press, 1990), 12, 185-186 (the overman is proposed as the hero of a nihilistic age); Alan Schrift, "Putting Nietzsche to Work," in *Nietzsche: A Critical Reader*, ed. Peter R. Sedgwick (Cambridge, MA: Blackwell, 1995), 262-264 (the overman is the name given to the process of accumulating strength and exerting mastery outside the limits of external authority); Richard Schacht, "Zarathustra/Zarathustra as Educator" in Sedgwick, *Nietzsche*, 237 (the overman is the notion of attainable higher humanity); Keith Ansell-Pearson, *An Introduction to Nietzsche as Political Thinker* (Cambridge: Cambridge University Press, 1994), 123, 125-126 (the notion of the overman is not an ideal for this would be humanely unattainable. Instead, the overman is inseparable from the notion of eternal recurrence); Kathleen Higgins, *Nietzsche's Zarathustra* (Philadelphia: Temple University Press, 1987), 81, 125 (the overman is an emblem for the goal of human development toward greatness); Walter Kaufmann, *Nietzsche: Philosopher, Psychologist, Antichrist*, 4th ed. (Princeton: Princeton University Press, 1974), 309, 312-313, 316 (the overman, who is valuable in himself, cannot be dissociated from the conception of overcoming.).
12. See, for example, Conway, "Overcoming the übermensch," 214.
13. Peter Berkowitz, *Nietzsche* (Cambridge, MA: Harvard University Press) 111.
14. Ibid., 112.
15. Ibid., 113.

16. See, for example, Bart D. Ehrman, *Jesus: Apocalyptic Prophet of the New Millennium* (New York: Oxford University Press, 1999); E.P. Sanders, *The Historical Figure of Jesus* (London: Allen Lane/Penguin Books, 1993): John P. Meier, *A Marginal Jew* (New York: Doubleday, 1994).

Four: The Perfectionism of Jesus

1. The section on the interpretation of the parable has been informed by Klyne R. Snodgrass, *Stories with Intent* (Grand Rapids, MI: William B. Eerdmans Publishing Company, 2008); Craig L. Blomberg, *Interpreting the Parables* (Downers Grove, IL: InterVarsity Press, 1990); Richard N. Longenecker (ed.), *The Challenge of Jesus' Parables* (Grand Rapids, MI: William B. Eerdmans Publishing Company, 2000); Kenneth E. Bailey, *Poet & Peasant Through Peasant Eyes* (Grand Rapids, MI: William B. Eerdmans Publishing Company, 2000).
2. Bailey, *Poet & Peasant*, 165.
3. Ibid., 177.
4. Jonathan Haidt, *The Righteous Mind* (New York: Pantheon Books, 2012), 245, 265.
5. Soren Kierkegaard, *Works of Love*, trans. Howard and Edna Hong (New York: Harper and Brothers, 1962), 72.
6. Henry Sidgwick, *The Methods of Ethics* (London: MacMillan and Company, 1874, 7th ed. 1907), 382.
7. Peter Singer, "Famine, Affluence, and Morality," in Peter Singer, *Writings on an Ethical Life* (New York: HarperCollins, 2000), 105-117.
8. Ibid., 107.
9. Ibid., 337 n.2.
10. Ibid., 107.
11. Ibid., 109.
12. Ibid., 115.
13. Peter Singer, *Practical Ethics* (Cambridge: Cambridge University Press), 180.
14. Ibid, 181.
15. Singer also famously enlarges his circle of concern to include the interests of non-human animals. See, for example, Peter Singer, *Animal Liberation* (New York: Random House, 1975).
16. Peter Singer, "Is Racial Discrimination Arbitrary?" *Philosophia* 8 (1978): 197.
17. William Godwin, "Enquiry Concerning Political Justice" (1798), quoted in Don Locke, *A Fantasy of Reason* (London: Routledge, 1980), 168.
18. Sidgwick, *The Methods of Ethics*, 498.
19. James Rachels, "Morality, Parents, and Children," in James Rachels, *Can Ethics Provide Answers?* (Lanham, MD: Rowman & Littlefield, 1997), 213-233, 215.
20. Ibid., 213.
21. Ibid., 215.
22. Ibid., 223.
23. Ibid., 230.
24. Ibid., 231.
25. Ibid.
26. Bart D. Ehrman, *Jesus: Apocalyptic Prophet of the New Millennium* (New York: Oxford University Press, 1999), 171.
27. See, for example, John Dominic Crossan, *Jesus: A Revolutionary Biography* (San

Francisco: HarperSanFrancisco, 1994); *The Historical Jesus: The Life of a Mediterranean Jewish Peasant* (San Francisco: HarperSanFrancisco, 1991); F. Gerald Downing, *Jesus and the Threat of Freedom* (London: SCM Press Ltd., 1987); B. Mack, *A Myth of Innocence* (Philadelphia: Fortress, 1988).
28. See, for example, J.J.C. Smart and Bernard Williams, *Utilitarianism: For and Against* (Cambridge: Cambridge University Presss, 1973), 116.
29. John Cottingham, "Ethics and Impartiality," *Philosophical Studies* 43 (1983): 90.
30. See, for example, John Kekes, "Morality and Impartiality," *American Philosophical Quarterly* 18 (1981): 298-299.
31. Rachels, "Morality, Parents, and Children," 231.

Five: The Perfectionism of Nietzsche

1. Thomas Hurka, *Perfectionism* (New York: Oxford University Press, 1993), 70.
2. Ibid., 70-71.
3. Ibid., 76-77.
4. Robert Unger, *Passion: An Essay on Personality* (New York: The Free Press, 1984), 3-5, 7-10, 20-39, 53-55, 57-62, 65-67, 69-76, 95-100.
5. Robert Nozick, *Philosophical Explanations* (Cambridge, MA: Harvard University Press, 1981), 571-619.

BIBLIOGRAPHY

Allais, Lucy. "Forgiveness and Mercy." *South African Journal of Philosophy* 27:1 (2008), pp. 1-9.
Altieri, Charles. "Ecco Homo." In *Why Nietzsche Now?* ed. Daniel O'Hara. Bloomington: Indiana University Press, 1985.
Altizer, T.J.J. *The Contemporary Jesus*. Albany, NY: State University of New York Press, 1997.
Ansell-Pearson, Keith. *An Introduction to Nietzsche as Political Thinker*. Cambridge: Cambridge University Press, 1994.
Aristotle. *Nicomachean Ethics*, trans. by Martin Ostwald. Indianapolis, IN: Bobbs-Merrill, 1962.
Badhwar, Neera Kapur. "Friends as Ends in Themselves." In *On Love and Friendship*, ed., Clifford Williams. Boston: Jones and Bartlett Publishers, 1995.
Bailey, Kenneth E. *Poet & Peasant Through Peasant Eyes*. Grand Rapids, MI: William B. Eerdmans Publishing Company, 2000.
Barry, Brian. *Political Argument*. London: Routledge & Kegan Paul. 1965.
Belliotti, Raymond Angelo. *Seeking Identity: Individualism versus Community in an Ethnic Context*. Lawrence, KS: University Press of Kansas, 1995.
_____. *Good Sex: Perspectives on Sexual Ethics*. Lawrence, KS: University Press of Kansas, 1993.
_____. *Justifying Law: The Debate over Foundations*, Goals, and Methods. Philadelphia: Temple University Press, 1992.
_____. "Honor Thy Father and Thy Mother and to Thine Own Self Be True," *Southern Journal of Philosophy* 24:2 (1986), pp. 149-162.
_____. "Parents and Children: A Reply to Narveson," *Southern Journal of Philosophy* 26:2 (1988), pp. 285-292.
_____. "Blood is Thicker Than Water: Don't Forsake the Family Jewels," *Philosophical Papers* 18:3 (1989), pp. 265-280.
Berkowitz, Peter. *Nietzsche*. Cambridge: Harvard University Press, 1995.
Betz, Hans Dieter. "Jesus and The Cynics," *The Journal of Religion* 74:4 (1994), pp. 453-475.
Blomberg, Craig L. *Interpreting the Parables*. Downers Grove, IL: InterVarsity Press, 1990.
Brandon, S.G.F. *Jesus and the Zealots*. New York: Scribner Books, 1967.
Brien, Andrew. "Mercy Within Legal Justice." *Social Theory and Practice* 24 (1) (1998), pp. 83-110.
Buchanan, G.W. *Jesus: The King and His Kingdom*. Macon, GA: Mercer University Press, 1984.
Butterfield, Herbert. *Christianity and History*. London: Bell, 1949.
Camus, Albert. *The Myth of Sisyphus and Other Essays* (1942), trans. Justin O'Brien. New York: Vintage Books, 1960.
Cole, W. G. *Sex in Christianity and Psychoanalysis*. New York: Oxford University Press, 1955.
Combee, Jerry H. "Nietzsche as Cosmologist." *Interpretation* 4 (1974): 38-47.
Conway, Daniel W. "Overcoming the *übermensch*: Nietzsche's Revaluation of Values," *Journal of the British Society for Phenomenology* 20 (1989): 211-224.

Copleston, Frederick. *A History of Philosophy*, vol. 7, pt. 2. Garden City, NY: Doubleday, 1946-1965)
Cottingham, John. "Ethics and Impartiality," *Philosophical Studies* 43:1 (1983), pp. 83-99.
Crossan, John Dominic. *Jesus: A Revolutionary Biography*. San Francisco: HarperSanFrancisco, 1994.
―――. *The Historical Jesus: The Life of a Mediterranean Jewish Peasant*. San Francisco: HarperSanFrancisco, 1991.
Cupitt, Don. *Jesus & Philosophy*. London: SCM Press, 1988.
Danto, Arthur C. *Nietzsche as Philosopher*. New York: Columbia University Press, 1965.
Derrett, J. Duncan M. *Law in the New Testament*. London: Darton, Longman and Todd, 1970.
Desmond, William. *Cynics*. Berkeley: University of California Press, 2008.
Detwiler, Bruce. *Nietzsche and the Politics of Aristocratic Radicalism*. Chicago: University of Chicago Press, 1990.
Diodorus Siculus. *The Library of History*, trans. C.H. Oldfather. Cambridge, MA: Harvard University Press, 1933.
Diogenes Laertius. *Lives of the Eminent Philosophers*, trans. R.D. Hicks. Cambridge, MA: Harvard University Press, 1925, 11th edition, 2005.
Dole, Andrew and Andrew Chignell, eds. *God and the Ethics of Belief*. Cambridge: Cambridge University Press, 2005.
Downing, F. Gerald. *Jesus and the Threat of Freedom*. London: SCM Press Ltd., 1987.
Eddy, Paul Rhodes. "Jesus as Diogenes? Reflections on the Cynic Jesus Thesis," *Journal of Biblical Literature* 115:3 (1996), pp. 449-469.
Ehrman, Bart D. *Jesus: Apocalyptic Prophet of the New Millennium*. New York: Oxford University Press, 1999.
Feinberg, Joel. *Harm to Others*. New York: Oxford University Press, 1984.
―――. *Doing and Deserving*. Princeton: Princeton University Press, 1970.
Feldman, Fred. "Desert: Reconsideration of Some Received Wisdom," *Mind* 104 (1995), pp. 63 – 77.
Fiorenza, Elisabeth Schussler. *In Memory of Her*. New York: Crossroad, 1983.
Freud, Sigmund. *Civilization and Its Discontents*. New York: Norton, 1930.
―――. *A General Introduction to Psychoanalysis*. New York: Pocket Books, 1971.
Funk, Robert W., and the Jesus Seminar. *The Acts of Jesus: The Search for the Authentic Deeds of Jesus*. San Francisco: HarperSanFrancisco, 1998.
Gardinier, Patrick. Schopenhauer." In *The Encyclopedia of Philosophy*, ed. Paul Edwards, vol. 7. New York: Macmillan, 1967.
Gemes, Ken. "Nietzsche's Critique of Truth." *Philosophy and Phenomenological Research* 52 (1992): 47-65
Geuss, Raymond. "Nietzsche and Genealogy." *European Journal of Philosophy* 2 (1994): 274-292.
Goldstein, Morris. *Jesus in the Jewish Tradition*. New York: Macmillan, 1950.
Haidt, Jonathan. *The Righteous Mind*. New York: Pantheon Books, 2012.
Hales, Steven D. and Robert C. Welshon. "Truth, Paradox, and Nietzschean Perspectivism." *History of Philosophy Quarterly* 11 (1994): 101-119.

Heidegger, Martin. "Tragedy, Satyr-Play, and Telling Silence in Nietzsche's Thought of Eternal Recurrence," trans. David Krell. In *Why Nietzsche Now?* ed. Daniel O'Hara. Bloomington: Indiana University Press, 1985.
Higgins, Kathleen. *Nietzsche's Zarathustra*. Philadelphia: Temple University Press, 1987.
Hillman, Robert A."Debunking Some Myths About Unconscionability," *Cornell Law Review* 67 (1981), pp. 1-49.
Hobsbawn, E. J. *Primitive Rebels*. New York: Norton & Company, 1959.
Hoistad, Ragnar. *Cynic Hero and Cynic King*. Uppsala: Bloms, 1948.
Hoover, Roy W., ed. *Profiles of Jesus*. Santa Rosa, CA: Polebridge Press, 2002.
Horsley, Richard A. *Jesus and the Spiral of Violence*. Minneapolis, MN: Fortress Publishers, 1987.
_____. *Bandits, Prophets & Messiahs*. Harrisburg, PA: Trinity Press International, 1985.
Hunt, Lester J. "The Eternal Recurrence and Nietzsche's Ethic of Virtue." *International Studies in Philosophy* 25 (1993): 3-11.
Hurka, Thomas. *Perfectionism*. New York: Oxford University Press, 1993.
Jaspers, Karl. *Nietzsche: An Introduction to the Understanding of His Philosophical Activity* (1935), trans. Charles F. Wallraff and Frederick J. Schmitz. Tucson: University of Arizona Press, 1965.
Josephus. *Jewish Antiquities*, trans. Louis H. Feldman. Cambridge, MA: Harvard University Press, 1965.
Kaufmann, Walter. *Nietzsche: Philosopher, Psychologist, Antichrist*, 4th ed. Princeton: Princeton University Press, 1974.
Kekes, John. "Morality and Impartiality," *American Philosophical Quarterly* 18:4 (1981), pp. 295-303.
Kierkegaard, Soren. *Works of Love*, trans. Howard and Edna Hong. New York: Harper and Brothers, 1962.
Kleinig, John. "The Concept of Desert," *The Philosophical Quarterly* 8:1 (1971), pp. 71 - 78.
Kloppenborg, John S. *Q Parallels: Synopsis, Critical Notes and Concordance*. Sonoma, CA: Polebridge Press, 1988.
Kosko, Bart. *Fuzzy Thinking: The New Science of Fuzzy Logic*. New York: Hyperion, 1993.
Lamont, Julian. "The Concept of Desert in Distributive Justice," *The Philosophical Quarterly* 44 (1994), pp. 45 - 64.
Lampert, Laurence. *Nietzsche's Teaching*. New Haven: Yale University Press, 1986.
Locke, Don. *A Fantasy of Reason*. London: Routledge, 1980.
Longenecker, Richard N., ed. *The Challenge of Jesus' Parables*. Grand Rapids, MI: William B. Eerdmans Publishing Company, 2000.
MacIntyre, Alasdair. *After Virtue*. 2d ed. Notre Dame: University of Notre Dame Press, 1984.
Mack, B. *A Myth of Innocence*. Philadelphia: Fortress, 1988.
MacMullen, Ramsay. *Enemies of the Roman Order: Treason, Unrest, and Alienation in the Empire*. Cambridge, MA: Harvard University Press, 1966.
Malherbe, Abraham J. *The Cynic Epistles*. Missoula, MT.: Scholars Press, 1977.
Meier, John P. *A Marginal Jew*. New York: Doubleday, 1994.

Middleton, Christopher, ed. and trans. *Selected Letters of Friedrich Nietzsche.* Indianapolis: Hackett, 1996.
Miller, David. *Social Justice.* Oxford: Oxford University Press, 1976.
Mo Tzu. *Basic Writings*, trans. Burton Watson. New York: Columbia University Press, 1963.
Moser, Paul, ed. *Jesus and Philosophy.* Cambridge: Cambridge University Press, 2009.
Murphy, Jeffrie G. "Remorse, Apology, and Mercy," *Ohio State Journal of Criminal Law* 4: 2 (2007), pp. 423-453.
_____ and Jean Hampton. *Forgiveness and Mercy.* Cambridge: Cambridge University Press, 1988.
Nehamas, Alexander. *Nietzsche: Life as Literature.* Cambridge: Harvard University Press, 1985.
_____. "Who Are 'The Philosophers of the Future'?" In *Reading Nietzsche*, ed. Robert Solomon and Kathleen Higgins. New York: Oxford University Press, 1988.
Norton, David. L. *Personal Destinies.* Princeton: Princeton University Press, 1976.
Nozick, Robert. *Anarchy, State, and Utopia.* New York: Basic Books, 1974.
_____. *The Examined Life: Philosophical Meditations.* New York: Simon & Schuster, 1989.
_____. *Philosophical Explanations.* Cambridge, MA: Harvard University Press, 1981,
Nussbaum, Martha C. "Equity and Mercy." *Philosophy & Public Affairs* 22:2 (1993), pp. 83-125.
Nygren, Andres. "Agape and Eros." In *On Love and Friendship*, ed., Clifford Williams. Boston: Jones and Bartlett Publishers, 1995.
Outka, Gene. *Agape.* New Haven: Yale University Press, 1972.
Parent, David J., trans. *Conversations with Nietzsche.* New York: Oxford University Press, 1987.
Plato, *Collected Dialogues.* 7th ed., ed. Edith Hamilton and Huntington Cairns. Princeton: Princeton University Press, 1973.
Rachels, James. *Can Ethics Provide Answers?* Lanham, MD: Rowman & Littlefield, 1997.
Rajak, Tessa. *Josephus: The Historian and His Society.* London: Duckworth, 1983.
Rawls, John. *A Theory of Justice.* Cambridge, MA: Harvard University Press, 1971.
Reginster, Bernard. *The Affirmation of Life.* Cambridge, MA; Harvard University Press, 2006.
Rosen, Stanley. *The Limits of Analysis.* New York: Basic Books, 1980.
Roth, Robin. "Nietzsche's Metaperspectivism." *International Studies in Philosophy* 22 (1990): 66-77.
Russell, Bertrand. *A History of Western Philosophy.* New York: Simon & Schuster, 1945.
Sanders, E.P. *The Historical Figure of Jesus.* London: Allen Lane/Penguin Books, 1993.
_____. *Jesus and Judaism.* Philadelphia: Fortress, 1985.
Sayre, Farrand. *The Greek Cynics.* Baltimore: J.H. Furst Company, 1948.
Schacht, Richard. "Zarathustra/*Zarathustra* as Educator." In *Nietzsche: A Critical Reader*, ed. Peter R. Sedgwick. Cambridge, Mass.: Blackwell, 1995.

Schlag, Pierre. "Missing Pieces: A Cognitive Approach to Law." *Texas Law Review* 67 (1989): 1195-1247.
Schrift, Alan. "Putting Nietzsche to Work." In *Nietzsche: A Critical Reader*, ed. Peter R. Sedgwick. Cambridge, Mass.: Blackwell, 1995.
Schwartz, Tony. *What Really Matters*. New York: Bantam Books, 1995.
Scott, James C. *Domination and the Arts of Resistance*. New Haven, CT: Yale University Press, 1990.
Shakespeare, William. *The Merchant of Venice* in eds. Hardin Craig and David Bevington, *The Complete Works of Shakespeare*. Glenview, Il: Scott, Foresman and Company, 1973.
Sher, George. "Effort, Ability, and Personal Desert," *Philosophy and Public Affairs* 8:4 (1979), pp. 361 - 376.
Sidgwick, Henry. *The Methods of Ethics*. London: MacMillan and Company, 1874, 7th ed. 1907.
Singer, Irving. *The Nature of Love, Volume 3: The Modern World*. Chicago: University of Chicago Press, 1989.
Singer, Peter. *Writings on an Ethical Life*. New York: HarperCollins, 2000.
_____. *Practical Ethics*. Cambridge: Cambridge University Press, 180.
_____. *Animal Liberation*. New York: Random House, 1975.
_____. "Is Racial Discrimination Arbitrary?" *Philosophia* 8: 2-3 (1978), pp. 185-203.
Slote, Michael A. "Desert, Consent and Justice," *Philosophy and Public Affairs* 2:4 (1973), pp. 323 - 347.
Small, Robin. "Three Interpretations of Eternal Recurrence," *Dialogue* 22 (1983): 91-112.
Smart, J.J.C. and Bernard Williams. *Utilitarianism: For and Against*. Cambridge: Cambridge University Press, 1973.
Smith, Morton. *Jesus the Magician*. San Francisco: Harper & Row, 1978.
Snodgrass, Klyne R. *Stories with Intent*. Grand Rapids, MI: William B. Eerdmans Publishing Company, 2008.
Solomon, Robert C. *Love: Emotion, Myth, and Metaphor*. Garden City: Anchor Books, 1981.
_____. *The Passions*. New York: Anchor Press, 1976.
_____. *About Love: Reinventing Romance for Our Times*. New York: Simon & Shuster, 1988.
_____. *From Hegel to Existentialism*. New York: Oxford University Press, 1987.
Stanton, Graham. *The Gospels and Jesus*. Oxford: Oxford University Press, 1989.
Steiker, Carol S. "Murphy on Mercy: A Prudential Reconsideration." *Criminal Justice Ethics* 27 (2008), pp. 45-54.
Tanner, Michael. *Nietzsche*. New York: Oxford University Press, 1994.
Tasioulas, John. "Mercy." *Aristotelian Society* 103:1 (2003), pp. 101-132.
Thiele, Leslie Paul, *Friedrich Nietzsche and the Politics of the Soul*. Princeton: Princeton University Press, 1990.
Thiering, B. *Jesus and the Riddle of the Dead Sea Scrolls*. San Francisco: HarperSanFrancisco, 1992.
Torrey, Charles. C. *Our Translated Gospels*. New York: Harper, 1936.
Unger, Roberto. *Passion: An Essay on Personality*. New York: The Free Press, 1984.

White, Richard. "Zarathustra and the Progress of Sovereignty." *International Studies in Philosophy* 26 (1994): 107-115.

Wilcox, John T. *Truth and Value in Nietzsche*. Washington, D.C.: University Press of America, 1982.

Wilkens, Michael J. and J.P. Moreland, eds. *Jesus under Fire*. Grand Rapids, MI: Zondervan Publishing House, 1995.

Williams, Clifford, ed. *On Love and Friendship*. Boston: Jones and Bartlett Publishers, 1995.

Wilson, Bryan R. *Magic and the Millennium*. New York: Harper & Row, 1973.

Wolterstorff, Nicholas. "Jesus and Forgiveness." In *Jesus and Philosophy*, ed. Paul K. Moser. Cambridge: Cambridge University Press, 2009.

Wright, N. T. *Jesus and the Victory of God*. Minneapolis: Fortress, 1996.

Zaitchik, Alan. "On Deserving to Deserve," *Philosophy and Public Affairs* 6:4 (1977), pp. 370 - 388.

Zemach, Eddy M. "Love My Neighbor as Thyself or Egoism and Altruism," *Midwest Studies in Philosophy* 3:1 (1978), pp. 148-158.

INDEX

absolutism, 52–55, 59–60
acts, supererogatory, 34
    and Jesus, 36–37, 39, 42, 162
ad hominem attack, 109
agape, 94–95, 119–123
    and abstractness, 157–159
    and Parable of the Prodigal Son, 115–119, 125–126
    and parental love, 123–126
    and perfectionism, 151–157
    See also unconditional love.
ahistoricism, 100, 109
amor fati, 65, 78, 80, 86–89, 92–99, 138, 146
analytic mode, 101–102, 104
anti-Semitism, 5, 6, 7, 112
aphorism, 1, 7, 9, 102, 104, 109
Apollo, 111–113
Archimedean point, 200, 205
    and Jesus, 15, 48
    and Nietzsche, 51, 77, 108, 113
aristocracy, 187–194
aristocratic privilege, 187–194
Aristotle, 25, 34, 208
Augustine, St., 142
autobiography and philosophy, 5, 7, 61, 63, 100–101, 107, 136, 138

Badhwar, Neera Kapur, 120–121
Baumler, Alfred, 7
Bayreuth, 6
becoming, 65, 105, 111–113, 131, 193
begging the question, 53, 57
being, 89–90, 111–113
Berkowitz, Peter, 137, 141–142
beyond good and evil, 80–84
"blond beast," 82–83
Buddhism, 109
Buffalo Bills, 21–22

Cabrini, Mother, 161

Caesar, Julius, 145
Callicles, 76
Calvin, John, 142
camel, 64–65, 131
child, 64–65, 131
community, 114, 177
    and individualism continuum, 10–11, 48–49, 195, 205–207
contract
    and procedural unconscionability, 26
    and proportionate reward, 26, 27
    and substantive unconscionability, 26
    and unequal bargaining power, 26
    freedom of, 26
Copleston, Frederick, 134
Cottingham, John, 171–172
Crossan, John Dominic, 2, 14
Cupitt, Don, 2, 33
Cynic philosophy, 1–3, 144, 147

Dean, James, 188
deconstructive mode, 103
Derrida, Jacques, 9
desert, principle of, 21–31, 38
Detwiler, Bruce, 112–113
Dionysus, 111–113
dogmatism, 57, 59–60, 75–76
dualism, 71

egalitarianism, radical, 18, 48, 161, 179, 208
Ehrman, Bart, 3
entitlement, principle of, 21–31, 38
Essenes, 2, 20
eternal recurrence, 84–99
    as cosmological doctrine, 84–85, 87–89
    as moral hypothesis, 85–88
    as psychological test, 86–99
experience machine, 197–198

experimentalism, 56–57
fallibalism, 59–60
final judgment, 5, 19, 71, 206
forgetting, 18, 26
forgiveness, 34–49
 and repentance, 38–42
Forster, Elisabeth Nietzsche, 5, 7, 9
Foucault, Michel, 9
friendship, 31
 and Aristotle, 25
Freud, Sigmund, 103
fundamental themes (of Nietzsche).
 See also themes (of Nietzsche), broad

genealogy, 7, 74, 104–105, 109
genetic fallacy, 53–54
God, death of, 66–69
Godwin, William, 165, 169, 175
Graham, Billy, 34
grand striver, 195–205
gravity, spirit of, 62, 89, 138, 148

Haidt, Jonathan, 78, 79, 157
happiness, 65, 75, 80, 92
 and contemporary philosophy, 169, 175
 and Nietzsche, 92, 128, 130–132, 181, 185
Heidegger, Martin, 9
herd morality, 69–79
Homer, 34, 69, 74, 111
humans, higher, 86–99, 126–131, 181–195
hyperbole, 104, 109

ideal observer, 48, 113, 165, 166, 178, 202
individualism, 114, 177
 and community continuum, 10–11, 48–49, 195, 205–207
intuitive mode, 102
impartialism, 167–169, 171–179

Jesus, 13–49, 115–126, 151–180

Jesus
 and contemporary philosophy, 161–179
 and disciples, 3, 8, 13, 19, 31–37, 142, 186
 and engagement in this world, 145–149
 and family relations, 13–17
 and final judgment, 5, 19, 206
 and forgiveness, 34–49
 and friendship, 25
 and identifying with undesirables, 17–19
 and interrogating prevailing norms, 20–31
 and Kingdom of God, 2–3, 14–15, 18, 145–149, 168–169, 178–179, 209
 and material minimalism, 31–34
 and mercy, 34–49
 and moral message, 34–49, 179–180, 205–209
 and Nietzsche, 10–12, 113–114
 and normative ideals, 149
 and Parable of the Good Samaritan, 13–14, 19–20, 151–157, 162, 164, 178
 and Parable of the Prodigal Son, 41–42, 48, 115–119, 125–126
 and Parable of the Unforgiving Servant, 38
 and perfectionism, 151–157, 159–161, 179–180
 and principle of desert, 21–31
 and Socrates, 31–32, 14
 and Son of Man, 3–5, 14, 19, 31, 143, 146
 and Sermon on the Mount, 32
 and synthesis with Nietzsche, 205–209
 and unconditional love, 47–48, 157–159
 and unsettling established rituals, 19–20
 as apocalyptic prophet, 1–3
 as Cynic philosopher, 1–3, 169

Jesus
    as interpreted by Nietzsche, 136–141, 142–145
    as Son of God, 1–4
Jews, 151–154
John the Baptist, 18

Kant, Immanuel, 153
Kaufmann, Walter, 9, 113
Kierkegaard, Soren, 158–159
Kingdom of God, 2–3, 14–15, 18, 145–149, 168–169, 178–179, 209

last men, 84, 91–92, 131–136, 191, 207
laughter, 138, 182–183
Leonardo standard (of perfectionism), 192–193
lion, 64–65, 131
literary style, 104–109
logic, bivalent and multivalent, 56–58
love, unconditional, 94–95, 119–123
    See also agape.
Luther, Martin, 142

MacIntyre, Alasdair, 134
Magnus, Bernd, 9
Marx, Karl, 103, 187, 203
material minimalism, 31–34
mercy, 34–49
metaphors, 104, 109
metaphysical foundations, and realism, 62–64
Miami Dolphins, 21–22
morality, 69–79
    master, 69–79 and slave, 69–79
    See also herd morality.

Nachlass, 8–9, 84
Nietzsche, 5–9, 51–114, 126–149, 181–209
    and aristocratic privilege, 187–194
    and contemporary philosophy, 195–205

Nietzsche
    and crafting a worthy soul, 64–65
    and death of God, 66–69
    and eternal recurrence, 84–99
    and genealogical critique, 7, 63–64, 74, 104–105, 109
    and interpretation of Christianity, 66–69, 69–79, 85, 141–142
    and interpretation of Jesus, 136–141, 142–145
    and interpretation of St. Paul, 137, 141–142
    and Jesus, 10–12, 113–114
    and last man, 84, 91–92, 131–136, 191, 207
    and love, 183
    and master-slave moralities, 69–79
    and nihilism, 67–69
    and normative ideals, 149
    and overman, 131–136
    and perfectionism, 181–195
    and perspectivism, 51–63
    and principle of nobility, 189–191
    and psychology, 99–104
    and solitude, 184
    and style and rhetoric, 104–109
    and synthesis with Jesus, 205–209
    and tragic view of life, 109–113
    and transvaluation of values, 80–84
    and value, 65–66, 72–73, 75–77, 80–84
    and will to power, 8–9, 126–131, 184
nihilism, 67–69
    active, 67–69, 80–84, 133, 182, 193
    deconstructive, 68
    passive, 67–69, 81
    pathetic, 67, 68, 81

Nozick, Robert, 11–12, 195–199, 201–205
Nygren, Andres, 121, 122, 123

Overbeck, Franz, 7
overman, 131–136

Parables, 159–160
  of the Good Samaritan, 13–14, 19–20, 151–157, 162, 164, 178
  of the Laborers in the Vineyard, 20–21, 25–30, 179
  of the Prodigal Son, 41, 42, 48, 115–119, 125–126
  of the Unforgiving Servant, 38
partialism, 169–179
Paul, St., 4, 137, 141–142
perfectionism
  and contemporary philosophy, 195–205
  and Jesus, 151–157, 159–161, 179–180
  and Nietzsche, 181–195
  and principle of nobility, 189–191
  and unconditional love, 151–157
  and will to power, 184
perspectivism, 51–63
Pharisees, 20, 136–137, 141, 142, 152
pity, 184–185
Plato, 75–76, 203
power, 110–111
  life-affirming, 69–79
  life denying, 69–79
  See also will to power.
pragmatic mode, 102
pragmatic theory of truth, 102
Presley, Elvis, 188
principle of nobility, 189–191
punishment, 43–46
  as deterrence, 43, 46
  as incarceration, 43, 46
  as rehabilitation, 43, 46
  as restitution, 43–44
  as retribution, 43–46

Pythagoras, 31–32

Rachels, James, 11, 161, 167–169, 174–176, 179
recurrence, eternal. See eternal recurrence.
redemption, 134–136
Ree, Paul, 6–7, 106
relations, family, 13–17
repentance, 38–42
ressentiment, 70–71, 78, 80, 86, 88–89, 96, 99
rhetoric, and style, 104–109
  and strategic modes, 101–104
  warrior, 81–84, 107.
  See also analytic mode; deconstructive mode; intuitive mode; pragmatic mode; substructuralist mode.
Ritschl, Friedrich Wilhelm, 5
Romans, 83, 119, 140
Rorty, Richard, 9
Russell, Bertrand, 134

Sadducees, 20, 142, 143
Salome, Lou, 6–7, 106
Schopenhauer, Arthur, 109–110, 204–205
self, 15–17
self-overcoming, 88–89, 130–131, 132–136
self-reference, paradox of, 58–60
Sidgwick, Henry, 161, 166, 178
Singer, Peter, 11, 161–166, 174, 176–178, 179
Sisyphus, myth of, 68, 89, 111, 132, 182, 201
Socrates, 31–32, 147
solitude, 184
Son of Man, 3–5, 14, 19, 31, 143, 146
spiritualization, 84
state, 83–84
substructuralist mode, 102–103, 104
suffering, 127–131, 185
synthesis, of Jesus and Nietzsche, 205–209

Teresa, Mother, 161, 190
themes (of Nietzsche), broad, 8, 11, 77, 86–87, 187–188
    casting suspicion on dominant ideas, 8
    deconstruction, reimagination, re-creation, 8, 52, 64–65, 131
    denial of absolutism, 8
    immediacy of life, 8
    imposing order, meaning, and value, 8, 77
    inner conflict, 8
    limits of language and logic, 8
    perspectivism, 8, 51–63
    psychology and truth, 8
    self-overcoming, 8, 88–89, 130–131, 132–136
    tragedy and contingency, 8
    writing and life, 8
Thrasymachus, 75–76
tragedy, 109–113
Trampedach, Mathilde, 6
transcendence, 149, 195–205
truth, 55–56

Ubermensch, 131–136
Unger, Roberto, 11–12, 195–197, 199–205

value, 80–84
    fact-value distinction, 75–76
    imposing, 8, 77
    See also Themes (of Nietzsche), broad.

Wagner, Cosima, 6
Wagner, Richard, 6, 106, 112
war, 81–84, 107
    See also Rhetoric, warrior
Weber, Max, 103
Whatley, George, 34
Will to power, 8–9, 126–131, 184
Wolterstorff, Nicholas, 37–38

About the Author

Raymond Angelo Belliotti is SUNY Distinguished Teaching Professor of Philosophy at the State University of New York at Fredonia. He received his undergraduate degree from Union College in 1970, after which he was conscripted into the United States Army where he served three years in military intelligence units during the Vietnamese War. Upon his discharge, he enrolled at the University of Miami where he earned his Master of Arts degree in 1976 and Doctorate in 1977. After teaching stints at Florida International University and Virginia Commonwealth University, he entered Harvard University as a law student and teaching fellow. After receiving a Juris Doctorate from Harvard Law School, he practiced law in New York City with the firm of Barrett Smith Schapiro Simon & Armstrong. In 1984, he joined the faculty at Fredonia.

Belliotti is the author of thirteen other books: *Justifying Law* (1992); *Good Sex* (1993); *Seeking Identity* (1995); *Stalking Nietzsche* (1998); *What is the Meaning of Human Life?* (2001); *Happiness is Overrated* (2004); The *Philosophy of Baseball* (2006); *Watching Baseball Seeing Philosophy* (2008); *Niccolò Machiavelli* (2008); *Roman Philosophy and the Good Life* (2009); *Dante's Deadly Sins: Moral Philosophy in Hell* (2011); *Posthumous Harm: Why the Dead are Still Vulnerable* (2011); and *Shakespeare and Philosophy: Lust, Love, and Law* (2012). *Good Sex* was later translated into Korean and published in Asia. *What is the Meaning of Human Life?* was nominated for the *Society for Phenomenology and Existential Philosophy*'s Book of the Year Award. He has also published 70 articles and 25 reviews in the areas of ethics, jurisprudence, sexual morality, medicine, politics, education, feminism, sports, Marxism, and legal ethics. These essays have appeared in scholarly journals based in Australia, Canada, Great Britain, Italy, Mexico, South Africa, Sweden, and the United States. Belliotti has also made numerous presentations at philosophical conferences, including the 18th World Congress of Philosophy in England, and has been honored as a featured lecturer on the Queen Elizabeth-2 ocean liner.

While at SUNY Fredonia he has served extensively on campus committees, as the Chairperson of the Department of Philosophy, as the Chairperson of the University Senate, and as Director of General Education. Belliotti also served as United University Professions local Vice President for Academics. For six years he was faculty advisor to the undergraduate club, the Philosophical Society, and he has served that function for *Il Circolo Italiano*. Belliotti has been the recipient of the SUNY Chancellor's Award for Excellence in Teaching, the William T. Hagan Young Scholar/Artist Award, the Kasling Lecture Award for Excellence in Research and Scholarship, and the SUNY Foundation Research & Scholarship Recognition Award. He is also a member of the New York State *Speakers in the Humanities* Program.

VIBS

The **Value Inquiry Book Series** is co-sponsored by:

Adler School of Professional Psychology
American Indian Philosophy Association
American Maritain Association
American Society for Value Inquiry
Association for Process Philosophy of Education
Canadian Society for Philosophical Practice
Center for Bioethics, University of Turku
Center for Professional and Applied Ethics, University of North Carolina at Charlotte
Central European Pragmatist Forum
Centre for Applied Ethics, Hong Kong Baptist University
Centre for Cultural Research, Aarhus University
Centre for Professional Ethics, University of Central Lancashire
Centre for the Study of Philosophy and Religion, University College of Cape Breton
Centro de Estudos em Filosofia Americana, Brazil
College of Education and Allied Professions, Bowling Green State University
College of Liberal Arts, Rochester Institute of Technology
Concerned Philosophers for Peace
Conference of Philosophical Societies
Department of Moral and Social Philosophy, University of Helsinki
Gannon University
Gilson Society
Haitian Studies Association
Ikeda University
Institute of Philosophy of the High Council of Scientific Research, Spain
International Academy of Philosophy of the Principality of Liechtenstein
International Association of Bioethics
International Center for the Arts, Humanities, and Value Inquiry
International Society for Universal Dialogue
Natural Law Society
Philosophical Society of Finland
Philosophy Born of Struggle Association
Philosophy Seminar, University of Mainz
Pragmatism Archive at The Oklahoma State University
R.S. Hartman Institute for Formal and Applied Axiology
Research Institute, Lakeridge Health Corporation
Russian Philosophical Society
Society for Existential Analysis
Society for Iberian and Latin-American Thought
Society for the Philosophic Study of Genocide and the Holocaust
Unit for Research in Cognitive Neuroscience, Autonomous University of Barcelona
Whitehead Research Project
Yves R. Simon Institute

Titles Published

Volumes 1 - 223 see www.rodopi.nl

224. Hugh P. McDonald, *Creative Actualization: A Meliorist Theory of Values*. A volume in **Studies in Pragmatism and Values**

225. Rob Gildert and Dennis Rothermel, Editors, *Remembrance and Reconciliation*. A volume in **Philosophy of Peace**

226. Leonidas Donskis, Editor, *Niccolò Machiavelli: History, Power, and Virtue*. A volume in **Philosophy, Literature, and Politics**

227. Sanya Osha, *Postethnophilosophy*. A volume in **Social Philosophy**

228. Rosa M. Calcaterra, Editor, *New Perspectives on Pragmatism and Analytic Philosophy*. A volume in **Studies in Pragmatism and Values**

229. Danielle Poe, Editor, *Communities of Peace: Confronting Injustice and Creating Justice*. A volume in **Philosophy of Peace**

230. Thorsten Botz-Bornstein, Editor, *The Philosophy of Viagra: Bioethical Responses to the Viagrification of the Modern World*. A volume in **Philosophy of Sex and Love**

231. Carolyn Swanson, *Reburial of Nonexistents: Reconsidering the Meinong-Russell Debate*. A volume in **Central European Value Studies**

232. Adrianne Leigh McEvoy, Editor, *Sex, Love, and Friendship: Studies of the Society for the Philosophy of Sex and Love: 1993–2003*. A volume in **Histories and Addresses of Philosophical Societies**

233. Amihud Gilead, *The Privacy of the Psychical*. A volume in **Philosophy and Psychology**

234. Paul Kriese and Randall E. Osborne, Editors, *Social Justice, Poverty and Race: Normative and Empirical Points of View*. A volume in **Studies in Jurisprudence**

235. Hakam H. Al-Shawi, *Reconstructing Subjects: A Philosophical Critique of Psychotherapy*. A volume in **Philosophy and Psychology**

236. Maurice Hauriou, *Tradition in Social Science.* Translation from French with an Introduction by Christopher Berry Gray. A volume in **Studies in Jurisprudence**

237. Camila Loew, *The Memory of Pain: Women's Testimonies of the Holocaust..* A volume in **Holocaust and Genocide Studies**

238. Stefano Franchi and Francesco Bianchini, Editors, *The Search for a Theory of Cognition: Early Mechanisms and New Ideas.* A volume in **Cognitive Science**

239. Michael H. Mitias, *Friendship: A Central Moral Value.* A volume in **Ethical Theory and Practice**

240. John Ryder and Radim Šíp, Editors, *Identity and Social Transformation, Central European Pragmatist Forum, Volume Five.* A volume in **Central European Value Studies**

241. William Sweet and Hendrik Hart, *Responses to the Enlightenment: An Exchange on Foundations, Faith, and Community.* A volume in **Philosophy and Religion**

242. Leonidas Donskis and J.D. Mininger, Editors, *Politics Otherwise: Shakespeare as Social and Political Critique.* A volume in **Philosophy, Literature, and Politics**

243. Hugh P. McDonald, *Speculative Evaluations: Essays on a Pluralistic Universe.* A volume in **Studies in Pragmatism and Values.**

244. Dorota Koczanowicz and Wojciech Małecki, Editors, *Shusterman's Pragmatism: Between Literature and Somaesthetics.* A volume in **Central European Value Studies**

245. Harry Lesser, Editor, *Justice for Older People,* A volume in **Values in Bioethics**

246. John G. McGraw, *Personality Disorders and States of Aloneness (Intimacy and Aloneness: A Multi-Volume Study in Philosophical Psychology, Volume Two),* A volume in **Philosophy and Psychology**

247. André Mineau, *SS Thinking and the Holocaust.* A volume in **Holocaust and Genocide Studies**

248. Yuval Lurie, *Wittgenstein on the Human Spirit.* A volume in **Philosophy, Literature, and Politics**

249. Andrew Fitz-Gibbon, *Love as a Guide to Morals.* A volume in **Ethical Theory and Practice**

250. Ronny Miron, *Karl Jaspers: From Selfhood to Being.* A volume in **Studies in Existentialism**

251. Necip Fikri Alican, *Rethinking Plato: A Cartesian Quest for the Real Plato.* A volume in **Philosophy, Literature, and Politics**

252. Leonidas Donskis, Editor, *Yet Another Europe after 1984: Rethinking Milan Kundera and the Idea of Central Europe.* A volume in **Philosophy, Literature, and Politics**

253. Michael Candelaria, *The Revolt of Unreason: Miguel de Unamuno and Antonio Caso on the Crisis of Modernity.* A volume in **Philosophy in Spain**

254. Paul Richard Blum, *Giordano Bruno: An Introduction.* A volume in **Values in Italian Philosophy**

255. Raja Halwani, Carol V. A. Quinn, and Andy Wible, Editors, *Queer Philosophy: Presentations of the Society for Lesbian and Gay Philosophy, 1998-2008.* A volume in **Histories and Addresses of Philosophical Societies**

256. Raymond Angelo Belliotti, *Shakespeare and Philosophy: Lust, Love, and Law.* A volume in **Philosophy, Literature, and Politics**

257. Jim Kanaris, Editor, *Polyphonic Thinking and the Divine.* A volume in **Philosophy and Religion**

258. Michael Krausz, *Oneness and the Displacement of Self: Dialogues on Self-Realization.* A volume in **Interpretation and Translation**

259. Raymond Angelo Belliotti, *Jesus or Nietzsche: How Should We Live Our Lives?* A volume in **Ethical Theory and Practice**

www.ingramcontent.com/pod-product-compliance
Lightning Source LLC
Chambersburg PA
CBHW030110010526
44116CB00005B/176